INNOVATION RENAISSANCE

T0384255

Innovation is not easy. Understanding the liability of newness but the potential for greatness is the central theme of this work. *Innovation Renaissance* explores and debunks the myths that have arisen from the proliferation of misleading and often confusing popular press treatments of creativity and innovation. Examples include the notion that successful entrepreneurs are winners because they are innovative—whereas creativity and business start-up acumen are not the same, and are rarely paired—or the idea of disruptive technology, which has now become the buzzword equivalent to radical new technology products or services, despite the fact that new technologies tend to offer simple, limited-capability products or services to satisfy overlooked customer demand. The popularity of open innovation has spawned assumptions, like the idea that crowdsourcing will increase the number of truly new ideas—but in fact the more novel these ideas, the less likely they are to be adopted by incumbent firms because they are less familiar.

Starting by defining innovation and the theories that have arisen surrounding it, Ettlie considers individual creativity and innovativeness, radical innovation, new products, new services, process innovation, and information technology. There is special emphasis on neglected topics such as the dark side of the innovation process—the unintended consequences of new ventures. Finally, the last chapter of the book summarizes a prescriptive model of the innovation process and attempts to answer the question: what causes innovation? Three major constructs are explored: leadership, enhancing capabilities, and integration.

This informative and unique text is designed as a resource for postgraduate students, academics, and professionals deeply committed to understanding and working through the innovation process. The book includes an introduction to the subject before moving on to an in-depth study of emerging evidence and topics in the field.

John E. Ettlie is executive education professor at the Saunders College of Business, Rochester Institute of Technology, USA. He earned his PhD at Northwestern University and has held appointments since then at the University of Illinois Chicago, De Paul University, and the University of Michigan. He has been ranked among the top ten leading scholars in innovation management globally.

INNOVATION RENAISSANCE

Defining, Debunking, and Demystifying Creativity

John E. Ettlie

Routledge
Taylor & Francis Group

LONDON AND NEW YORK

First published 2020
by Routledge
2 Park Square, Milton Park, Abingdon, Oxon OX14 4RN

and by Routledge
52 Vanderbilt Avenue, New York, NY 10017

Routledge is an imprint of the Taylor & Francis Group, an informa business

British Library Cataloguing-in-Publication Data
A catalogue record for this book is available from the British Library

Library of Congress Cataloging-in-Publication Data
Names: Ettlie, John E., author.
Title: Innovation renaissance : defining, debunking, and demystifying
creativity / John E. Ettlie.
Description: Abingdon, Oxon ; New York, NY : Routledge, 2020. |
Includes bibliographical references and index.
Identifiers: LCCN 2019038506 (print) | LCCN 2019038507 (ebook) | ISBN
9781138392151 (hbk) | ISBN 9781138392175 (pbk) | ISBN
9780429402326 (ebk)
Subjects: LCSH: Technological innovations--History. | Creative
ability--History. | Entrepreneurship--History.
Classification: LCC HC79.T4 E88 2020 (print) | LCC HC79.T4 (ebook) |
DDC
658.4/063--dc23
LC record available at https://lccn.loc.gov/2019038506
LC ebook record available at https://lccn.loc.gov/2019038507

ISBN: 978-1-138-39215-1 (hbk)
ISBN: 978-1-138-39217-5 (pbk)
ISBN: 978-0-429-40232-6 (ebk)

Typeset in Bembo
by Lumina Datamatics Limited

CONTENTS

PREFACE

The idea for this book is the result of the confluence of several strong professional and personal influences. First, and perhaps foremost, my former editor, Sharon Golan, has never given up on me as the current custodian of my first two textbooks in the field. But she knew and I knew all along that just a third edition of my text was not the best use of our joint efforts. I use cases and readings in my innovation classes, which are refreshed for every new semester and every new executive program. Even with digital printing, this makes the concept of a textbook seem archaic.

Second, and very importantly, my colleagues have pushed me, perhaps at times unknowingly, in the direction of this book. It is shorter than a textbook, and is focused on the enduring answers to the most important question in our field today: so what?

Some of these notable influences include Andy Hoffman's iconoclastic notion that senior scholars in any field ought to be obligated to stand back and ask: what does this all mean? The alternative is to continue pursuit of a junior scholar research agenda, one article after one small article. Time lags alone, between actual defensible contributions and publication, probably mandate a publication agenda shift for tenured faculty and senior researchers. I have been at this for 40+ years, so I'm overdue in that respect.

Another recent and primary professional influence that brought me to the brink of shifting priorities in my writing queue came from Nada Sanders. Her presentation at Morgan Swink's conference at TCU in June of 2015 on innovative supply chains was a wake-up call for me. Our recent paper with the same title as this book was the result of that meeting and association. That paper is a modest road map for changing the way we approach our innovation research philosophies and methodologies. The current orthodoxy has led to gross mistakes in the top journals of our field. These errors have resulted from a closed-form approach to science, which is discipline-bound, and myopic in attendance to details that no longer serve the purpose they were initially adopted to correct. We have reached a troubling plateau of irrelevance, especially because of the eclectic nature of innovation studies and its management, which uniquely challenges single-discipline approaches to complex problems.

Another primary source of my deflection to a new writing regimen were two emails from colleagues responding to my draft paper on a very risky research topic related to creativity: the power of the nocturnal versus diurnal thought process in changing a person's innovation intentions. My interest in the dream state was rekindled by Veronica Tonya and her work on creativity and dreams, but until my sabbatical at RIT I did not have the time or the patience to seriously pursue the project. Feedback on the first draft of my paper "Dreams Become You," from Rick Bagozzi, made me believe in this unorthodox project and gave me guidance going forward. Rick continues to be a great mentor and provider of detailed feedback on our work, for which we are most appreciative. Then there was that meeting with Sharon Golan, my editor in May. That was the final straw. The mantra began as a drum beat in my head: be honest, be bold, and try to answer big questions, not just a series of small questions. I am in debt to Sophia Levine, her nice replacement as editor, for continuing this tradition of able guidance through to the end of this project. In the end, we agreed to be focused on foreshadowing the future, not preoccupied with the past.

My current and recent co-authors continue to make me believe that there is hope that we can go beyond the titles of articles and conference presentations that promise the world and deliver very, very small improvements on the past: Peter Gianiodis, Rajendran Murthy, and Tingting Yang and Morgan Swink; Nada Sanders, Celine Abecassis-Moedas, Don Wilson, Chris Tucci, Ron Hira, Charlie Vance and Ken Groves; Jose Urbina, Steve Rosenthal, Sandy Rothenberg, Matthew Kubarek, Jorge Elsenbach, Paul Pavlou, Francisco Veloso, Muammer Ozer, Vic Perotti, Mark Cotteleer, and Dan Joseph; Mohan Subramaniam, Kannan Sethuraman, Mike Johnson, Germain Boer, and Joan Penner-Hahn.

The very words "innovation" and "creativity," and their cousins like "disruptive technology" and "open innovation," have been hijacked by the popular press, the trade publications, and CEOs in cheerleading pronouncements at the beginning of annual reports everywhere. In part, this book is an attempt to repatriate the terms associated with true novelty. The myth is spreading that all individuals, all groups, and all companies are or can be innovative is real. That myth stops here. Innovation is a rare and difficult achievement. Much of the first part of the book is devoted to debunking "common" knowledge on this subject, which simply doesn't agree with the facts.

So the idea of the book was clear: make your view of the innovation world easily available to a wide audience of readers. In the book, I have taken the enduring themes, models, empirical findings, and conclusions of my work, often co-authored, which have accumulated almost five decades of research on innovation and its management. I have my students to thank for continuing to challenge my world view, week in and week out, on every possible aspect of the innovation process. Chapter 12 came about as a direct result of a suggestion of one my students who had the courage to ask after a 14-week semester: what causes innovation? I am deeply indebted to Al Rubenstein and Gil Krulee, my mentors at Northwestern, for encouraging me to become involved in research in the field, and colleagues like Bob O'Keefe for making it a reality. Reviews of earlier drafts of the book helped immensely, especially comments from Phil Anderson, Karen Schnatterly, Dave Welemon, Don Wilson, Mary Tripsas, and Carsten Dreher.

My student editors, Brad Boise, Kate Ferguson, and my professional editor, Pat Scanlon, and my graduate research assistants, Arjun Ruhatiya, Nahn Do and Sri Velamuri, as well as my undergraduate research assistant, Danny Keirsbilck, all deserve a special round of applause, because they were there at the finish line to help me break the tape. Holly Yates, helped with some challenging tables and figures that needed to be redone. My life partner, Gail Hunsberger, will finally see light at the end of this tunnel, and my daughter, Gretchen Ettlie, took the cover art to heart and produced a perfect cover for the theme of the book. Without Gretchen, this book would never had made it to print since she organized and did most of the permission work. Leigh Onorato, Gail's daughter, proofed the entire book draft. The project was a unique family affair.

My father, Joseph, lives on in these pages; he knew what questions to ask. I hope my answers matter. My time in his employ working in his machine-tool business, specifically installing a part called the historically, third-ever numerically controlled boring bar, would ultimately inspire my most important career research stream. Like Susanne Langer, he had a knack for asking great questions. I am still struggling to answer some of those questions after all these years. Without him, none of this would have happened. Nor can I ever forget the support of my persevering mother, Catherine, for her inspiration all along. Alas, the mistakes that remain, by omission or commission, are mine alone.

John E. Ettlie
Oceanside, California and Rochester, New York

The house my father built, circa 1958.

1

INTRODUCTION

In 2010, the McKinsey Global Survey (N = 2,240) results on innovation and commercialization reported the following sobering statistics: "84% of executives say innovation is extremely or very important to their companies' growth strategy"; however, only 10% of respondents say their corporate venture capital is effective, 13% say their global centers of innovation are effective, and 13% are satisfied with outsourcing R&D and innovation to another organization or geographical location.[1]

It appears that little has changed since 2010. In 2013, the PwC survey reported that "three-quarters of CEOs regard innovation as at least equally important to operational effectiveness."[2] Further, "93% of executives indicate that organic growth through innovation will drive the greater proportion of their revenue growth."[3]

Similarly, the 2016 Deloitte survey[4] on digital technologies (see Chapters 7 and 8) found similar CEO concerns:

- "87% of respondents believe digital technologies will disrupt their industry to a great or moderate extent, but only 44% agree or strongly agree that their company is adequately preparing."[5]
- "Companies that are more digitally advanced...place a strong emphasis on innovation and are over twice as likely to be investing in innovation than are early-stage entities—87% versus 38%."[6]
- "Digitally maturing companies also take a longer-term view of strategy compared to early-stage companies (50% versus 34%)."[7]
- "Digitally maturing companies also place a premium on leadership. More than 70% of respondents from digitally maturing organizations say their leaders have sufficient knowledge and ability to lead the company's digital strategy versus 22% of early-stage business respondents."[8]

There is an additional Deloitte survey on boards of directors and radical technology that is quite useful, in particular for both Chapters 3 and 5, but the results are consistent with these other C-level opinions: innovation is challenging and sought after with difficulty.

Digital manufacturing is an evolutionary development merging enterprise resource planning (ERP), design-thinking concepts, product data management, logistics, and even marketing concepts. In other words, it offers complete integration of the value-added chain, more or less controlled by or directed from a major link in this chain, typically a multinational enterprise (MNE) or global manufacturer like Microsoft, Toyota, or Siemens.[9] Here are some examples of the digital manufacturing challenges continued in Chapter 7.

The headline in the *Economist*[10] read: "Amp my ride" and the subheading read: "In its biggest deal yet, Samsung bets on connected cars as a driving force" (running headline: Samsung buys Hartman). This was another established and well-known multinational corporation leaping into unaligned diversification, based on current convergent mobility trends. Although Samsung was not the first to "converge," they are hardly the most "unaligned." Google, Apple ("Project Titan"), Xiaomi (Chinese smartphone maker), and all of the major automobile and on-demand ride companies like Uber and Lyft are already on the dance floor, with more arrivals at the mobility ball surely to arrive soon.

Samsung paid $8 billion for Hartman, which is a company known for internet audio, information technology, and security systems, located in Stamford, CT. This sector is one of the gateways to autonomous vehicles. Samsung has already invested in Vinli and nuTonomy, both of which make software for connected cars. Samsung supplies lithium-ion batteries for cars through its affiliate Samsung SDI. Samsung's earlier (late 1990s) entry into automobile OE went under and was ultimately purchased by the French company Renault.

Samsung's smartphone division recently suffered a major setback due to exploding batteries in its recent Galaxy Note phone offering. This, coupled with the convergence trends in mobility, illustrates two important themes of this book. First, discontinuous change in innovation management, such as the convergence occurring in the personal transportation industry, occurs infrequently and challenges even the best of incumbents, as well as new entrant firms (start-ups and otherwise). Second, radical change takes a long time to stabilize and is extremely challenging.

A recent article in the *Harvard Business Review*[11] argues that the greater the industry investment in R&D, the greater the unfolding uncertainty. An understanding of the amount of uncertainty ahead and one's ability to manage that uncertainty in different ways is essential to success. For example, the authors show medical equipment has 8.2% R&D/sales and 90.7% revenue volatility, whereas precious metals have a 0.1% R&D ratio and 40.7% revenue volatility. These industry differences are significant.

This type of recurring discontinuous change involves both new products and new process innovations, including new information technology changes. Each one of these elements requires a different set of technology orchestration skills and is based on different economic and strategic theories that are recurring with perpetual themes and paradigms. This is the Innovation Renaissance: the understanding of lasting and accumulated knowledge in the innovation field. This book is devoted to sharing these enduring lessons of technological change and debunking and exposing the shortfall of most popular treatments of this sea change. The obfuscation that has resulted in the popular press to try to make "easy to understand" sense of current trends has, for the most part, done more harm than good.

The faster things change, the more mistakes are made in the popular press in trying to understand these recurring themes. In the first Industrial Revolution, a very similar convergence occurred in the making of the textile industry in England. Simple machines to convert cotton cloth eventually were combined and integrated into more complex, but more efficient factory systems, requiring fewer "hands." No one person, firm, or enterprise had the complete answer, and the solution often morphed to meet the context. The Industrial Revolution in America was powered by water, not steam. Herein lays the plausible explanation of why simple treatments of sea change end up being confusing. Understanding technological change is not the purview of one discipline of engineering, or even one field of science. Sociology has as much to contribute to our understanding of technological trajectories as physics. It is ultimately not the technology itself but the understanding and implementation of technology in society that matter most. Clayton Christensen has often correctly said that when an industry like health care is disrupted, everyone is better off.[12] Medical research and treatment can concentrate on the most difficult health issues like cancer. Emerging fields of science and medicine can concentrate on delivering large-scale health care to many, many more needy patients. Disruptive technology is probably among the most misused terms applied in the popular press, all the way up to and including annual reports today. The singular important purpose of this book is to debunk these simplified pronouncements that contribute to the confusion and replace platitudes with enduring, theory-based empirical research that has been applied over and over for the betterment of everyone.

Where have we been? Where are we going?

It would be difficult to argue that what has persisted in any field of inquiry is independent of the state-of-the-art comparisons. Therefore, it is necessary to review assessments of the technology and innovation management-applied research field as well as practitioner reports of challenges. A selection of both are included here with one caveat: it is very difficult to predict where a field is going based on what informed opinion suggests is the state-of-the-art and to chronicle the past contributions in any domain related to the innovation process.

Nonetheless, boldly we go forward. Perhaps the most recent review of the management of technology field, as of this writing, is the special issue of *Production and Operations Management*.[13] In spite of the comprehensive coverage of topics in this special issue, the editors rightfully admit that a field as eclectic as technology management "…focuses on the entire gamut of issues that arise as firms transform newly developed scientific or technological knowledge into new products, services, and business models to impact the marketplace."[14] Therefore, it would not be possible to cover the entire field but rather a sampling based, in part, on editors' solicitations and choices of topics by contributors. The range of topics and experience of authors is impressive in this special issue. Creativity, ideation, organizational learning, value chains, information technology, co-production, digital goods, and new product development are all featured prominently. For the most part, the articles all beg to be read, depending upon your own particular interests in the field. Further, the issue has a noble objective: to focus attention on "multidisciplinary knowledge on management of technology." The consequences of not taking this view are many. One documented case in Ettlie and Sanders[15] is the absence of manufacturing scope considerations in flexible innovation theory development.

The articles generally do a good job of reviewing where we have been but fall short, for the reason stated earlier, on where we are going, which is what lead researchers are grappling with right now. Good journals only publish new ideas, which are yet to be determined. So-called "gaps" in knowledge rarely produce breakthroughs in knowledge. This is easy to evaluate by just examining the theory section of this book or any book on the subject.

Focus first on the limitations of the special issue as they relate to the present volume. Ken Kahn[16] has published a concise introduction to the subject whereby innovation is really one of three things: outcome, process, and mind-set. Nearly all the contributions that appear in journals and the trade press focus on strong appropriation conditions,[17] where knowledge is protected or potentially protectable by secure intellectual property acquisition, like patents, and the focus is almost exclusively on outcomes. The current volume is targeting the interface between product and operations management and management of technology, but most operations and information technology are adopted from outside the firm. Without deep understanding of weak appropriation conditions, and with only one article focused on the implementation of information technology,[18] the result is a very large piece of the intellectual pie being absent from this special issue. This exact topic (managing production and operations under conditions of weak appropriation) is featured in Chapters 7 and 8. Managing under weak appropriation conditions is quite different from managing under strong appropriation conditions. The paradox of standardization and innovation taken up by several of the special issue authors should have been rigorously addressed by contributions in this regard.

The special issue addresses many interfaces but conspicuous by its absence is the marketing discipline and function of the firm. Errors of omission could have been avoided if this path had been taken. A prime example is the fine contribution by Loch[19] on creativity and risk taking. Loch devotes much of his contribution to behavioral issues in the stage-gate process and project management, but only one reference to Robert Cooper is cited and no references to the marketing literature appear. His review of the stage-gate process and its shortcomings relative to the novelty of the technology involved[20] has actually been addressed in marketing literature. For example, Ettlie and Elsenbach[21] hypothesized that the stage-gate process was more suited to incremental rather than radical product technology in new product development projects. Using a sample of 72 new products in the automotive industry, the authors replicated the general finding in the marketing literature that 60% of new products are commercially successful once launched and that the stage-gate process is modified 30% of the time in firms. What they found was that firms modify the stage-gate to improve the efficiency of the new product development process while not significantly sacrificing product novelty, or new-to-the-world or new-to-the-industry technology. There was no significant variance in the new product development (NPD) process by novelty; in fact, firms do quite well with radical technology projects managed by stage-gate and virtual teams.

Another example of a missed opportunity for want of marketing contributions is the discussion of competition in the marketplace and decisions to share information of a co-operative nature having an impact on competitor behavior.[22] The entire body of marketing literature on signaling behavior was excluded from this treatment.[23]

Finally, placing emphasis on understanding managing risk to achieve success excludes a better understanding of the unintended negative consequences of the innovative process. This topic is taken up in depth later.

We begin the journey in the next chapter by attempting to set aside the confusion about what entrepreneurship has to do with technological innovation: very little, it turns out. We are not talking about what should be the relationship between innovation and entrepreneurship, but what the relationship is. As it turns out, only a relatively small percentage of entrepreneurial start-ups are high technology. Elon Musk is the rare, celebrated exception to the rule. Further, the trend is toward new business models that emphasize social entrepreneurship, or doing well by doing good—a societal disruption that is way overdue.

The other issue addressed in the next chapter is the misuse of terms introduced by scholars and then misinterpreted by casual readers and applied for their own purposes. *Disruptive* technology is not radical technology—actually it is just the opposite. Innovation and creativity are not the same but are often used interchangeably. Innovation is typically the commercialization of a creative idea. Open innovation is not working more with suppliers or other entities outside the firm in order to reduce spending on R&D. Finally, and perhaps most importantly, innovation is not the proven, fast route to becoming rich. Innovation doesn't always pay, and being first is risky. R&D investments do not guarantee successful products and services. Chapter 2 is meant to be a serious challenge to the ongoing pirating of the innovation and creativity fields of study by those who publish glib, half-baked, typically incorrect, and misleading statements about an important academic and applied combination of disciplines.

In subsequent chapters, radical technology (Chapter 3) is explored, and the rare birth of a new-to-the-world product is examined. Not only is radical innovation uncommon, it takes a long time to emerge, and often there is great societal resistance to what is truly new and different.

Chapter 4 introduces theories of innovation, but the chapter is not meant to be a comprehensive treatment of the subject. The remarkable theoretical developments that are emerging are discussed, as well as several important empirical studies. This includes: disruptive technology, dynamic capabilities, open innovation (in its various forms), and organizational ambidexterity.

In Chapter 5, state-of-the-art and enduring principles of new product development are covered. In Chapter 6, new services take center stage, including many of the new disruptive entrants like Uber and Airbnb.

Chapter 7 features the beginning of the centerpiece of the book: successful adoption of new process technology and enduring advantageous models of synchronous innovation. This theme is applied and echoed in Chapter 8, which covers the efficacious adoption of information technology. The theme of these two chapters is the unique theoretical lens of the simultaneous enactment of technological and organizational innovation. Adoption of technology has taken a back seat to the more popular new product and service introduction as a result of strong appropriation models, which occupy much of the economic, R&D, and marketing literature. The operations management and information technology disciplines have taken an unfortunate low status in the technology management literature when the resources needed to sustain these adoptions are often greater than new product investments. A new product plant might require $1 billion to procure. Billions of dollars, euros, and so on are spent on new production and information systems every year in the modern and emerging economic world.

Chapter 9 addresses the misconceptions concerning creativity and innovation introduced here. We conclude this individual and group-focused chapter with a bold prediction that the day may come when creativity enhancement will not be dominated by waking exercises to promote an individual's ability to advance new ideas, and will take its place alongside a better understanding of the dream state and subconscious creativity enhancement.

In Chapter 10, we revisit the important emerging topic of the dark side of the innovation process: the unintended, negative consequences of innovating.

Chapter 11 is the summary chapter where the book is encapsulated and illustrated by capstone-type cases that currently exemplify the overriding purpose of the book: to debunk the superficial treatment of the innovation subject with a durable and sustainable understanding of the causes and consequences, intended and otherwise, of technological change.

Chapter 12, is the marquee chapter that focuses on vital questions: what causes innovation? What can we do about it? This is the only prescriptive chapter in the book, which boils recommendations down to just three things: leadership, capabilities, and integration.

How to use this book

If you have read this far, you probably don't need to be convinced of the importance of the subject. Some of the topics here have been dealt with before, including by me. You can skip those if you are in a hurry or know most of this content already. So, go directly to Chapter 2 to see my take on how the field of innovation studies has been pirated by folks who only want to skip stones on the surface of the water and have not taken time to understand the depth and nuances of the field.

Then proceed to Chapter 9 and see some truly novel ideas about creativity, especially our own work on the dream state and innovation. Then read Chapter 10 on the dark side of the innovation process—an emerging topic—and then skip to Chapter 12, where there is actually some advice that should work for any situation, strong or weak appropriation. In the end, Chapters 2, 9, 10, and 12 are the new legacy of this volume; the rest takes care of itself.

Notes

1 Capozzi, M. M., Gregg, B., & Howe, A. (2010). *Innovation and commercialization.* New York: McKinsey & Company.
2 PWC. (2013). Business models: Back to basics. PricewaterhouseCoopers, London. Retrieved from www.pwc.com/mx/es/gobierno-corporativo/archivo/2013-07-articulo-business-model.pdf
3 Ibid., p. 5.
4 Thanks to Mark Cotteleer for providing early access at the time of this writing to their survey results.
  Kane, G. C., Palmer, D., Phillips, A. N., Kiron, D., & Buckley, N. (2016). Aligning the organization for its digital future. *MIT Sloan Management Review, 58*(1), 7–8.
5 Ibid., p. 6 (Deloitte).
6 Ibid., p. 10 (Deloitte).
7 Ibid., p. 9 (Deloitte).
8 Ibid., p. 11 (Deloitte).
9 Lee, C., Leem, C. S., & Hwang, I. (2011). PDM and ERP integration methodology using digital manufacturing to support global manufacturing. *The International Journal of Advanced Manufacturing Technology, 53*(1–4), 399–409. https://doi.org/10.1007/s00170-010-2833-x.
10 The Economist (2016). Samsung buys Hartman. *The Economist.* November 19, 2016, pp. 57–58.
11 Dyer, J. et al. (2014). Leading your team into the unknown. *Harvard Business Review,* December 2014 Issue.
12 Christensen, C., & Hwang, J. (2008). Disruptive innovation in health care delivery: A framework for business-model innovation. *Health Affairs, 27*(5), 1329–1335.
13 Gaimon, C., Hora, M., & Ramachandran, K. (2017). Towards building multidisciplinary knowledge on management of technology: An introduction to the special issue. *Production and Operations Management, 26*, 567–578. doi:10.1111/poms.12668.
14 Ibid.
15 Ettlie, J. E., & Sanders, N. R. (2017). Discipline boundaries in innovation studies: Operations management and allied fields. *Journal of Strategic Innovation and Sustainability, 12*(1), 41–54.
16 Kahn, K. B. (2018). Understanding innovation. *Business Horizons, 61*, 453–460.
17 Teece, D. J. (2006). Reflections on "profiting from innovation." *Research Policy, 35*(8), 1131–1146.

18 Schoenherr, T., Bendoly, E., Bachrach, D. G., & Hood, A. C. (2017). Task inter-dependence impacts on reciprocity in IT implementation teams: Bringing out the worst in US, or driving responsibility? *Production and Operations Management, 26*(4), 667–685. doi:10.1111/poms.12671.
19 Loch, C. H. (2017). Creativity and risk taking aren't rational: Behavioral operations in MOT. *Production and Operations Management, 26*, 591–604. doi:10.1111/poms.12666.
20 Ibid., pp. 594–595.
21 Ettlie, J. E., & Elsenbach, J. M. (2007). Modified stage-gate regimes in new product development. *Journal of Product Innovation Management, 24*(1), 20–33.
22 Ibid (Gaiman).
23 Heil, O., & Robertson, T. S. (1991). Toward a theory of competitive market signaling: A research agenda. *Strategic Management Journal, 12*(6), 403–418.

2

DEFINING, DEBUNKING, AND DEMYSTIFYING INNOVATION

Perhaps the supreme irony of any article, book, or publication on innovation today is that this subject has become so popular that we are drowning in misinformation and partial understanding: a little knowledge can be fatal when it comes to technological innovation. There are several dimensions to the debunking process in this chapter, all popular or misunderstood, or misrepresented and buried ideas that are inconvenient to writers. Entrepreneurship is one such subject. Benchmarking is another, along with "radical" innovation, which is extremely rare. The dark side of innovation is also introduced in this chapter and taken up later as a separate subject in its own chapter.

Entrepreneurship is not what you might think it is, especially as it applies to high technology entrepreneurship. Just a few statistics to get started and then we'll launch into the back story. The following statistics that are referenced from several sources by Mansfield[1] might be surprising to most readers:

- 9% of all businesses close each year, and only 8% are opened or restarted.
- Slightly more than 50% of small businesses fail during the first four years.
- The leading cause of business failure: incompetence (46%) followed by lack of experience (30%).
- Having two founders instead of one increases the odds of raising money by 30%, and these start-ups have a threefold growth potential.
- Start-up success varies significantly by industry: finance, insurance, and real estate have a 58% probability of still operating after four years.
- Small-business accounting, tax preparation, bookkeeping, and payroll services have an 18.4% net profit margin; while specialized design services have only an 11.4% net profit margin.
- Not a single high-technology small business is in the top 12 of most-profitable small businesses. Previously successful founders of a business have a 30% chance of next success while only 18% of first-time entrepreneurs succeed.

What can we learn by examining the entrepreneurship and innovation studies fields simultaneously? The innovation studies field has evolved significantly in the last 20 years and has enjoyed an intense popularity in all camps, such as academic, practitioner, and government. There are many dimensions to this peaking frenzy, and confusion and muddy waters have been attendant to this spiked interest. The purpose of this chapter is to chronicle this new wave of interest in the context of the development of this challenging, eclectic field as well as to set the record straight on what innovation theories, practices, and policies actually confer on decision-making.

Entrepreneurship is not innovation and vice versa

Part of the purpose of this introductory chapter is to debunk an unfortunate growing list of misconceptions about the innovation management field. Perhaps the most important generalization that leads to misunderstanding about this complex subject is that entrepreneurship is the same as innovation. Innovation is the actual bringing to market or implementing of a new product, service or process which makes someone's life better. It is not creativity, which is the spawning of ideas that have the potential to be innovations.

Let's start with a celebrated example: SpaceX, short for Space Exploration Technologies, which is a private satellite launch firm founded by the now famous entrepreneur, Elon Musk.[2] SpaceX is probably the less well-known start-up next to Elon Musk's Tesla automotive company devoted to electric vehicles like the Tesla-S.[3] Herein we confront the challenge. Celebrated cases like Elon Musk's start-up firm, in industries dominated by old-line, incumbent companies like Ford Motor Company or well-known governmental agencies like NASA, tend to mask the more general understanding about how many entrepreneurs start high-tech firms in any industry, and the success and failure rates of those start-ups. As an illustration of the first important topic of this chapter, Elon Musk did not invent the electric vehicle (EV) or the orbital insertion rocket.

Many famous entrepreneurs didn't invent, but rather commercialized a concept originated by someone else. Walt Disney didn't invent animation. Steve Jobs didn't invent the personal computer. Henry Ford didn't invent the automobile but was inspired by the way Karl Benz had his production decentralized in many small mechanics' garages. Ford visited meat-packing plants and thought cars could be made the way meat was processed: on a moving assembly line. Sam Walton didn't invent the supermarket. Larry Page didn't invent the search engine; he and Sergey Brin brought Robin Li's sit-scoring algorithm to market. Bill Gates didn't invent MS-DOS. Invention, creativity, and innovation are not the same. Entrepreneurship, on the other hand, is nearly always commercially driven.

The best idea is not always the one to survive. Why did VHS surpass Betamax, clearly the better-quality video tape format? Sony insisted on a closed innovation system with Betamax even though it was considered by many to be the superior technology. As a consequence, VHS was adopted by equipment makers as the best value product for the money.

The state of US entrepreneurship

What is not well-known about entrepreneurship in the US is that start-ups per capita have been in steady decline for many decades. Kaufman Foundation data[4] on per-capita start-ups is one reliable source documenting this trend (their Figure 2.1) reproduced with permission below.

Job creation has also declined in new establishments.[5]

> The number of jobs created by establishments less than 1 year old has decreased from 4.1 million in 1994, when this series began, to 3 million in 2015…This trend combined with that of fewer new establishments overall indicates that the number of new jobs in each new establishment is declining.[6]

Although there are still debates about whether small firms create more jobs, small firms (5–249 employees) performed only 11% of the total private sector R&D in 2016, where the average R&D ratio was 7.8%. They employed 20% of the 1.5 million employees in businesses performing R&D in the US. Most R&D is performed by larger firms in the US, period.[7]

There is no consensus on whether or not small, sometimes start-up, firms are more innovative based on the type of project—radical or incremental—that leads to the introduction of a new product or service. Some authors have published findings showing small firms are more innovative. For example, Breitzman and Hicks[8] found that small firms outperform larger firms on patent performance (e.g., patents per employee). Most patents are not commercialized or licensed. Although there is disagreement on what percentage of patents are commercialized (2%–50%) and the return on these patents, there may be a problem using this metric to compare firms. Patent citations and other indicators like abnormal returns, market share, and revenue growth might be more valid measures. One study found that 42% of US innovative firms (those with 15+ patents between 2005 and 2009) are small firms with 500 or fewer employees. Artz et al. found that "larger firms are proportionally less innovative than smaller firms."[9]

Similar results were reported in a study of Institute of Electrical and Electronics Engineers (IEEE) citations:

> Small firms tend to get patents for new inventions rather than incremental improvements at a higher rate than large firms. This is because of their limited resources. They concentrate their patenting on their most important innovations while large firms are likely to patent incremental improvements as well as their most important innovations.

The IEEE study contends that "in each of the 11 categories small firm patents tend to perform better in a variety of metrics including citation impact, current citation impact, as well as patent generality and originality." Others have found for new products medium-sized firms are the true innovators, although very large firms tend to introduce just incremental products.[10]

We do know that the best recent evidence[11] indicates that not only does innovation pay off in financial performance for firms, but also:

> ... innovativeness has direct positive effects on the financial position and... while larger firms appropriate greater returns in terms of market and financial positions, smaller firms are in a better position to reap the benefits of their innovative efforts in stock markets. Our meta-analysis also confirms that radical innovations consistently generate more positive performance outcomes than incremental innovations. We found a positive interaction effect between radical versus incremental innovations and advertising intensity on market position and firm value....[12]

Further context for understanding the complexity of entrepreneurship is worth noting briefly. Per capita, entrepreneurship based on business start-ups has been in decline in America since after World War II. Further, high-technology entrepreneurship has been in decline since the 1980s. US census data indicate that the "...high-tech entrepreneurship rate fell from a high of nearly 60% in 1982 to a low of 38% by 2011." This is shown in Figure 2.1 from the Census Bureau. High technology and innovation are not the same things, but it is a safe assumption that most new-to-the-world products and services, not one-off or incremental improvements of existing ideas, come from the high-technology sectors. The most successful product ever featured on *Shark Tank* was a new, resilient cleaning sponge.

Economists Ian Hathaway and Robert Litan documented that the percentage of US firms that were less than a year old fell by almost half between 1978 and 2011. There was a precipitous decline during the Recession of 2007–2009 with only a slow recovery afterward, based on US Census Bureau data from 1982 through 2012.[13]

"Subsistence" entrepreneurship is in decline and only a small number (about 15%) of new businesses are "transformational"; that is, they add jobs at a rate of

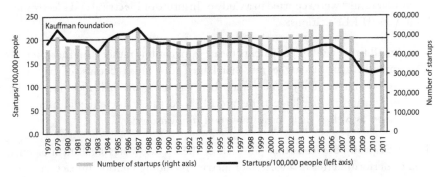

FIGURE 2.1 Start-ups: volume and per capita (Reproduced from State of Entrepreneurship Address. Ewing Marion Kauffman Foundation: Kansas City, 2014. With permission.)

more than 25% a year. These new businesses account for roughly 50% of total jobs created, and invest more, proportionately, in R&D than older ones. Further, they are concentrated in areas like the San Francisco Bay area. The downside of this geographic concentration is that it puts great pressure on housing and other local service markets. In other words, both decline and concentration in high technology have exaggerated the notion that entrepreneurship and innovation are the same.

About 20%–25% of the California population works in the high-technology sector. The median income in Silicon Valley was $94,000 in 2013 as compared to the national average of $53,000, and 31% of jobs there pay less than $16 per hour. The poverty rate that year in Santa Clara County was approximately 19%. However, not all concentration data prove a causal connection between high-technology activity (like venture capital locations) and income inequality, so there is a complex relationship embedded in these concentration data.[14]

The angel investor market is relatively stable at about $26 billion, but again the concentration of these investments in a few sectors can be complicating and misleading in concluding innovation and entrepreneurship are identical twins. Software, health, and biotech accounted for nearly one-half (47%) of angel investments in 2014.

It is important to keep in mind that so-called innovative start-ups are relatively concentrated geographically. This geographic concentration profile of start-ups is somewhat similar to a recent ranking of the best cities for entrepreneurs published by *Entrepreneur Magazine*.[15] This list is led by Boulder, CO, and Austin, TX, and not a single California city is ranked in the top 50.

The authors[16] rank cities based on the number of start-ups and employees, (2011–2015), unemployment rates, venture capital (VC) deals in the previous ten years, business tax rates, proportion of college educated in the area, cost of living, commute times, access to high-speed broadband, projected household income to 2020, concentration of spending, and growth of jobs in high-income positions, as well as a rating of overall quality of life. Note the proximity to a major university appears in most of the top locations. Boulder, CO; Austin, TX; Chapel Hill, NC; Ann Arbor, MI; State College, PA; Minneapolis, MN; Columbus, OH; Lincoln, NE; and Ithaca, NY, are all in the top ten spots on the list. The relativity broad regional distribution of cities softens the proportional impact of concentration, although the actual metric of concentration does not appear in this list. That is, we don't know if the first city on the list (Boulder, CO) is 2× or 10× or 100× more favorable to entrepreneurs than the last city on this list (Bellevue, WA).

There is an upside to this concentration. In many urban areas, with the involvement of government, centers and regions of development have resulted in creating jobs and making calculated risk-taking a celebrated example of one way forward. Antonine van Agtmael and Fred Bakker have documented many of these innovation zones in their book *The Smartest Places on Earth*.[17] They call these new innovation regions "brain belts"—replacing "rust belts"—and survey many examples of how collaboration between universities, government, and the private sector can accelerate the pace of high-technology investments. In the US, these zones include old standby stars like Silicon Valley, where the focus on information technology (IT), EVs, and wearable technology is fairly well-known, in contrast with the less well-known examples like Albany's Hudson Tech Valley's focus on semiconductors involving two universities (RPI and SUNY). Akron, OH, the old center of tire manufacturing, has become a hub of investment in polymers and other new materials. In Minneapolis/St. Paul, MN, the university there is a partner in medical device and bioscience R&D. Carnegie Mellon is the anchor of a brain belt in Pittsburgh, PA, focused on robotics and IT, and in Rochester, NY, a consortium is partnering with photonics. There are no fewer than 35 such examples in the US and a total of 59 examples worldwide, including in Canada and Mexico.

Although an entrepreneur's initial strategy choices have a critical impact on a new venture's survival, growth, and long-term performance, few studies have explored how pre-founding experience influences these choices. Founders who over-rely on their historical industry experiences may simply replicate the strategies of legacy firms. In turn, little is known about how founders can break these experience-based constraints if they exist. In an empirical analysis of 120 prospective entrants in air transportation from 1995 to 2005, Fern et al.[18] report that a founder's past experience strongly constrains choices, and the effect depends on the form of experience and type of strategy choice. The diversity of experience, at the level of the founder and founding team, lessens these constraints.

In our own research[19] of haute cuisine entrepreneurs who succeeded in starting the top restaurants in the US, we found all these leaders in their industry "learn to innovate vicariously through observing competent models [especially parents] and innovation mediates the relationship between the observation of models and performance [of haute cuisine]." That is, social learning theory provides important insights into understanding successful entrepreneurship.[20]

Another qualification to the business-start-up/entrepreneurship-innovation generalization is the notion that much of the innovative activity documented is actually corporate entrepreneurship corporate new ventures (CNVs), not small business activity. Further, the open innovation movement is devoted primarily to incumbent firms changing their innovation strategies, which has had a great impact on commercialization of new products and services. CNVs have many outstanding published examples, and overview reading is widely available.

An example of this well-established literature is a study by Birkinshaw,[21] which found that corporate ventures (CVs) can help firms act ambidextrously and increase survival potential, but they also experience high failure rates. The authors examine why and how some CV units last significantly longer than others. Their success depends on their ability to develop and create strong relationships between parent firm executives, business unit managers, and the venture capital community.[22]

Another study published by Shrader and Simon[23] examined independent ventures (IVs), which are established by individual entrepreneurs and CVs. The findings show that these two types of ventures are quite different: CVs focused on internal capital, IP (intellectual property that was proprietary knowledge), and expertise in marketing. IVs focused on external capital, technical expertise, and building a brand. IVs also pursued broader strategies and customer service and specialty products, as compared to CVs that used narrower strategies, probably to steer clear of internal conflicts with other projects in the firm. These broad IV strategies increased their performance while the more narrow CV strategies resulted in a lower performance in spite of their greater access to resources.[24]

One of the most interesting new ideas concerning CVs is explored in a recent paper on their relationship to more traditional R&D operations, by Chesbrough, Tucci, and Van de Vrande.[25] What the authors found was that corporate venture capital (CVC) programs inside a firm have a significant complementary effect with internal R&D on corporate innovative initiatives. CVs and higher R&D were associated with higher firm performance.

Chemmanur, Loutskina, and Tian found that "CVC-backed firms are more innovative, as measured by their patenting outcome, although they are younger, riskier, and less profitable than IVC-backed firms."[26] Park and Steensma[27] used a sample of computer, semiconductor, and wireless ventures and found CVC funding is useful for new ventures when they require specialized complementary assets or depending upon their industry context.

At the end of this chapter, we take up the issue of innovation and firm performance asking: Does innovation pay?

Celebrated cases of entrepreneurs like Elon Musk ignore the statistics on the failure of start-ups. Failures run about 80% for new business start-ups after the first year, and half these firms that survive after the first year will be gone in five years—some by choice of the entrepreneur to take a better job or opportunity.[28] The reports of failure rates do vary in the published literature, regardless of sector or perhaps because of the sector, which is not taken into account in reporting failure rates. The SBA reports that about half of all new establishments survive five years or more, and about a third survive for ten years or more.[29]

Success depends on choosing the right sector and industry. Scott Shane[30] reports that:

> ...there is only [a] 38% four-year survival rate for [the] information sector whereas there is [a] 55% survival rate for [the] education and health service sector[s]. Hence, it means that the sector of the economy in which a business is started has a huge effect on the survival rate of the business.

The Kauffman Foundation focuses on two primary sectors: entrepreneurship and information, communication technology (ICT), and high technology—and they find that just focusing on the last three decades, the high-tech sector was 23% more likely and ICT 48% more likely than the private sector as a whole to register new business formation.[31]

The Bureau of Labor Statistics data echo this conclusion (Figure 2.2). Survival rates for establishments vary by industry. The health care and social assistance

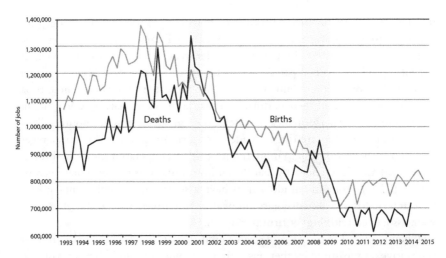

FIGURE 2.2 Quarterly employment gains and losses resulting from private sector establishment births and deaths, 1993–2015 (Reproduced from Bureau of Labor Statistics, U.S. Department of Labor, Entrepreneurship and the US Economy, 2016. With permission.)

industries consistently rank among the industries with the highest survival rates over time, while construction ranks among the lowest.

Breitzman and Hicks[32] found that if you rank technology in broad terms, small firms tend to specialize in health and information-related technologies. In health, this is biotechnology, pharmaceutical, and medical devices, and for information technologies this is communications/telecommunications, semi-conductors, and computer hardware and software.

Survival rates also vary, and the following data indicate that they are not all in the high-technology sector.[33]

It is also important to note the rate of start-up to failure in order to gain a complete picture of the context when examining the entrepreneurship-innovation relationship. Trend data from the US Census Bureau show that the net rate of survival (births to deaths ratio) varies by year and favors births one year (e.g., 2000) and deaths in other years (e.g., 2009, 2010, and 2011).

Job creation is also in decline (BLS data).[34] The number of jobs created from establishment births peaked in the late 1990s and has experienced an overall decline since then. The decrease in birth-related employment during the latest recession is the largest in the history of the series, followed closely by the period of "jobless recovery" after 2001, which is summarized in Figure 2.2.

Reshoring, economic sector, and firm size

There is some evidence in scattered reports that smaller firms benefit more than larger firms from reshoring in manufacturing directly,[35] although this varies by economic sector. For example, Walmart started a program in 2013 to spend

$250 million to create 250,000 manufacturing jobs after having been criticized for exporting jobs since the 1990s. Walmart said they would purchase more products from Dalen Products, specifically an owl with a rotating head, if they would make the product in the US for the same cost. Dalen came up with a new process to produce the owls, which allowed them to keep their plant in Knoxville, TN running year-round. The trend is for smaller firms to benefit most from these initiatives, with Walmart leading the way, creating about 7,000 reshoring jobs.

Other examples include Ford with 3,000 jobs repatriated in six years and GE and GM, with 2,000 reshored jobs each. It also appears to be clear that the technology is still not quite there to justify bringing all work back in large measure to the US. What Dalen reports is that some projects still cannot find the technology they need to offset the 10-to-1 labor cost advantage of operating in China for other product categories.[36]

In summary: entrepreneurship is not the same as innovation, and with rare exception, using the terms interchangeably is troubling, obfuscating, and dangerous, especially if it guides strategic action. Innovation is a risky business. The misconception about innovation and entrepreneurship is almost as troubling as what comes next in this chapter—a tale of the piracy of the common words we use in this diverse field of innovation management.

Disruptive technology is not radical technology

When Clayton Christensen published his first book (*Innovator's Dilemma*) on disruptive technology (DT) in 1997, little did anyone know the resultant bow wave of activity that would follow, including applause, criticism, and confusion. The most recent challenge to the theory published by Andy King[37] concludes that only about 9% of the cases Christensen cites stand up to objective, empirical examination. To Clayton's credit, as we'll see in subsequent chapters, he has clarified his construct. He admits that exceptions do exist to incumbents being successfully challenged by newcomers that start with simple technology and grow to satisfy markets overshot by leaders in an industry. Innovation and technology have become such buzzwords in the last decade that if you don't have a key general manager like a CEO repeating the DT mantra, no one will believe anything else they say.

DT is not radical innovation. We document this contention with Clayton's own data on disc drives, whereby new technology in emerging markets actually has a payoff potential greater than existing technology.

The most common misconception resulting from all the hype about how innovation is required to get ahead, no matter what, is that radical departures (new-to-the-world) from the past are the same as disruptive technology. The opposite is actually true: DT is not for the most demanding customers wanting the latest technology (radical or otherwise), but rather for those who seek solutions that are easy to implement, typically (but not always) less costly, and likely to solve problems for people in great need of attention but considered to be "unworthy" of attention by the market leaders. Words matter, as do basic definitions and concepts. People tend to lunge at any new-sounding term to get attention and make a case for something they are already doing—basic advertising with no knowledge of what is being advertised.

Mistaken definitions for DT, or what it has more commonly come to be referred to as disruptive innovation, continue unabated today, even in refereed journals. Take for example the following sentence in a 2019 article on radical technology. "Contrary to incremental innovations, in the radical technological innovation camp disruptive innovations happen based on technological breakthroughs that are discontinuous and radical in nature...."[38] Of course, Christensen has said the incumbent firms will use either incremental or radical technology to satisfy their best customer needs and "sustain" their advantage, not disrupt their best customers—the two dimensions of innovation are orthogonal or independent.

There is some research on the "optimistic overconfidence" (OO) of entrepreneurs. Simon and Shrader studied...55 small companies and found that... product success was positively related to introducing products that required more resources and were more pioneering. Furthermore, satisfaction with company performance had a curvilinear (U-shaped) relationship with overconfidence. Both high and low levels of satisfaction were associated with greater OO in product introductions. In addition, the bias was positively correlated with entering hostile environments; that is, environments that are characterized by intense competition that threatens a firm and its introductions.[39]

Innovation is not creativity and creativity is not innovation

A recent visit to one of our finer institutions of higher learning revealed the following unveiling of a new business school strategy: creativity is the cornerstone of the future. The entire college will pull together in all ways to become more creative—more creative courses, more faculty research on creativity, and so on. This is a business school that had been dedicated to innovation in those areas that matter, like course content and typical faculty vitae, for decades. Now, suddenly, it is creativity. This business school is not alone, but the general lesson here can be gleaned from an answer to the following question.

Has anything changed? Well, things do change, of course, but anyone who knows universities also knows proposals to change come with the clichés of "like moving a cemetery, one bone at a time" and "asking faculty to work together is like herding cats." Why did things change? The term "innovation" was worn out, like a threadbare tweed sports coat with no arm patches to protect the elbow pop outs. So what has changed is our understanding of what creativity and innovation are and the critical difference between them? Creative ideas are not new products, services, and processes. Innovation, like a new product, comes well after the original idea is born, and the real work begins when the creative idea is implemented or embodied in a new product or service. Ken Kahn[40] has published a concise introduction to the subject whereby innovation is really one of three things: outcome, process, and mind-set. So did that set the record straight? Sadly, this was not the case. Creativity is now the sexy term; it's vogue, new-sounding, with a ring of authentic commitment to something that takes place in the future, and it seems to have real meaning. This smacks of coining a new word which is not a new concept and merely defects critical thinking away from deep understanding of nuanced theory."

Open innovation is NOT working more with suppliers and less with R&D

When Chesbrough[41] made the distinction between open and closed innovation, a cottage industry emerged to study open innovation (OI), and then morphed into open service innovation, even more got lost in translation. There are four basic types of OI:

- Working with suppliers.
- Working with customers (like lead users) or competitors ("coopetition").
- Mergers and acquisitions (M&A).
- Crowdsourcing.

Ironically, only crowdsourcing in its modern form (like contests or *Shark Tank*) is really new on the scene. The other types of innovation, like working with other firms (suppliers, customers, competitors), have been around for a long time. Furthermore, what is often forgotten is that it takes a minimum amount of internal capability to work with outsiders—open ideas are not "free." We return to OI later in the book. Simply acquiring new ideas is obviously not the way OI really works, and there are alternative theories to explain why it works when it does—like market signaling.

Strategy and entrepreneurship

Corporate strategy used to be a subject fought over between economics and business strategy faculty at universities. Now, corporate strategy is relevant because it includes entrepreneurship, due in great measure to the work of Danny Miller[42] who proposed the original theory of entrepreneurial orientation (EO) for incumbent firms. Much work on the strategy-innovation-success causal connection has been done since Miller's original thesis, such as that by Jeff Covin and his colleagues at Indiana University. However, what has been forgotten about the original EO framework is that Miller predicted that too much innovation was not productive. We revisit these theories in later chapters of the book, but in order to digest a comprehensive view of the innovation subject, one has to be patient and tolerant to many misconceptions out there. Nearly every academic discipline and every manager or entrepreneur who ever thought innovation was important has something to say about this subject.

Take for example the case of Toyota, a leading R&D performer and industry giant in global vehicle production, and the apparent reluctance of Toyota to enter the electric vehicle market. Despite not having a single electric vehicle in its lineup or any publicized plan to produce one, Toyota must be flexible enough to introduce the cars to markets in which regulations mandate them or the infrastructure is best suited to them, a senior company executive said. "EVs do have many challenges," Executive Vice President Takahiko Ijichi said. "But different countries and regions have different energy policies, and depending on infrastructure availability, we would like to have a structure that allows us to consider the introduction of EVs."[43]

Ijichi's comments show greater openness to pure electric vehicles, which Toyota has long held at arm's length, citing their high cost, limited driving range, and lengthy recharging time. Instead, Toyota has positioned hydrogen fuel cells as its long-term bet on green drivetrains. Ijichi, speaking at Toyota's quarterly earnings announcement, didn't waver from that stance. "If you ask the question, What is the ultimate environmentally friendly vehicle?—we'll say it will be fuel cell vehicles." Ijichi has indicted that Toyota's idea has not changed: they are a full-line automaker, and must cover all alternative drivetrains, including battery-powered electric vehicles.

Ijichi's comments came a day after Japan's *Nikkei* newspaper reported that Toyota was planning to jump into mass production of long-range EVs by 2020. Toyota will set up a team next year to develop EVs that can cruise more than 300 km (186 miles) on a single charge and sell them in Japan and other markets that promote EVs, such as California and China.

On the eve of the Beijing auto show, Hiroji Onishi, head of Toyota's China operations, said China's fuel economy regulations will make it tougher for the company to reach its China sales goal of two million vehicles by around 2025. The rules are forcing Toyota to deviate from its product strategy centered around conventional hybrids. Those do not qualify for what China's regulators count as "new energy vehicle" credits for plug-in electric vehicles. Toyota pulled the plug on its EV program in 2014 when it said it was ending a two-year deal to build electric Toyota RAV4 crossovers with Tesla Motors, Inc. The company declared the same year that it would end deliveries of its pint-sized eQ, a battery-driven car based on the Scion iQ three-seater.[44]

Toyota spent over ¥1 trillion on R&D in 2016,[45] has increased R&D spending every year since 2010 and was the leading R&D performer before 2008. How is it that an industry leader in quality and R&D spending is not in the lead on EVs and autonomous vehicles? Toyota had a relationship with Tesla, the industry leader in EVs, which was terminated in 2014, and now Toyota plans to go ahead, apparently alone. Their lead in hybrid vehicles seems to have deflected any redirection of R&D into EVs, and their problems in recalls were likely caused by global market overreach and have been a complicating factor. There is little evidence in any company history that there is a linear, simple path from innovation investment in technology to industry sales leadership. Innovation is not easy, nor is it straightforward, and that is part of the reason that while it appears to be newsworthy, is not always well understood by news producers.

Innovation payoffs

Cutting to the chase, yes, innovation does pay off, and the more radical the innovation, the bigger the risk but so is the payoff. It can benefit not only the originators and the followers, but society in general. However (you knew there was a "however"), innovation is not easily achieved or easily appropriated. Although the "how" of innovation pay offs is reserved for subsequent chapters, here is a brief review of extant empirical findings on the topic.

Earlier literature on innovation performance[46] was important in setting the tone for research on this performance-link topic: the payoff from investing in R&D (i.e., applied science) was complex and not easily understood. The general consensus, especially in the corporate strategy literature, has been that, as challenging as it might seem, new technology embodied in products and services, does matter, and the impact of capturing the benefits of innovation can be quite large. Continuous improvement is still a challenge for most applied research on R&D management and practice.

A good place to start in the more recent literature on innovation performance is the Sood and Tellis[47] study, which is summarized next. Overall, the authors reject stock price as a valid measure of innovation, and they propose tracking all sets of activities associated with innovation projects, like initiation, development, and commercialization. Here is a summary of their major findings[48]:

- Total market returns to an innovation project are $643 million, substantially greater than $49 million, the returns to an average event in the innovation project.
- Of three sets of activities of innovation (initiation, development, and commercialization), returns to the development activities are consistently the highest across and within categories and the returns to commercialization the lowest. Moreover, returns to initiation occur, on average, 4.7 years ahead of launch.
- Returns to the new product launch are the lowest among all eight events tracked.
- Returns to negative events are higher in absolute value than those to positive events.
- Returns are consistently higher for small firms than for lag and for those that focus on a few rather than may technologies.
- Returns to the announcing firm are substantially greater than those to competitors across all stages.
- Number of prior announcements of time since the last announcement has no effect on the market returns to innovation.
- Returns to the first announcement of an innovation project are not different from returns to later announcements. Similarly, results for older technologies and projects are not different from those for newer ones (footnote 56 in their original text).

A longitudinal study reported by Artz, Hatfield, and Cardinal[49] found:

> ...that a firm's R&D spending is a very good predictor of its patenting and new product announcements, although not always in the anticipated direction. Another surprising result is the negative relationship between patents and performance. As expected, R&D spending was positively related to patents.

However, there were some unexpected results as well: "Negative relationship was found between patents and both ROA and sales growth." They also found a positive association between patents and new product announcements. In addition, larger firms had more patents, product announcements, and R&D spending, as one would expect.

Finally, and not surprising, new product introductions impact market value of the introducing firms with an average impact of the announcement of a new product resulting in an approximate 0.75% increase in the market value of the firm. The impact is concentrated nearly exclusively during the three days surrounding the announcement of the new product. Industry matters slightly, and by year, but is sensitive to the type of product.

The dark side of innovation

Perhaps it all began with the often-now-forgotten Danny Miller model of Entrepreneurial Orientation.[50] He predicted there was a downside—maybe even a dark side—of innovation. Too much of a good thing is a bad thing. There is such a thing as optimal innovation. We return to this seminal article again and again throughout this text. Even though it is taken as an organizing assumption that creativity is a desirable trait in individuals and a valuable resource in organizations, there is evidence that creativity increases dishonesty.

Other studies confirm these findings:

> This paper explores the relationship between self-reported innovative characteristics and dysfunctional personality traits. Participants ($N = 207$) from a range of occupations completed the Innovation Potential Indicator (IPI) and the Hogan Development Survey (HDS). Those who reported innovative characteristics also reported the following dysfunctional traits: Arrogant, Manipulative, Dramatic, Eccentric; and lower levels of Cautious, Perfectionist and Dependent. A representative approximation of the higher order factor "moving against people" (Hogan & Hogan, 1997)[51] was positively associated with innovative characteristics. It is concluded that innovation potential may be viewed as a positive effect of some otherwise dysfunctional traits, most notably those encompassed under the second-order HDS factor "moving against people."[52]

Journals have devoted special issues to the topic. In 2004, the *Journal of Organizational Behavior* did just that:

> This introduction essay proposes a challenging program for researchers eager to explore factors and process mechanisms contributing to the benefits and costs individuals and groups incur from pursuing innovative approaches. With respect to individual innovation, such moderating factors might be found in the characteristics of the innovative idea, the innovator, co-workers, supervisors, the broader organizational context, and in national culture…<factors>beneficial and detrimental outcomes of group innovation include knowledge, skills and ability of group members, group tenure, diversity among group members, group processes (clarifying group objectives, participation, constructive management of competing perspectives), and external demands on groups.[53]

Returning to the Danny Miller hypothesis[54] that too much of a good thing is a bad thing, one might imply that the nature of the relationship between underlying variables drives innovation. Take trust, for example. Most would assume trust is behind good relationships, especially under the stress of producing in high-risk situations—like a new, untested problem solution. We found evidence of a curvilinear relationship in trust between the information technology function and R&D in virtual engineering projects.[55] Others have found similar results to support:

> …the positive and negative impact of trust on the innovation performance of firms in industrial districts… Some level of trust is beneficial because it enables transfer of tacit knowledge and risk taking, but firms that over invest in trust, trust too much, or invest in trusting relationships that have little value for the firm, may be misallocating precious resources and/or taking unnecessary risks that could have substantial negative effects on their innovation performance. Drawing on a sample of 156 manufacturing firms from different industrial districts in Valencia we find, that beyond an optimum threshold level, additional increases of trust bring diminishing benefits and may even decrease innovation returns for the firm involved.[56]

What better way to illustrate the emerging importance of the unintended consequences of the innovation process than to review the case of Uber: personal transportation on demand?

Uber is the poster child for the American cultural characteristic of turning a blind eye and deaf ear to the unintended negative consequences of the innovation process. We revisit the dark side of the innovation process in Chapter 10, and we add more firms to this poster: Airbnb, Snapchat, and many more.

At least two more celebrated cases of the damaging side of the innovation process are worth including as we finish this important part of the debunking process. The first is Volkswagen's well-documented Emissions Scandal of 2015. VW installed a software program in their vehicles that enabled their cars to "pass" emission testing by fooling the test equipment. They knew performance would suffer if they were not able to defeat the trade-off between power train performance and air quality performance. According to Rhodes,[57] "The Volkswagen scandal shows how established organizational practices of corporate business ethics are no barrier and can even serve to enable, the rampant pursuit of business self-interest through well-orchestrated and large-scale conspiracies involving lying, cheating, fraud and lawlessness." The author goes on to point out that society does eventually rectify this problem, but unintended consequences disrupt corporate sovereignty.

In another evaluation of the VW fraud case, Oldenkamp, van Zelm, and Huijbregts[58] estimate that on-road emissions, measurement of which was avoided by the software dodge of air quality testing, amounted to:

> 526 ktons of [nitrogen oxides] (in the U.S. and Europe) more than was legally allowed...[causing] 45,000 disability adjusted life years (DALYs) and a value of life lost of at least 39 billion U.S. dollars...which is 5.3 times larger than the 7.3 billion U.S. dollars that VW group has set aside to cover worldwide costs related to the diesel emission scandal.[59]

The second and final illustration of the dark side of the innovation process goes far beyond the well-documented case of women underrepresented in technical fields working in Silicon Valley. Justin Wolfers[60] summarizes a thesis from University of California Berkeley by Alice H. Wu, advised by Professor David Card, which attempts to explain the underrepresentation of women in top universities in economics departments. Ms. Wu created a virtual water cooler to document over one million anonymous online message board posts. Among the top 30 words most "uniquely associated with discussions of women" were "hotter" and "lesbian." The innovation of the online water cooler had essentially created an open forum where misogynistic messages could proliferate. We return to the role of academe in the dark side of the innovation process in Chapter 10.[61]

Benchmarking is the answer. What was the question?

In my university, and likely in many others, faculty are regaled with presentations of standing committee reports, policy change proposals, and carefully researched and well-documented plans for new programs that will enhance the reputation of our campus. It is likely that this is the case in all organizations, including planning meetings for new products, supplier evaluation reviews, etc.

However, there is one aspect of these presentations that continues to be troubling: data on benchmarking. There are two questions that leap to mind when benchmarking data are presented. How were the comparison universities or programs selected? How were these data sampled and collected? It turns out the real issues underlying benchmarking go much deeper and are much more complex.

Benchmarking is "…an external focus on internal activities, functions, or operations in order to achieve continuous improvement,"[62] but without strategic focus and flexibility in achieving goals, it is unlikely to achieve its purpose. Strategic alignment is the first principle in making benchmarking useful.[63] Therefore, if the strategy is not abundantly clear to all involved, benchmarking is likely to be deflected from its true purpose.

The common errors of benchmarking—that is, benchmarking exclusively in your own industry—can be avoided by not restricting the search for benchmark partners geographically or by product or service.[64] One case example in specialized industrial products included four benchmarks of direct competitors, one non-competitor, and one best sales force in the nation.[65]

Central to the benchmarking creed is that best practices can be identified and copied or emulated. So called "best practices" are probably the most typical of the assumption fallacies of benchmarking. First, it is typically easy to identify an example of "best practices." However, what can be identified as a best practice is typically obsolete when it becomes known. Exemplars are always on the move. It is not a coincidence that C.K. Prahalad was fond of saying (I paraphrase), we are not interested in best practices (that are already obsolete), but we are interested in NEXT practices. Second, if one could emulate a best practice, one would have to emulate the culture that produced the practice. An often-cited example of this issue is the Toyota production system, which other car companies have been chasing for 35 years. An example closer to home is that of Northeastern University. When NEU tried to copy best practices identified at Boston University, it was a costly misadventure, and it took years to redirect efforts toward the true cultural strengths that made NEU strong in the first place.[66]

Generating targets is often the beginning of the exercise of change management, not the end. The barriers may be formidable in achieving a goal of continuous improvement. The key to understanding the real value of benchmarking can get lost when organizations that have prevailed in the face of similar barriers were not on the list of easily identified "best" practice examples.[67] Think of the paradox: on the one hand, benchmarking requires partnering, and on the other, its purpose is to improve competitive position.[68]

This brings us to the last concern about benchmarking in this chapter. Is benchmarking enough? Well, you guessed the answer: no. As one can see from even the very limited literature cited here, the capability to change is at the heart of making benchmarking useful. Other methods may have to be employed to achieve the desired ends. For example, business process reengineering (BPR) has often been shown to be necessary to capture the benefits of enterprise resource planning (ERP) systems.[69]

Summary

Smaller firms maybe more efficient innovators, but larger firms perform the most R&D and often organize for internal entrepreneurial activity like smaller firms. Larger firms report the lion's share of the outcomes of the innovation process like new products and resulting revenues. Patenting tends to follow predictable patterns, but actual accounting performance (like ROA) doesn't always follow. Small, entrepreneurial firms tend to concentrate activity in health and computer-related industries like software, and they are in the minority of all start-ups and concentrated in certain parts of the country. Overall, start-ups per capita in general, and high technology in particular, have been in decline for many years. Entrepreneurship and innovation are not the same, and although innovation pays off, it is a complex process that yields high returns on R&D and patenting activity.

As we'll see in the subsequent chapters, evidence of actionable policies and practices like structuring for innovation to increase the odds of success is very much a topic that has a rich, multi-disciplinary publication history. There are better ways to think about, strategize, and implement plans to capture the payoffs of innovation. The challenge of fruitful innovation management continues to be a significant issue in most organizations, in large measure due to the confusion created by the partial understanding and hype reviewed here. Now that you know "what not to do," the next chapters will capture the "what to do," ideas gathered from the sources that made an impact on successful innovators.

As a preview to these actionable theory-based empirical findings, a recent study of pay for performance on innovation[70] found in a lab experiment that:

> …the combination of tolerance for early failure and reward for long-term success is effective in motivating innovation. Subjects under such an incentive scheme explore more and are more likely to discover a novel business strategy than subjects under fixed-wage and standard pay-for-performance incentive schemes. We also find evidence that the threat of termination can undermine incentives for innovation, whereas golden parachutes can alleviate these innovation-reducing effects.

Notes

1 Mansfield, M. (2018). Startup statistics—the numbers you need to know. *Small Business Trends*. Retrieved from https://smallbiztrends.com/2019/03/startup-statistics-small-business.html.

2 Park, K., Cooper, C., & Lee, J. (2016). High hopes for satellites. *Bloomberg Businessweek*, pp. 19–20.

3 Kessler, A. M. (2015). Elon musk says self-driving tesla cars will be in the U.S. by summer. *New York Times*. Retrieved from https://www.nytimes.com/2015/03/20/business/elon-musk-says-self-driving-tesla-cars-will-be-in-the-us-by-summer.html.

4 The Kauffman Foundation. (2014). State of entrepreneurship address. *The Kauffman Foundation*. Retrieved from https://www.kauffman.org/~/media/kauffman_org/research%20reports%20and%20covers/2014/02/state_of_entrepreneurship_address_2014.pdf.

5 Ibid.

6 Bureau of Labor Statistics. (2016). Entrepreneurship and the US Economy: Business establishment age. *Bureau of Labor Statistics*. Entrepreneur Weekly, Small Business Development Center, Bradley University of Tennessee Research (2016, January 24); Startup Business Failure Rate by Industry. Retrieved from http://www.statisticbrain.

com/startup-failure-by-industry; Hathaway, Ian. (2013). Tech starts: High-technology business formation and job creation in the United States. *Ewing Marion Kauffman Foundation Research Paper.*

7 NSF InfoBriefs, NSF 18–312, September 25, 2018, by Raymond M. Wolf, especially p. 6 of 16.

8 Breitzman, A., & Hicks, D. (2008). An analysis of small business patents by industry and firm size. *Faculty Scholarship for the College of Science & Mathematics, 335*, 8–9.

9 Artz, K. W., Norman, P. M., Hatfield, D. E., & Cardinal, L. B. (2010). A longitudinal study of the impact of R&D, patents, and product innovation on firm performance. *Journal of Product Innovation Management, 27*(5), 725–740.

10 Ettlie, J., & Rubenstein, A. (1987). Firm size and product innovation. *Journal of Product Innovation Management, 4*(2), 89–108.

11 Rubera, G., & Kirca, A. (2012). Firm innovativeness and its performance outcomes: A meta-analytic review and theoretical integration. *Journal of Marketing, 76*(3), 130–147.

12 Ibid., p. 130.

13 Hathaway, I., & Litan, R. (2014). What's driving the decline in the firm formation rate? A Partial Explanation. *Economic Studies at Brookings.*

14 Florida, R. (2014, December 9). Tech culture and rising inequality: A complex relationship. *City Lab.*

15 Carter, C. et al. (2016). The Best 50 Cities for Entrepreneurs. *Entrepreneur, 44*(8), 30–41. Retrieved from http://search.ebscohost.com/login.aspx?direct=true&db=bsh&AN=116681633&site=ehost-live.

16 Ibid.

17 Van Agtmael, A., & Bakker, F. (2016). *The smartest places on earth: Why rustbelts are the emerging hotspots of global innovation.* New York: PublicAffairs.

18 Fern, M. J., Cardinal, L. B., & O'Neill, H. M. (2012). The genesis of strategy in new ventures: Escaping the constraints of founder and team knowledge. *Strategic Management Journal, 33*, 427–447. doi:10.1002/smj.1944.

19 Abecassis-Moedas, C., Sguera, F., & Ettlie, J. (August 2016). Observe, innovate, succeed: A learning perspective on innovation and performance of entrepreneurial chefs. *Journal of Business Research, 69*(8), 2840–2848.

20 Ibid.

21 Birkinshaw, J. (1997). Entrepreneurship in multinational corporations: The characteristics of subsidiary initiatives. *Strategic Management Journal*, 18, 207–229. doi:10.1002/(SICI)1097-0266(199703)18:3<207::AID-SMJ864>3.0.CO;2-Q.

22 Ibid., p. 47.

23 Rodney S., & Simon, M. (1997). Corporate versus independent new ventures: Resource, strategy, and performance differences. *Journal of Business Venturing, 12*(1) 47–66. https://doi.org/10.1016/S0883-9026(96)00053-5.

24 Ibid.

25 Chesbrough, H. W., Vanhaverbeke, W., West, J., & (Firm). (2006). *Open innovation: Researching a new paradigm.* Oxford, UK: Oxford University Press; Tucci, C. L., Chesbrough, H., & Van de Vrande, V. (2013). Corporate venture capital in the context of corporate R&D. EPFL Scientific Publications.

26 Chemmanur, T., Loutskina, E., & Tian, X. (2014). Corporate venture capital, value creation, and innovation. *The Review of Financial Studies, 27*(8), 2434–2473. doi: https://doi.org/10.1093/rfs/hhu033.

27 Park, H. D., & Steensma, H. K. (2013), Role of corporate investors on new venture innovativeness. *Strategic Entrepreneurship Journal*, 7, 311–330. doi:10.1002/sej.1165.

28 Mason, M. K. (2010). Research on small businesses. *MKM Research Website.* Retrieved from http://www.moyak.com/papers/small-business-statistics.html.

29 U.S. Small Business Administration Office of Advocacy. (2018). Frequently asked questions about small business. pp. 1–2.

30 Shane, S. (2008). Startup failure rates vary—Choosing the right industry matters. *Small Business Trends.*

31 The Kauffman Foundation (2014).

32 Breitzman and Hicks (2008).

33 Bureau of Labor Statistics (2016).

34 Ibid.

35 Pettypiece, S. (2016, July). If wal-mart can't bring manufacturing back to America, how can Trump? *Bloomberg, Economics Section.*

36 Ettlie, J. E., & Hira, R. (2018). Reshoring and nearshoring manufacturing. Chapter 2 In Vol. 2, J. Ettlie & R. Hira (Eds.), *Engineering globalization reshoring and nearshoring: Management and policy issued* (pp. 11–25). Hackensack, NJ: Chief, Donald Siegel, World Scientific Reference on Innovation.

37 King, A., & Baatartogtokh, B. (2015). How useful is the theory of disruptive innovation? *MIT Sloan Management Review, 57*(1), 77.

38 Ringberg, T., Beihlen, M., & Ryden, P. (2019). The technology-mindset interactions: Leading to incremental, radical or revolutionary innovations. *Industrial Marketing Management, 79,* 102–113, quote is on the top of page 107.

39 Simon, M., & Shrader, R. (2012). Entrepreneurial actions and optimistic overconfidence: The role of motivated reasoning in new product introduction. *Journal of Business Venturing, 27*(3), 291–309.

40 Kahn, K. (2018). Understanding innovation. *Business Horizons, 61*(3), 453–460.

41 Chesbrough, H. *Open innovation: The new imperative for creating and profiting from technology.* Boston, MA: Harvard Business School Press.

42 Miller, D. (1984). A longitudinal study of the corporate life cycle. *Management Science, 30*(10), 1161–1183.

43 Greimel, H. (2016, November 16). Toyota warming to the idea of electric vehicles. *Automotive News, 90*(6751) p. 31. Retrieved from https://ezproxy.rit.edu/login?url=https://search.proquest.com/docview/1840801664?accountid=108 Longtime electric-car skeptic Toyota Motor Corp. is cracking the door for battery-powered vehicles to join its lineup -- at least for compliance purposes.

44 ibid.

45 https://www.statista.com/statistics/279648/research-and-development-spending-at-toyota/

46 Linder, J. C. (2006). Does innovation drive profitable growth? new metrics for a complete picture. *Journal of Business Strategy, 27*(5), 38–44.

47 Sood, A., & Tellis, G. (2009). Do innovations really pay off? Total stock market returns to innovation. *Marketing Science, 28*(3), 403–615. https://doi.org/10.1287/mksc.1080.0407.

48 Sood, A., & Tellis, G. (2009). Innovation does pay off—if you measure correctly. *Research-Technology Management, 52*(4), 13–15.

49 Artz et al. (2010).

50 Miller, D. (1984). A longitudinal study of the corporate life cycle. *Management Science, 30*(10), 1161–1183.

51 Hogan, R., & Hogan, J. (1997). *Hogan development survey: UK edition manual.* Tunbridge Wells, UK: Psychological Consultancy Limited.

52 Zibarras, L. D., Port, R. L., & Woods, S. A. (2008). Innovation and the "dark side" of personality: Dysfunctional traits and their relation to self-reported innovative characteristics. *The Journal of Creative Behavior, 42*(3), 201–215.

53 Janssen, O. (2004). The bright and dark sides of individual and group innovation: A special issue introduction. *Journal of Organizational Behavior, 25*(2), 129–145. https://doi.org/10.1002/job.242.

54 Miller (1984).

55 Ettlie, J., Tucci, C., & Gianiodis, P. (2017). Trust, integrated information technology and new product success. *European Journal of Innovation Management, 20*(3), 406–427. https://doi.org/10.1108/EJIM-12-2015-0128.

56 Molina-Morales, F. X. et al. (2011). The dark side of trust: The benefits, costs and optimal levels of trust for innovation performance. *Long Range Planning, 44*(2), 118–133. doi:10.1016/j.lrp.2011.01.001.

57 Rhodes, C. (2016). Democratic business ethics: Volkswagen's emissions scandal and the disruption of corporate sovereignty. *Organization Studies, 37*(10), 1501–1518. https://doi.org/10.1177/0170840616641984.

58 Oldenkamp, R., van Zelm, R., & Huijbregts, M. (2016). Valuing the human health damage caused by the fraud of Volkswagen. *Environmental Pollution, 212,* 121–127. https://doi.org/10.1016/j.envpol.2016.01.053.

59 Ibid., p. 121.

60 Wolfers, J. (2017). Evidence of a toxic environment for women in economics. *New York Times.*

61 Hossfeld, K. (1990). Their logic against them: Contradictions in sex, race, and class in silicon valley. *Women Workers and Global Restructuring, 149,* 178; Phillips, L. (2011). Gender mainstreaming: The global governance of women? *Canadian Journal of Development Studies, 26,* 651–653. https://doi.org/10.1080/02255189.2005.9669 104; Shih, J. (2006). Circumventing discrimination: Gender and ethnic strategies in Silicon Valley. *Gender & Society, 20*(2), 177–206.

62 Elmuti, D., & Kathawala, Y. (1997). An overview of benchmarking process: A tool for continuous improvement and competitive advantage. *Benchmarking for Quality Management & Technology, 4*(4), 229–243.

63 Merrill, P. (2016). Benchmarking innovation. *Quality Progress, 49*(9), 43–45.

64 Pryor, L. S., & Katz, S. J. (1993). How benchmarking goes wrong (and how to do it right). *Planning Review, 21*(1), 6–53.

65 Armour, M. (2015–2016). Talking about a (business continuity) revolution: Why best practices are wrong and possible solutions for getting them right. *Journal of Business Continuity and Emergency Planning,* 9, 103–111; and on internal capabilities and evolution of methods: Francis, G., & Holloway, J. (2007). What have we learned? themes form the literature on best-practice benchmarking. *International Journal of Management Reviews, 9*(3), 171–189.

66 Wiarda, E. A., & Luria, D. (1998). The best-practice company and other benchmarking myths. *Quality Progress, 31*(2), 91–94.

67 Cox, J. R. W., Mann, L., & Samson, D. (1997). Benchmarking as a mixed metaphor: Disentangling assumptions of competition and collaboration. *Journal of Management Studies, 34*(2), 285–314. doi:10.1111/1467-6486.00052.

68 Thor, C. G., & Jarrett, J. R. (1999). Benchmarking and reengineering: Alternatives or partners? *International Journal of Technology Management, 17*(7–8), 786–796.

69 Ibid. Ettlie, J. E., Perotti, V., Cotteleer, M. J., & Joseph, D. (2005). Strategic predictors of successful enterprise system deployment. *International Journal of Operations and Production Management. 25*(9/10), 953–1153.

70 Ederer, F., & Manso, G. (2013). Is pay for performance detrimental to innovation? *Management Science, 59*(7), 1496–1513.

3

RADICAL INNOVATION

What's new?

There are very few literature reviews on radical innovation. One of the exceptions[1] emphasizes leadership, organizational culture, and organizational characteristics (like structure, reliance on partnerships, cross-functional integration, and a marketing performance management system). We return to leadership and integration in Chapter 12. Green and Cluley[2] support culture as a predictor of radical innovation using longitudinal data from a small to medium (SME) digital design agency that developed a radical innovation in the market research industry. In the next chapter, Ken Kahn will argue that technological innovation often falls on a spectrum from slight improvements to drastic departures from the past. We will consider all types in this chapter but focus on the latter.

In Chapter 5 of this book, the July 2017 special issue of the *Journal of Product Innovation Management* (JPIM) is introduced, as it was devoted to organizing for radical innovation. The editors say radical innovation is fraught with risk but brings extensive economic rewards, and that most problems stem from the inadequate organizational arrangements to support radical innovation processes.[3] This is the essence of synchronous innovation for weak appropriation conditions, which is a major theme of Chapter 7, as well as new products typical of strong appropriation regimes.

Two of the contributions to the JPIM special issue are noteworthy here. Ironically, they are the last two articles in this special issue. Perra, Sidhu, and Volberda ask: how do established firms produce breakthrough innovations?[4] Their answer is that established firms can produce breakthroughs if they can manage to change their "product-market scope,"[5] which is very similar to Christensen's notion of establishing a separate unit for disruptive technology.

The authors also found, unexpectedly, that formalization actually strengthens the possible change potential in product-market scope, which is consistent with the strategy-structure linkages found in previous studies, which segregate radical from incremental formal linkages.[6]

The last article in the special JPIM issue was by Dong, McCarthy, and Schoenmakers.[7] The authors ask a perennial practical question: how central is too central for breakthrough innovation? They write:

> Using longitudinal data from the U.S. pharmaceutical industry, we build alliance networks in the period 1985–2001 [and find], for breakthrough innovation, collaborating with more partners that are more central in alliance networks the better, but only to a point. Beyond that point, we find that the likelihood of achieving breakthrough innovation drops. Furthermore, and looking at the kinds of knowledge provided by the partners in each firm's alliances, we report that firms with a greater share of private partners, relative to public partners, suffer less from the diminishing benefits of collaboration with central partners when developing breakthrough innovation.[8]

What's missing here is how to structure internally for radical innovation, and we already know that successful radical and incremental innovation follow from different structures. More recently, Fores and Camison[9] add to our knowledge on this subject by adding absorptive capability to the causal mix. Using data from 952 Spanish firms they found: (1) incremental innovation performance is positively affected by internal knowledge creation and absorptive capabilities, (2) absorptive capability affects radical innovation performance positively, (3) size has a direct positive effect on incremental innovation performance, and (4) size has a direct positive effect on internal knowledge creation capability. What they do not find is a curvilinear relationship between size and radical new product introduction. However, they do report that larger firms have hierarchies that contribute to conservatism, and managers become risk averse, favoring improvement of existing products.

There are indications from European data of a link between intellectual capital and radical innovation. Delgado-Verde and Martín-de Castro[10] studied 251 Spanish high- and medium-tech firms and found that:

> While the technological capital-radical innovation link loses intensity once a certain endowment of technological capital is reached, the relationship between vertical social capital and radical innovation increases exponentially and grows more intensively once a certain endowment of vertical social capital is attained. Conversely, the relationship between human capital and radical innovation is linear and positive.[11]

It seems that SMEs follow a similar pattern.[12]

Firms can prepare to launch radical innovation. Roy and Sarkar[13] studied the robotics industry and found that "'preadapted' firms—the ones with prior relevant technological knowledge and with access to internal users of 'brainy' robots—were the innovation leaders in the emerging new technology but were laggards in the old technology."[14] However, the R&D portfolio matters. Caviggioli[15] found using patent data that mergers are more frequent if the technologies involved are closely related, often through collaboration. The more complex the technology is, the less likely it is that convergence and fusion will occur.

Industry leaders cause imitation in followers. Giachetti and Lanzolla[16] studied the mobile phone industry (1997–2008) and found that:

> …product technologies launched by market leaders are copied more quickly than ones launched by non-market leader firms; product technologies launched by members of a focal firm's own strategic group are copied more quickly than ones launched by outsiders; and substitute technologies are copied more quickly than functionality-defining technologies.[17]

In regulated industries like telecom, it is probably important to note that public policy has a differential impact on type of innovation. Beck, Lopes-Bento, and Schenker-Wicki[18] found that while "…privately motivated R&D expenditures are significant for both types of innovation, the policy-induced part is significant only for radical innovation"[19] but does not encourage collaboration among firms.

Large, incumbent firms dominate the chemical industry, but smaller newcomers are increasing the fund of environmental technology. The US government has traditionally played an important role in fostering these technologies and signaling their importance.[20] This echoes the signaling behavior of private sector firms. One study found that the quality of this information improves the relationship between innovativeness and stock market returns.[21] Younger firms realize greater benefits from R&D but also face greater risk if their growth rates are slower, based on data from Spain.[22]

Ownership and scale continue to matter. Covin, Eggers, Kraus, Cheng, and Chang[23] sampled 1,671 firms in four countries and found only one of six configurations of behavioral tendencies common between family and non-family firms in predicting radical innovativeness. Market pull versus technology push also continues to be of interest to researchers. Kyriakopoulos, Hughes, Hughes[24] found that "…market knowledge resources appear to hurt both radical innovation activity and its financial rewards."[25] Another recent study builds on this trend. Hao and Song[26] report on a study of 146 US new ventures and found:

> …that technology-driven strategy is positively related to technology capabilities and information technology capabilities, but negatively related to marketing capabilities and market-linking capabilities. Their other work is noteworthy for continued investigation of the EO (entrepreneurial orientation construct).[27] Furthermore, all types of strategic capabilities are positively related to firm performance.[28]

These studies on functions and technology are often directly related to the research on strategy and technology. A recent contribution was published by Wang,[29] who found:

> ...a positive association between a firm's capabilities and the earliness of its deployment timing. A faster pace of frontier advancement exacerbates the impact of a firm's capabilities on technology deployment timing. We draw empirical evidence from the thin film transistor-liquid crystal display (TFT-LCD) industry between 1995 and 2010.[30]

Emerging interest in design thinking is appearing in the literature, but the results from one study are not encouraging. Roper, Micheli, Love, and Vahter[31] studied 1,300 Irish firms and found that:

> ...while discourse and perceptions over design's role in NPD have certainly changed over time, suggesting a much more widespread and strategic use of design, our findings provide a more static picture, showing that design engagement with the NPD process has not changed significantly over the last two decades.[32]

Further, the impact of design thinking appears to be captured primarily by larger firms. Another study found mixed results for design thinking in new product development (NPD). Candi[33] surveyed managers of 176 technology-based service firms and found "that design emphasis and design resources both contribute to market performance [but] design excellence is not found to contribute to market performance."[34] We return to the issue of strategic design of the innovation process in Chapter 12.

This does not negate the longstanding finding that formalization of the NPD process improves performance. Eling, Griffin, and Langerak[35] sampled 161 firms from members of the Product Development and Management Association and found that:

> ...the highest idea success rate (i.e., the proportion of selected ideas that are eventually launched as new products and are successful in the marketplace) is associated with firms' use of formal processes to select the vast majority of both incremental and radical new product ideas for advancement.[36]

Burgeoning interest in open innovation (OI) also continues unabated. For example, Rubera, Chandrasekaran, and Ordanini[37] used data from 239 firms, with secondary data on innovation and financial outcomes, with results supporting the notion that there is a critical need to distinguish different types of OI practices in order to understand the nature of their rule in the NPD process and capabilities. Datta[38] used patent filings between 1996 and 2009 from the information technology (IT) industry from the Standard & Poor's (S&P) 500 databases and found that "there is an optimum recombination of exterior sourcing and technology distinctness in which radicalness is maximized."[39]

We have found in our own research on the Iberian banking industry that inside-out OI impacts the efficiency of a bank, and that outside-in OI promotes growth.[40] We used longitudinal and multisource data on a sample of firms engaged in R&D alliances in the information technology industry and found that:

> ...knowledge acquisition is on average positively associated with firms' numbers of new products...[and has a greater impact] for new product development both when firms and their partners are active in similar technology domains and when they operate in distinct product markets.

These findings are consistent with other studies that have recently appeared. This type of OI study begins to suggest that ecosystem research will eventually sort out some of these somewhat divergent research findings.[41]

Another way of studying OI is to differentiate between strong and weak appropriation. Krzeminska and Eckert[42] used cross-sectional firm-level data of the German manufacturing sector from 2001, 2005, and 2009 and found "... evidence for significant complementarities between internal and external R&D for product innovations but find limited existence of complementarity for process innovations."[43] These issues are revisited in Chapter 7 on process innovation, which typically is adopted from outside the firm.

One of the most interesting emerging research streams is on coopetition or collaboration among competitors for NPD. One study of 1,049 NPD alliances in German medical and machinery industries found that "...while coopetition is advantageous for incremental innovation in both pre-launch and launch phases, radical innovation benefits from coopetition in the launch phase only."[44]

Special case: supply chain innovation

Although easily appropriate for inclusion in Chapter 7 on new process technology, perhaps the alert on the state of the art of innovation studies needs to be included here. There is no greater need for a renaissance than for supply chain innovation in operations management. A recent survey published by Chen et al.[45] of members of the Council of Supply Chain Management Professionals (CSCMP) is a prime example of the challenge of understanding and managing change driven by new technology.

In the CSCMP survey, innovation in process—like reverse logistics, new case picking automation, green packing, and a procurement risk management program—dominates the supply chain at 74%. A total of 76% of the cases were incremental innovations, and only 5% of the cases were "new-to-the-world," which is comparable to the other ratios reported concerning new products, etc.[46] It is extremely rare to see a firm simultaneously adopt a new organizational structure to implement these changes, but there is some evidence of synchronous innovation (Chapter 7).

What endures

First and foremost, new products are quite different from new services, so these two topics are dealt with separately in subsequent chapters. Radical technology can be incorporated into new products, which we'll focus on for now, and examples abound of how this process takes a long time and, as a result, is quite rare. It took 13 years for Gillette to introduce the Sensor Razor. There are a number of recent case histories illustrating how radical technology products are so very different from all the rest.

The Boeing 787 Dream Liner is a near perfect example of how challenging the launch of a radically new technology product can be, especially in durable goods. Accounts of the delayed launch of this new commercial aircraft and subsequent problems vary somewhat. Perhaps the most important point of agreement in these summary treatments is the conclusion that converting a development effort from in-house R&D and delegated delivery to meet original specification and outsourced R&D was the primary underlying cause of resulting issued. This included both late and technical issues with brakes, computers, and—worst of all—battery fires, which prompted the FAA to ground the plane in January 2013. Senior management at Boeing wanted to save development costs and share 30%–70% in the development effort with suppliers (30% Boeing, 70% suppliers, of course). The bitter lesson that so many other firms have learned in durable goods is that cost cutting in new technology development projects is a recipe for disaster.[47]

There is also an excellent Harvard case study on the Dream Liner, titled "Boeing 787: Manufacturing a Dream," by Professor Rory McDonald and Suresh Kotha (9-615-048, Rev. May 29, 2015), which is highly recommended and gives some of the details of how Boeing attempted to fix the broken supply chain to launch this radically new, carbon fiber aircraft. Later, the case of a follower that attempts to emulate this product, the Airbus A350, is an excellent comparative basis to understand what it truly means to launch a radically new durable goods offering. Suffice it to say that any company embarking on such a development challenge cannot afford to manage any exceptional new program the way the more typical incremental product improvements are handled.

Another recent case illustrates why managing a radical new product development and launch is so very different from an incremental product improvement. This case history is the story of the Pratt & Whitney PurePower GTF commercial jet engine, which took an unprecedented 30 years to develop.[48] The new engine, destined for the narrow-body commercial segment, already had orders and needed the backing of customers to make it through the long development cycle, as well as $10 billion in development investment.

These examples of radical technological change are not limited to high technology. The Chicago stockyards in the early twentieth century are the historical home of the meat-packing industry. The stockyards were made infamous by Upton Sinclair's novel of 1906, *The Jungle*.[49] President Teddy Roosevelt was so revolted by the book that he took swift action to regulate the industry to avoid the types of outrageous work practices prevalent in meat processing at the time.[50]

One of the misconceptions about the innovation process is that unless it is some new, leading-edge technology project or case example, it is not relevant to our understanding. However, there should be an echo in an autonomous EV (electric vehicle) project to what has come before, and there is. In 1900, there were 30,000 electric cars registered in the US.[51] So, why are EVs just now becoming a viable alternative to internal combustion cars, like the Tesla S? The answer is that markets and technology must be reconciled in order to have successful firms and an industry of durable goods. Battery technology had to improve to meet modern demands for distance travel in a safe vehicle.

Perhaps the most important feature of radical or discontinuous technology products and services that is overlooked by superficial, uninformed treatments of the subject is how long it takes for these alternatives to emerge as practical solutions to problems. Tushman and Anderson[52] originally defined a technological discontinuity as a "technical advance so significant that no increase in scale, efficiency, or design can make the older technologies competitive with the technology." They went on to study such discontinuous innovations as commercial aircraft, showing how the relative performance of breakthroughs like the wide-body jet (Boeing 747) had a significant, long-lasting impact on the industry. They also show how infrequently these discontinuities occur, as depicted in Figure 3.1, and how difficult they are to predict before emergence. When this process is rushed, the Boeing 787 was delayed and the 737 Max disaster resulted.[53]

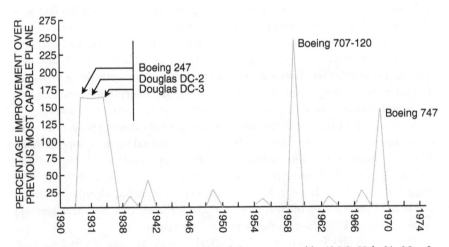

FIGURE 3.1 Seat-miles-per-year capacity of the most capable (ASQ Vol. 31, No. 3, September 1986) Plane Flown By U.S. Airlines, 1930–1978 (From Tushman, M. L., & Anderson, P. *Adm. Sci. Q.*, 31, 439–465, 1986.)

Rothaermel and Hill[54] studied discontinuities in four industries and showed how two types of complementary assets (generic and specialized) predict outcomes in commercialization. How do we know these were discontinuities? First and foremost, look at the examples they picked. Cellular telephony was first conceived in Bell labs in 1947 but not introduced until 1984, in Chicago. There are many other examples. DNA technology was "pioneered in 1973…however, this change did not become obvious for at least a decade, as illustrated by the abortive attempts of many biotechnology firms to establish themselves as fully integrated pharmaceutical companies."[55]

Next, we take a detailed look at one of the most significant discontinuities of the late twentieth century in a non-obvious industry: food processing and packaging. What is significant about this industry example is that this pattern of strategy-structure adaptation is repeated in so many industries, regardless of R&D ratios.

Packaging technology discontinuity

What a remarkable coincidence it was that my colleagues and I at DePaul University and the University of Illinois-Chicago would land an NSF grant to study the transition of the food-packaging industry from heavy, rigid metal cans to flexible, light packing material, all being located in Chicago, the historical home of the meat-packing industry. We began background interviews with a number of well-known food companies in the Chicago area and found out almost immediately that there were really two stories to be told about this sea-change in food packaging. At the time, about two-thirds of the cost of food came from packaging, advertising, and shipping. So the promise of a lighter, easier packaging format for advertising and shipping was very attractive.

Packaging technology is an extremely interesting innovation in that it seems to affect everything in a food production plant. Flexible packaging adoption causes a completely radical rethinking and redesign of how food is processed and stabilized for safe shipment and consumption. We had companies working on technology to keep fish fresh for 20 days. This was a radical change in the ecosystem.

Firms were making the leap into new packaging types, such as retortable pouches, aseptic packaging, and many other forms of new containers. A trip to McCormick Place at the Food Packaging Exposition was a day well spent and an exhaustive exposure to the wide array of new options being offered by packaging equipment manufacturers.

The second part of the emerging story to be told was about the career path of individuals in the industry. We'd follow engineers from one firm to another, all in rapid pursuit of new jobs in firms adopting flexible packaging options and some new and incumbent firms bidding on government contracts for Meals Ready to Eat (MREs), which were replacing C/K-rations for GIs. The study of individuals involved in this transition was spun off a second project about creativity and innovation. This focus on individual creativity and innovation is a second research stream taken up in Chapter 9.

The study and published papers that resulted from this research are among the most quoted in my article count.[56] This project significantly influenced our subsequent work, leading to the synchronous innovation model elaborated in Chapter 7. It appears in reverse chronological order for the simple reason that it has broad appeal in the innovation studies community of scholars beyond the operations management and information technology disciplines. Its influence on others' research is more important than its enduring prescriptive impact.

We tested a differentiated model of process (i.e., packaging) technology adoption and new product introduction. Here is what we found.[57] The purpose of our study was to test a model of the organizational innovation process. We hypothesized that the strategy-structure causal sequence is differentiated by radical versus incremental innovation. That is, unique strategy and structure will be required for radical innovation, especially process adoption. More traditional strategy and structure arrangements will tend to support new product introduction and incremental process adoption. This differentiated theory was strongly supported by data from the food-processing industry. We found that radical process and packaging adoption are significantly promoted by an aggressive technology policy and the concentration of technical specialists. Incremental process adoption and new product introduction were promoted in large, complex, decentralized organizations that have market-dominating growth strategies.

We return to this intimate connection between product and process in Chapter 5, and how it differs from new service development and introduction in Chapter 6. Chapter 5 also includes some teaching materials on new product development—again focusing on what endures. The new product development exercise presented there continues to be very useful, especially for executive programs.

Campbell Soup's attempt to develop a microwavable soup package is another case that nearly perfectly reflects the outcomes of our food-packaging study, embodied in one firm's journey into new packaging technology. Even though it is an older case, it exemplifies the results of our study. Yes, you can buy a Campbell Soup package that actually works today. But during the 1980s, this was an R&D experiment that had a difficult uphill battle to make it even to the pilot plant stage. Published in 1990, the case is still available under the Campbell Soup name, written by Steven Wheelwright and Geoffrey Gill.[58]

There are some modern cases worth examining, many of which are multimedia cases, and those will be included or referenced throughout the book. However, I take advantage now of YouTube video clips from classic performances. For the food-processing industry, the video clip from the I Love Lucy show that takes place in the candy factory is not only entertaining for the audience but makes a point: volume production is the key in any food-processing plant.[59] If you can't get quality out of a mass production line, you can't be in this business.

Managing the radical innovation process

Why all the fuss about radical versus incremental technological innovation? Easy: they are both essential for the success of any innovation program in any organization, but you can't manage the two types the same way if capturing the benefits of your efforts is your goal.

In subsequent chapters, it is clear to see how managing a new incremental project improvement is quite different from adopting a radically new process like an advanced manufacturing system or information technology like an enterprise system. Further, the standard approaches to managing an incremental product improvement like a phased process (sometimes called stage-gate or platform approach) are quite different from launching a product that is new-to-the-world, like the new virtual reality (VR) product streams or autonomous vehicles.

Andy Van de Ven's case history of cochlear implants for the hearing impaired is another fascinating example.[60] Developers came to one dead end after another. Based on typical criteria used in R&D management, they should have given up dozens of times, but they carried on, "irrationally," until the technical problems were solved.

The current and in-process example of the need for a breakthrough outside of medicine is battery research, especially for mobility (e.g., like cars and trucks). Time after time, when it appeared the answer to better energy storage was upon us, it escaped final successful testing. Rapid, wireless recharging of high-capacity batteries is another related problem with lots of interest.

Another historical case that is very emblematic of the differences between radical product and process development is Pilkington float glass. Motivated by a rumor that a competitor in the United States was testing a chemical float method of making high-quality plate glass, Pilkington embarked on a development to defy the odds and change the way glass had been produced...well, forever. The solution was actually discovered by accident when a pouring spout broke and the rate of capture on the molten tin batch from the hearth changed enough to "discover" the process. When the team replaced the spout, they could not reproduce the discovery and had to backtrack through trial and error to rediscover the float-glass method. Luck had another role to play in this story because the glass floats in stable fashion at the width required by high-quality construction installations. Given that many predictive regression equations in the field of innovation management at this level of aggregation only explain about 35%–40% of the variance in relevant performance outcomes, it is no wonder that chance factors and risk play a major role in the radical innovation process.

Chapter 2 has already introduced the idea that very large companies are typically not radical innovators (Tesla's Model S EV is an exception, but is risky). There are a number of ways incumbent firms have attempted to get off the treadmill of incremental change. The most popular, proven method is the use of internal corporate new venture (CNV) groups. In Chapter 4, theories will be introduced that suggest other ways of incorporating both radical and incremental innovation into successful organizational strategies. Ambidextrous organizations and crowdsourcing have both been shown to be successful alternatives to the more well-known methods of kick-starting breakthrough technology investments like M&A and CNVs. The emergence of autonomous vehicles as a radical technology provides a great opportunity to study the process of discontinuous change.[61]

Notes

1 Slater, S. F., Mohr, J. J., & Sengupta, S. (2013). Radical product innovation capability: Literature review, synthesis, and illustrative research propositions. *Journal of Product Innovation Management, 31*(3), 522–566.
2 Green, W., & Cluley, R. (2014). The field of radical innovation: Making sense of organizational cultures and radical innovation. *Industrial Marketing Management, 43*(8), 1343–1350.
3 Perra, D., Sidhu, J., & Volberda, H. (2017). How do established firms produce breakthrough innovations? Managerial identity-dissemination discourse and the creation of novel product-market solutions. *Journal of Product Innovation Management, 34*(4), 509–525.
4 Ibid.
5 Ibid., p. 520.
6 Ettlie, J., Bridges, W., & O'Keefe, R. (1984). Organization strategy and structural differences for radical versus incremental innovation. *Management Science, 30*(6), 682.
7 Dong, J., McCarthy, K., & Schoenmakers, W. (2017). How central is too central? Organizing interorganizational collaboration networks for breakthrough innovation. *Journal of Product Innovation Management, 34*(4), 526–542.
8 Ibid.
9 Fores, B., & Camison, C. (2016). Does incremental and radical innovation performance depend on different types of knowledge accumulation capabilities and organizational size? *Journal of Business Research, 69*(2), 831–848.
10 Delgado-Verde, M., Martín-de Castro, G., & Amores-Salvado, J. (2016). Intellectual capital and radical innovation: Exploring the quadratic effects in technology-based manufacturing firms. *Technovation, 54*, 35–47.
11 Ibid., p. 35.
12 Ibid.
13 Roy, R., & Sarkar, M. (2016). Knowledge, firm boundaries, and innovation: Mitigating the incumbent's curse during radical technological change. *Strategic Management Journal, 37*, 835–854. doi:10.1002/smj.2357.
14 Ibid., p. 835.
15 Caviggioli, F. (2016). Technology fusion: Identification and analysis of the drivers of technology convergence using patent data. *Technovation, 55–56*, 22–32.
16 Giachetti, C., & Lanzolla, G. (2016). Product technology imitation over the product diffusion cycle: Which companies and product innovations do competitors imitate more quickly? *Long Range Planning, 49*(2), 250–264.
17 Ibid., p. 250.
18 Beck, M., Lopes-Bento, C., & Schenker-Wicki, A. (2016). Radical or incremental: Where does R&D policy hit? *Research Policy, 45*(4), 869–883.
19 Ibid., p. 869.
20 Epicoco, M. (2016). Patterns of innovation and organizational demography in emerging sustainable fields: An analysis of the chemical sector. *Research Policy, 45*(2), 427–441.
21 Lee, R., Chen, Q., & Hartmann, N. (2016). Information quality enhances innovation's effect. *Journal of Product Innovation Management, 33*, 455–471.

22 Coad, A., Segarra, A., & Teruel, M. (2016). Innovation and firm growth: Does firm age play a role? *Research Policy, 45*(2), 387–400.
23 Covin, J., Eggers, F., Kraus, S., Cheng, C., & Chang, M. (2016). Marketing-related resources and radical innovativeness in family and non-family firms: A configurational approach. *Journal of Business Research, 69*(12), 5620–5627.
24 Kyriakopoulos, K., Hughes, M., & Hughes, P. (2016). Marketing resources and radical innovation activity. *Journal of Production Innovation Management, 33,* 398–417.
25 Ibid., p. 398.
26 Hao, S., & Song, M. (2016). Technology-driven strategy and firm performance: Are strategic capabilities missing links? *Journal of Business Research, 69*(2), 751–759.
27 Covin, J. G., & Miles, M. P. (2007). Strategic use of corporate venturing. *Entrepreneurship Theory and Practice, 31*(2), 183–207.
28 Hao and Song (2016, p. 751).
29 Wang, K. (2017). Technology deployment by late movers. *International Journal of Innovation Management, 21*(4), 1750040.
30 Ibid., p. 1.
31 Roper, S., Micheli, P., Love, J., & Vahter, P. (2016). The roles and effectiveness of design in new product development: A study of Irish manufacturers. *Research Policy, 45*(1), 319–329.
32 Ibid., p. 319.
33 Candi, M. (2016). Contributions of design emphasis, design resources and design excellence to market performance in technology-based service innovation. *Technovation, 55,* 33–41.
34 Ibid., p. 33.
35 Eling, K., Griffin, A., & Langerak, F. (2016). Consistency matters in formally selecting incremental and radical new product ideas for advancement. *Journal of Product Innovation Management, 33,* 20–33.
36 Ibid., p. 20.
37 Rubera, G., Chandrasekaran, D., & Ordanini, A. (2016). Open innovation, product portfolio innovativeness and firm performance: The dual role of new product development capabilities. *Journal of the Academy of Marketing Science, 44*(2), 166–184.
38 Datta, A. (2016). Antecedents to radical innovations: A longitudinal look at firms in the information technology industry by aggregation of patents. *International Journal of Innovation Management, 20*(7), 1650068.
39 Ibid., p. 1.
40 Gianiodis, P., Ettlie, J., & Urbina, J. (2014). Open service innovation in the global banking industry: Inside-out versus outside-in strategies. *Academy of Management Perspectives, 28*(1), 76–91.
41 Adner, R., & Kapoor, R. (2016). Innovation ecosystems and the pace of substitution: Re-examining technology S-curves. *Strategic Management Journal, 37,* 625–648. doi:10.1002/smj.2363.
42 Krzeminska, A., & Eckert, C. (2016). Complementarity of internal and external R & D: Is there a difference between product versus process innovations? *R&D Management, 46*(S3), 931–944.
43 Ibid., p. 931.
44 Bouncken, R. B., Fredrich, V., Ritala, P., & Kraus, S. (2018). Coopetition in new product development alliances: Advantages and tensions for incremental and radical innovation. *British Journal of Management, 29*(3), 391–410.
45 Chen, D., Preston, D., & Swink, M. (2015). How the use of big data analytics affects value creation in supply chain management. *Journal of Management Information Systems, 32*(4), 4–39, doi:10.1080/07421222.2015.1138364.
46 Ibid.
47 Stone, B., & Ray, S. (2013). Don't dream it's over. *Bloomberg Businessweek,* January 28–February 3, pp. 4 and 5.

48 Coy, P. (2015 October 19–25). The little gear that could. *Bloomberg Businessweek*, pp. 36–37.
49 Sinclair, U., & Lee, E. (2003). *Jungle: The uncensored original edition*. Tucson, AZ: Sharp Press.
50 See Dave Upton's Harvard case study on the meat packing industry in Australia, *Cypertech*.
51 Poole, S. R. (2016). *The surprising history of new ideas*. New York: Scribner.
52 Tushman, M. L., & Anderson, P. (1986). Technological discontinuities and organizational environments. *Administrative Science Quarterly, 31*(3), 439–465.
53 Nicas, J., Kitroeff, N., Gelles, D., & Glanz, J. (2019 June 2). Boeing built deadly assumptions into the 737 max, blind to a late design change. *New York Times*, Sunday, Front Page.
54 Rothaermel, F.T., & Hill, W. L. (2005). Technological discontinuities and complementary assets: A longitudinal study of industry and firm performance. *Organization Science, 16*(1), 52–70.
55 Ibid., p. 6.
56 Ettlie, J. E., Bridges, W. P., & O'Keefe, R. D. (1984). Organization strategy and structural differences for radical versus incremental innovation. *Management Science, 30*(6): 682–695.
57 Ibid.
58 Wheelwright, S. C. (1990). Campbell Soup Co. Harvard Business School Case 690-051.
59 Lucy, T. V. (2010). *Lucy's Famous Chocolate Scene*. Retrieved from: https://www.youtube.com/watch?v=8NPzLBSBzPI
60 Van de Ven, A., & Garud, R. (1989). Innovation and industry development: The case of cochlear implants. *Research on Technological Innovation, Management and Policy, 5*, 1–46.
61 Poo, B., & Dalziel, N. (2016, September). Consumer perceptions towards radical innovation: Autonomous cars. *British Academy of Management*.

4

THEORIES OF INNOVATION

This chapter introduces four major organizing constructs as they have appeared for the first time in the literature. It is not a comprehensive treatment of theory but rather a tour of the major constructs that serve as a doorway into theory development and testing.[1]

Many of these theoretical elements appeared under different banners earlier (e.g., the Utterback–Abernathy theory of evolution of the product segment is a part of disruptive technology). Here is the list: disruptive technology, dynamic capabilities, ambidextrous organization, and open innovation (OI) (in four parts). The chapter ends with the emerging hot topic in theory development for innovation studies: ecosystems.

Let's start with a great introduction via Ken Kahn's article from his abstract:[2]

> While innovation has become a pervasive term, many of today's organizations still find innovation elusive. One reason may be that much of what is being said about innovation contributes to misunderstanding. To truly manifest innovation and reap its benefits, one must recognize that innovation is three different things: innovation is an outcome, innovation is a process, and innovation is a mindset. Innovation as an outcome emphasizes what output is sought, including product innovation, process innovation, marketing innovation, business model innovation, supply chain innovation, and organizational innovation. Innovation as a process attends to the way in which innovation should be organized so that outcomes can come to fruition; this includes an overall innovation process and a new product development process. Innovation as a mindset addresses the internalization of innovation by individual members of the organization where innovation is instilled and ingrained along with the creation of a supportive organizational culture that allows innovation to flourish.

Disruptive technology: the poster child for innovation theory challenges

How do we reconcile inconsistencies and limitations of current theories? How do we merge research streams to create new theories of innovation? We begin the process of reintegrating and merging existing theory and research streams in this field by starting with the current dilemmas posed by the disruptive technology construct and then considering how the limitations of this model can be ameliorated by OI and dynamic capabilities.

A special issue of the *Journal of Product Innovation Management* edited by Erwin Danneels[3] was the last omnibus attempt to sort out the pros and cons of the Christensen's arguments concerning disruptive technology (DT): new entrants eventually displace incumbents because of the latter's focus on sustaining technology for their best customers and overshooting the much larger, overserved markets.

As of this writing, the most recent published reevaluation of Christensen's ideas appeared in the Wieners article in *Bloomberg-Business Week*.[4] Although the purpose of the article was to review Christensen's new book, *How Will You Measure Your Life?*,[5] at the end of the piece, the innovator's dilemma is revisited and critiqued. On page 68 of the article, the author says the following: "If there has been one knock against Christensen's theories, it's that they have been better as analysis than as a course of action." He further goes on to quote consultants saying the theory is an "incomplete idea."[6] There is rebuttal in the article, citing solid returns to an investment firm and venture capital enterprise based on the DT model, but the data are incomplete, with very short track records to date and with the questionable investment returns in earlier ventures.[7] Further to the point, Wieners quotes Larry Keeley, another consultant, as saying "the theory is more descriptive than prescriptive," and "there are very few robust intellectuals working on innovation."[8] We'll come back to this latter point and readers and reviewers will be tasked with either agreeing or disagreeing with this statement. It is clear all together that scholars like David Teece, Frank Rothaermel, Andrew King, and many others do not lack intellectual capacity. Among others, Gerald Tellis[9] has been very active in empirical testing relevant to the DT model and concludes the original theory was developed on flawed sampling methodology.[10] Further, the general confusion in the trade press and even business cases between radical innovation and disruptive technology, continues 15 years after the original article by Christensen and Bower.[11]

Certainly the original book, *The Innovator's Dilemma*, generated considerable interest in the field of innovation among practitioners and academics.[12] Christensen received the Distinguished Scholar Award bestowed by the Technology & Innovation Division of the Academy of Management in 2011. So many of our members of the academy seem to think his contributions have been significant. There have been a number of important articles published by good researchers on DT, but very few have challenged the original model or original data. Adner uses the example of the desktop computer model[13] to argue that lower unit price, not price/performance comparisons, caused disruption. This type of research clarifies the DT model but does not really offer an alternative comprehensive theory or even a satisfying theoretical fragment. It merely extends the original DT argument.

More substantial commentary has been forthcoming in articles like that published by Utterback et al.,[14] which give numerous counterexamples to refute the DT model by showing how they don't conform to the original DT pattern. These examples include: the compact disc, electronic calculator, components for fuel injection, wafer board, and oriented strand board construction panels. The authors argue that digital cameras, when first introduced, had superior performance on some dimensions to film, which refutes the DT model. Further, they argue that DT products actually enlarge and broaden markets and provide new functionality rather than displace established products.[15] They also say the DT model does not apply to services as Christensen contends but do not address that issue. The final suggestion in the article is that some combination of the theory of discontinuous innovation and theory of DT may ultimately be the answer to these inconsistencies.

Other authors have suggested similar resolutions to the "dilemma." For example, Yu and Hang suggest integration of the DT theory with other research domains such as OI.[16] In this book, an alternative approach is taken to explore and reevaluate where we stand on the "dilemma" and what to do about it. In the current view, we go back to the roots of the theory of disruption itself for clues. First, we examine the original data reported by Christensen[17] and a secondary and extended analysis of these data,[18] and then suggest a theoretical way forward in light of these findings.

Christensen originally reported that there was no relationship between radical technology and whether it sustained or disrupted an industry leadership pattern.[19] When the technology did disrupt industry leaders, "innovations were technologically straightforward, consisting of off-the-shelf components put together in product architecture that was often simpler...."[20] In a secondary analysis of these data, he shows that the greatest revenues and profit accrue to firms that enter new markets with new technologies, which is a direct contradiction of the original theory. Further, he says the way to avoid disruption by new entrants is to engage in careful self-disruption by establishing a separate organizational unit far away and removed for the incumbent's goals, metrics, and organizational routines the way HP introduced the disruptive inkjet printer. HP used an existing organizational unit to launch and successfully commercialize inkjet printers, eventually offshoring the production to Singapore. In his own original book, Christensen documents an exception to the rule of the demise of the market leader. In his example case of Micropolis, the incumbent "survived to become a significant manufacturer of 5.25-inch drives...accomplished only with Herculean managerial effort."[21] Exceptions that don't support a theory tend to be forgotten in the traffic jam of published ideas.

Reanalysis of the Christensen data by King and Tucci[22] demonstrated that even though leaders were toppled in the disk-drive industry by new entrants, these same firms went on to become even stronger competitors in other industry sectors. The idea that new entrants topple incumbents is not a novel observation—this finding has been in literature since the 1980s and introduced as a key point in the Utterback et al. article,[23] as well as by von Hippel in his early work on user innovation. There are alternative explanations for new entrant success, as advanced by Tushman and Anderson[24] and others involving theories of organizational inertia and various interpretations.

In this chapter, a new approach to resolving the "dilemma" of the innovator's dilemma is suggested using an extension of the dynamic capabilities framework.[25] We can draw on data of the economic downturn of 2008 in the auto industry to see how this approach can be extended. Integrating both the dynamic capabilities and OI[26] perspectives including user innovation, moves us ever closer to a general theory of the innovation process.[27]

First things first: disruptive technology it's not

Although Christensen's notion of integrating markets with technology is an original and significant contribution to literature, it is not independent of the work that preceded it and has followed since. His data on disk drives does not make sense in light of the current models of radical and incremental technology (or more recently, incremental, architectural, modular, and radical technology) (Henderson & Clark 1990).[28] Using Christensen's own recasting of his disk drive data (see Table 4.1), we can easily see that radical (new) technology versus proven (incremental) technology does make a difference in the established versus emerging market success categories of disk drives.

TABLE 4.1 What strategies generate growth

New Technology	0% Successful	38% Successful
	Total Accumulated Revenues $236.7 B	Total Accumulated Revenues $16,379.3 B
	Average per Company $15.8 B	Average per Company $2,047.4 B
Proven Technology	3% Successful	33% Successful
	Total Accumulated Revenues $3,056.2 B	Total Accumulated Revenues $35,734.7 B
	Average per Company $86.2 B	Average per Company $1,906 B
	ESTABLISHED MARKET	EMERGING MARKET
	Market Entry Strategy	

Source: Reprinted with permission from: Christensen, Clayton, M., *The Opportunity & Threat of Disruptive Technologies*, Boston, MA, Harvard Business School Publishing Class Lecture, 2003. Electronic. (Faculty Lecture: HBSP Product No. 1482°C.)

Clayton Christensen's term, "disruptive innovation" has become widespread. Unfortunately, Christensen's theory relies on far too narrow a conception of both disruption and innovation to be a central framework for thinking about low-carbon transitions. It is better understood as describing one specific mechanism of technological and industrial change that contributes to a broader framework of understanding transitions. The theory is better understood as a warning and reminder: businesses, policy analysts, and energy modelers alike are prone to overlook potential shifts in user demands, and the technological changes that chase and enable them.[29]

Integrating dynamic capabilities with disruptive technology

In their seminal article, Teece et al. (1997) use the economic theory of appropriation of rents to build a model of dynamic capabilities, which relies on learning, integration, and coordination to leverage innovation for competitive success.[30] Since then, Teece has added to this theory by emphasizing the notion of sensing, seizing, and reconfiguration.[31] What is perhaps most relevant to the integration of this dynamic capabilities framework with the disruptive technology model and OI is the type of capabilities that are most distinguishing for the ultimate transformation of the firm: intermediate appropriation conditions. Strong and weak conditions refer most generally to the degree to which ideas can be protected and captured for economic leverage. In the original article, Teece suggests that there is an intermediate condition as well.[32] What might this intermediate condition look like? We take that up next.

Why do firms engage differently in co-development of new products or services? Partial answers to this question do emerge in literature. Two answers have been documented in widely different literature streams.

First, there appear to be industry differences based on technology intensity (high tech versus low tech) in how dynamic capabilities impact the outcomes of joint development alliances in virtual engineering teams. Taking technology intensity into account is quite important when one examines Table 4.1, which shows that markets and technology both matter to the success of disruptive strategies, contrary to the DT theory.

Second, there appear to be industry differences in how firms use external access to dynamic capabilities. In discrete parts of manufacturing, there tends to be intensive, serial, but shorter-term engagements versus longer-term relationships in non-discrete parts manufacturing like chemicals. Ann Ridder studied dynamic capabilities in European firms and found the following:

> Indeed, I did check for industry differences in external sourcing of dynamic capabilities. Basically, I did a split group analysis (for "processing industries", "manufacturing industries", and "other industries"). While the significance levels remain largely the same, I do find some differences in the weights of the different paths. For instance, I find stronger effects of external dynamic capabilities in the processing industries.[33]

The importance of this type of empirical evidence is that it points to the way in which resource issues are resolved in overcoming the innovator's dilemma. In fact, if there were no resource issues, in theory, there should be no dilemma.[34] If resource issues were resolvable, general managers might spread their bets (real-option theory would also apply here) and prepare to self-disrupt on many promising and emerging, dominant design options. This does ignore the inertial factor in incumbent firms, but it is the first step down the path of self-disruption. If the trajectory of dynamic capability development is toward resolving intermediate appropriation issues in a path-dependency framework,[35] this would have very important theoretical implications. Our own findings suggest that there are differences between high- and low-technology firms, and the impact of information technology (IT) support on new product development (NPD) success is mediated by partnership capabilities.[36]

What are we left with so far? There is hope that Christensen was mistaken when he claimed the existing models and theories didn't make sense because dynamic capabilities had already taken hold at the time of his first book. In light of the disk drive data, the models do in fact make sense if one understands how they can be recast by taking into account the success of innovation and the type of technology market (see Table 4.1). Previous, as well as subsequent, research on the type of technology (radical vs. incremental) and product versus process technology, do matter. There is potential to integrate these two paradigms.

In search of a general theory of innovation

DT, dynamic capabilities, and organizational ambidexterity,[37,38] are three legitimate contenders for a general theory of the innovation process. All three frameworks have shortcomings, some of which have already been pointed out, including a more recent meta-analysis of ambidexterity.[39]

The conclusion of the research is that industry context is a significant moderator of the impact of ambidexterity on performance, methodological issues notwithstanding. Given the widespread challenges of these theories on the innovation process in the face of the apparent increasing importance placed on innovation among practitioners, it appears that the reconsideration of the way forward in theory-building for this (and perhaps other related fields like entrepreneurial orientation) would be timely.

There is a concern that the revitalization of the interdisciplinary approach to science and problem-solving is, at best, vague and misguided and, at worst, harmful to rethinking the theory-building process because of the indifference to the checkered history of interdisciplinary track records. While it may be true that the disciplinary structure of academe discourages interdisciplinary work, it is equally true that a "general" approach to any problem or science that vaguely advocates crossing discipline boundaries is also problematical. I offer an alternative to serious researchers and theory-builders here, which responds to the legitimate criticism of discipline-based science and avoids the trap of admonitions for more "inter-," "cross-," or "multi-" disciplinary approaches to improve our understanding of the innovation process.[40]

Open innovation

As mentioned in Chapter 1, OI comes in at least five flavors, examples of each follow below, as well as illustrative cases throughout the book, but the paradox of openness has still to be resolved in the literature—sharing ideas with outsiders can lead to technological spillovers.[41] OI types are divided here into five categories (covered in random order) below:

- Crowdsourcing and crowdfunding
- Customer co-development (user innovation)
- Mergers & acquisition (M&A)
- Supply chain innovation
- Coopetition

Crowdsourcing and crowdfunding

> Crowdsourcing, originally defined as "taking a job traditionally performed by a designated agent (usually an employee) and outsourcing it to an undefined, generally large group of people in an open call," is a distributed, collaborative, cross-organizational process seeing increased use among practitioners.[42]

Crowdsourcing is an extremely valuable component of OI. Crowdsourcing has been around for a very long time. A historical example of this practice is the contests sponsored by royalty in the Middle Ages, seeking the best and brightest guild members to compete for the commissions to provide products and services. Now many computer games are delegated to an elite crowd, and Lego changed the way they source ideas based on being hacked by an outsider.

Allan Afuah contends that information processing theory explains crowdsourcing effects and that the real benefit of the crowd is in the power of the tail of the distribution of provisions—radical outliers represent significant departures from current or incremental practice. There is a new book on the important topic.[43] Crowdfunding brings to mind Kickstarter, and there is an excellent article evaluating this method of funding start-ups worth examining closely.

User innovation

I first met Eric von Hippel at a conference at Northwestern University in 1977 funded by the National Science Foundation, as his work was beginning to appear in literature on user or lead-user innovation, as it was called then. There are several useful cases on user innovation, that is, your best customer has already invented your next radical innovation. One study in the banking industry does a great job of documenting the boundaries of user innovation depending on type of service and technology.[44]

There are caveats concerning this approach to the innovation process. First, it is not faster to work with a lead user, but actually it takes longer to develop a relationship with most new outsiders. Second, there is no guarantee that the "solution" to the problem will be a radical departure from existing practice, and, of course, there can be resistance to any radical idea, regardless of its source. Third, over the protestations of Eric who contends entrepreneurs don't care about intellectual property, this is a problem with any OI solution, and there is no accommodation for coopetition (working with competitors). Finally, where does the boundary occur in crowdsourcing? At least two studies suggest that the boundary is internal to the firm, not external.[45]

Mergers, Acquisitions and innovation

Mergers and acquisitions are not often thought of as a dimensional action alternative under the OI umbrella, but it's clear that they are. Two celebrated cases illustrate this axiom. Again, every approach to the innovation process can be theoretically useful and practically significant, but no one theory covers everything in this eclectic field.

Merck

The Merck transformation to OI is documented in "Merck (in 2009): *Open Innovation*."[46] In this teaching case summary, the historical context was that Merck had been unable to replicate its past successes for nearly two decades and needed a game-changing strategy. Merck acquired Schering–Plough (SP) in November 2009 in order to diversify and reap economies of scale. SP, and many other smaller Merck rivals such as Amgen, Genentech, and Genzyme, was already and seemed to be on their way to leveraging external research capabilities, which is one of the mainstays of an OI strategy. Since SP was far ahead of Merck in implementing an OI strategy, the post-reverse-merger challenge became how Merck would proceed from a closed, not-invented-here culture to a more OI strategy. Should the newly acquired SP take the lead in open initiatives? The protagonist in the case, Dr. Mervyn Turner, the chief strategy officer, was confronted with this dilemma.

The starting point on Dr. Turner's journey to implement an OI strategy was an examination of Merck's informal networks in the scientific community, including co-authorship of journal articles with external collaborators. He confronted the OI paradox, reporting that there is information in the case that he firmly believed that the need to foster connectivity with the external environment, even though there were potential losses associated with publication of once-proprietary intellectual knowledge. Dr. Turner believed the Merck track record of successful commercialization of new drugs and FDA approvals would attract new partners, and he wondered if the virtual lab was a way to do this.

The predicament in this case arose from the two alternative strategies being considered by Dr. Turner. Since SP had 55% of its new drugs originating from external sources, one clear path to follow would be to use SP as the spearhead for implementation of OI. However, there had always been a bias at Merck against mergers and acquisitions that might help in the short run but not really add much for long-term growth. This was a risky strategy, since Dr. Turner was aware of one study showing the lack of any significant association between the size of the R&D budget and productivity during the years 1993 and 1998 among 40 pharmaceutical firms. Another study had shown that after a merger, development projects declined by 34%. The implication of these studies was that the Merck/SP merger might actually hurt successful new drug development and impede an OI initiation rather than help it, at least in the short term. Dr. Turner even began to question the OI strategy, regardless of how this initiative would be implemented. The two R&D pipelines of Merck and SP were quite complementary and perhaps the best move would be to just develop synergies between the two pipelines rather than opening up these R&D efforts to outsiders.

P&G

P&G's transformation to OI, currently called "Connect & Develop," has received widespread exposure in the business and trade press.[47] It consists of a number of external partnerships used to both accelerate and shepherd breakthrough innovations across the company and around the globe and all of its brands. Bruce Brown, the chief technology officer, is often quoted as saying this version of OI has helped renew a growth strategy, but presenters from P&G often say that they are concerned about technology spillovers.

In 2000, P&G realized that the invent-it-ourselves approach to new products could not sustain a 4%–6% (~$4 billion) a year growth rate. Only 35% of new products met financial objectives, and stock prices declined from $118 to $52 a share. In 2002, the Pringles project came along, which produced sharp-imaged chips in multiple colors as a result of writing a tech brief and sending it "out there" for bids. The result: collaboration with a small bakery in Bologna and a university professor and double-digit growth in 2 years.

What is not reported in the recent accounts of Connect & Develop is the history of P&G's efforts to continue to grow in the face of large-scale, often mature product categories. What is perhaps the most interesting part of this story of OI is that the well-springs of this strategy go back two decades to the P&G investment in a corporate new venture group in Cincinnati. A multi-disciplinary team installed in the mid-1990s began experimenting with new ideas and new methods of bringing ideas to commercialization. The first new category product to emerge from this group was pet insurance. This new category was the result of leveraging the Iams pet food brand connection with veterinarians, and a partnership with an insurance carrier.

Supplier chain innovation and supply alliances

Supply chain management (SCM) has been traditionally preoccupied with cost and cost reduction. Now enter supply chain innovation. The original research sparked much of the current interest in this new phase of SCM research. Our results are based on the understanding of the dynamic capabilities of the partners and was inspired by earlier work of David Teece on the subject.[48]

We wanted to capture the dynamic capabilities that result from interfirm partnerships during the joint NPD process—the ability to build, integrate, and reconfigure existing resources to adapt to rapidly changing environments. These capabilities, in turn, would have a positive impact on NPD performance outcomes: proportion of new product success and superior new product commercialization. In contexts where the locus of innovation is rapidly changing, the impact of interfirm NPD dynamic capabilities would be diminished, especially for buyers (original equipment manufacturers) and to a lesser extent for suppliers. Still, technology-based interfirm NPD partnerships were predicted to ultimately outperform low-technology ones in both NPD performance outcomes. Finally, IT support for NPD was hypothesized to influence the interfirm NPD partnership's dynamic capabilities. Using survey data from 72 auto company managers and their suppliers, the proposed model in which IT support for NPD influences the success of interfirm NPD partnerships through the mediating role of interfirm NPD partnership dynamic capabilities in high- and low-technology contexts was generally supported. These findings show the nature of technology-based interfirm NPD partnerships.[49]

Coopetition[50]

Ford and GM have been developing automatic transmissions together for years, starting with six-speed transmissions and then nine and ten-speed transmission for niche markets. Coopetition is the simultaneous pursuit of cooperation and competition and high-tech examples like Sony–Samsung serve as exemplar examples of how this can work as the partners tend to appropriate value from the relationship based on their internal capabilities.[51]

Innovation ecosystems

The increase in interest in innovation ecosystems is rekindled from earlier days and suggests this is a topic to watch redevelop.[52] There isn't much in the literature yet, but some contributions are worth noting. The practical notion behind considering an innovation ecosystem is that most major innovations do not emerge in a vacuum.[53] For example, HDTV needed supporting systems to be developed into a usable product. Another current example is that sensor technology is not sufficiently developed to allow autonomous vehicles on the highway. Summarizing Gobble's definition of innovation ecosystems as interlocking communities requiring trust and co-development and complementary technologies reveals the complexity of modern development of new products and services.[54]

Gawer and Cusumano extend the concept to industry platforms:

> two predominant types of platforms…internal (company or product)
> platforms as a set of assets organized in a common structure from which
> a company can efficiently develop and produce a stream of derivative
> product…<and> external (industry) platforms as products, services, or
> technologies that act as a foundation upon which external innovators,
> organized as an innovative business ecosystem, can develop their own
> complementary products, technologies, or services.[55]

Examples with dozens or even thousands of partners include cell phones and
hardware-software products for computers.

Valkokari distinguishes three types of ecosystems: "relationships between
business, innovation, and knowledge ecosystems."[56] Oh, Phillips, Park and Lee
say that:

> The term "innovation ecosystems" has become popular in industry, academia,
> and government. It is used in corporate, national, or regional contexts, in
> idiosyncratic ways. It implies a faulty analogy to natural ecosystems and is
> therefore a poor basis for the needed multi-disciplinary research and policies
> addressing emerging concepts of innovation.[57]

The authors go on to provide a critical review of the subject, concluding that:

> It remains to broaden and refine their ideas to encompass the entire inno-
> vation system…clarifying whether and how innovation ecosystems differ
> from national and regional innovation systems; finding ways to measure
> innovation system performance; further detailing similarities and differ-
> ences between natural and innovation ecosystems; and reconciling the
> levels at which the term is used, such as within firms, cities, or supplier
> networks.[58]

The relaxation of the traditional biological definition of an ecosystem will be
necessary to make progress in this theoretical development research stream.

Innovation ecosystems and synchronous innovation

The appealing development of the emergence of ecosystems in the innovation
process is that this approach would include simultaneous consideration of strong
and weak appropriation systems. The potential lasting contribution of this book
is that there is an equal emphasis on both of these regimes, and it compensates for
the preoccupation in the literature on strong appropriation. In particular, service
innovation systems tend to be appropriated under weak conditions (Chapter 6). Most
hardware/software systems like digital manufacturing (Chapter 7) and information

technologies (Chapter 8) are adopted from suppliers and rarely developed in house. Therefore, the messages of these latter chapters are potentially unique in the consolidated literature of innovation studies as they present various examples of appropriation under weak conditions using the synchronous innovation framework.

Notes

1 For example, a Professional Development Workshop at the Academy of Management in Boston is planned for August 2019 titled "Pathways to Innovation: Lessons from Multiple Discoveries and Inventions," Friday, August 9, 8 AM–10.30 AM.
2 Kahn, K. (2018). Understanding innovation. *Business Horizons, 61*(3), 452–460.
3 Danneels, E. (2004). Disruptive technology reconsidered: A critique and research agenda. *Journal of Product Innovation Management, 21*(4), 246–258.
4 Wieners, B. (2012). Clay Christensen's life lessons. *Bloomberg-Businessweek*, May 7–13 (May 4 on line), https://www.bloomberg.com/news/articles/2012-05-03/clav-christensens-life-lessons.
5 Christensen, C. M. (2017). *How will you measure your life? (Harvard Business Review Classics)*. Boston, MA: Harvard Business Review Press.
6 Ibid.
7 Danneels (2004).
8 Wieners, p. 68.
9 Grover, R., & Vriens, M. (2006). *The handbook of marketing research: Uses, misuses, and future advances*. Thousand Oaks: Sage Publications.
10 Sood, A., & Tellis, G. J. (2013). Demystifying disruption: On the hazard of being replaced by new technology. *GfK Marketing Intelligence Review, 5*(1), 24–30.
11 Bower, J. L., & Christensen, C. M. (1995). Disruptive technologies: Catching the wave (pp. 43–53). Boston, MA: Harvard Business Review Press.
12 Christensen, C. M. (1997). *The innovator's dilemma: When new technologies cause great firms to fail*. Boston, MA: Harvard Business Review Press.
13 Adner, R. (2002). When are technologies disruptive? A demand-based view of the emergence of competition. *Strategic Management Journal, 23*(8), 667–688.
14 Utterback, J. M., & Acee, H. J. (2005). Disruptive technologies: An expanded view. *International Journal of Innovation Management, 9*(1), 1–17.
15 Ibid., p. 15.
16 Yu, D., & Hang, C. C. (2010). A reflective review of disruptive innovation theory. *International Journal of Management Reviews, 12*(4), 435–452.
17 Christensen, C. M. (1997). *The innovator's dilemma: When new technologies cause great firms to fail*. Boston, MA: Harvard Business School Press.
18 King, A. A., & Tucci, C. L. (2002). Incumbent entry into new market niches: The role of experience and managerial choice in the creation of dynamic capabilities. *Management Science, 48*(2): 171–186.
19 Christensen (1997, p. 13).
20 Ibid., p. 15.
21 Ibid., p. 20.
22 King and Tucci (2002).
23 Utterback et al. (2005).
24 Tushman, M. L., & Anderson, P. (1986). Technological discontinuities and organizational environments. *Administrative Science Quarterly, 31*(3), 439–465.
25 Christensen, C. M. (2003). *The opportunity & threat of disruptive technologies*. Boston, MA: Harvard Business School Publishing Class Lecture. Electronic. (Faculty Lecture: HBSP Product No. 1482C.)
26 Rothenberg, S., & Ettlie, J. E. (2011). Strategies to cope with regulatory uncertainty in the auto industry. *California Management Review, 54*(1), 126–144.

27 Anderson, P., & Tushman, M. L. (1990). Technological discontinuities and dominant designs: A cyclical model of technological change. *Administrative Science Quarterly, 35*(4), 604–633. doi:10.2307/2393511.

28 Henderson, R., & Clark, K. B. (1990). Architectural innovation: The reconfiguration of existing product technologies and the failure of established firms. *Administrative Science Quarterly, 35*, 9–28.

29 Christensen, C. M. (2002). The opportunity and threat of disruptive technologies. *MRS Bulletin, 27*(4), 278–282.

30 Teece, D. J., Piasno, G., & Shuen, A. (1997). Dynamic capabilities and strategic management." *Strategic Management Journal, 18*(7), 509–533.

31 Teece, D. J. (2009). *Dynamic capabilities and strategic management: Organizing for innovation and growth* (Vol. 4). Oxford, UK: Oxford University Press.

32 Teece, D. J. (2006). Reflections on "profiting from innovation." *Research Policy, 35*(8), 1131–1146.

33 Ridder, A. K. (2012). External dynamic capabilities: Creating competitive advantage in innovation via external resource renewal. *Academy Management Proceedings, 2013*(1), 10356–10356. doi:10.5465/AMBPP.2013.10356abstract.

34 McDowall, W. (2018). Disruptive innovation and energy transitions: Is Christensen's theory helpful? *Energy Research & Social Science, 37*, 243–246.

35 Garud, R., & Karnoe, P. (2012). *Path dependence and creation*. New York: Psychology Press, Taylor & Francis Group.

36 Ettlie, J. E., & Pavlou, P. A. (2006). Technology-based new product development partnerships. *Decision Sciences, 37*(2), 117–147.

37 O'Reilly III, C. A., & Tushman, M. L. (2008). Ambidexterity as a dynamic capability: Resolving the innovator's dilemma. *Research in Organizational Behavior, 28*, 185–206.

38 O'Reilly III, C. A., & Tushman, M. L. (2013). Organizational ambidexterity: Past, present, and future. *Academy of Management Perspectives, 27*(4), 324–338.

39 Junni, P., Sarala, R. M., Taras, V., & Tarba, S. Y. (2013). Organizational ambidexterity and performance: A meta-analysis. *Academy of Management Perspectives, 27*(4), 299–312.

40 Ettlie, J. E., & Sanders, N. R. (2017). Discipline boundaries in innovation studies: Operations management and related fields. *Journal of Strategic Innovation and Sustainability, 12*(1), 41–54.

41 West, J., & Gallagher, S. (2006). Challenges of open innovation: The paradox of firm investment in open-source software. *R&D Management, 36*(3), 319–331. After Kenneth Arrow (1962) seminal contributions.

42 Tarrell, A., Tahmasbi, N., Kocsis, D., Tripathi, A., Pedersen, J., Xiong, J., ... & de Vreede, G. J. (2013). Crowdsourcing: A snapshot of published research. *19th Americas Conference on Information Systems, AMCIS 2013 - Hyperconnected World: Anything, Anywhere, Anytime, 2*, 962–975.

43 Tucci, C. L., Afuah, A., & Viscusi, G. (Eds.). (2018). *Creating and capturing value through crowdsourcing*. Oxford, UK: Oxford University Press.

44 Oliveira, P., & Von Hippel, E. (2011). Users as service innovators: The case of banking services. *Research Policy, 40*(6), 806–818.

45 Miller, D. J., Fern, M. J., & Cardinal, L. B. (2007). The use of knowledge for technological innovation within diversified firms. *Academy of Management Journal, 50*(2), 307–325; and Ettlie, J. E., & Wilson, D. (2019). Boundary spanning, group heterogeneity and engineering project performance. *International Journal of Innovation and Technology Management, 16*(1), 36.

46 Horbaczewski, A., & Rothaermel, F. T. (2012). *Merck (in 2009): Open for innovation?* Boston, MA: Harvard Business Review Press.

47 Huston, L., & Sakkab, N. (2006). Connect and develop. *Harvard Business Review, 84*(3), 58–66; and Brown, B., & Anthony, S. D. (2011). How P&G tripled its innovation success rate. *Harvard Business Review, 89*(6), 64–72.

48 Teece et al. (1997).

49 Ettlie and Pavlou (2006).
50 Gnyawali, D. R., & Park, B.-J. (2011). Co-opetition between Giants: Collaboration with competitors for technological innovation. *Research Policy, 40*, 650–663.
51 Bunkley, N. (2016, June 27). Transmission is no truce for Camaro and Mustang. *Automotive News,* pp. 1/32.
52 Ander, R., 2006. Match your innovation strategy to your innovation ecosystem. *Harvard Business Review, 84*, 98–107.
53 Aaldering, L. J., Leke, J., &Song, C. H. (2019). Competition or collaboration? – Analysis of technological knowledge ecosystem within the field of alternative powertrain systems: A patent-based approach. *Journal of Cleaner Production, 212*, 362–371.
54 Gobble, M. M. (2014). Charting the innovation ecosystem. *Research-Technology Management, 57*(4), 55–59.
55 Gawer, A., & Cusumano, M. A. (2014). Industry platforms and ecosystem innovation. *Journal of Product Innovation Management, 31*(3), 417–433; Gnyawali, D. R., & Park, B.-J. (2011). Co-opetition between giants: Collaboration with competitors for technological innovation. *Research Policy, 40*, 650–663.
56 Valkokari, K. (2015). Business, innovation, and knowledge ecosystems: How they differ and how to survive and thrive within them. *Technology Innovation Management Review, 5*(8), 17.
57 Oh, D. S., Phillips, F., Park, S., & Lee, E. (2016). Innovation ecosystems: A critical examination. *Technovation, 54*, 1–6.
58 Ibid.

5

NEW PRODUCTS

State of the art of new product development

A wide range of issues permeates the recent literature on theory and practice of new product development (NPD). A survey of these contributions—a sampling of what appears in print—follows. We focus here on the key issues that are typical of the challenges in developing new ideas embodied in products to offer for sale: what the best sources of ideas are and how to realize these ideas successfully.

Entrepreneurial orientation

Cassia et al. (2011) found that:

> Family firms clearly emerge as more long-term oriented than non-family enterprises. The long-term orientation of family businesses vs. non-family companies seems to play a pivotal role in originating NPD projects with long-term thrust. If a company is long-term oriented it is reasonable to expect that it will put its long-term vision in NPD programs, thus reaching a NPD long-term thrust.[1]

The study begs the question: is it family or ownership that matters? In Europe there are many large family-controlled firms.

An alternative conceptualization, entrepreneurial orientation (EO), originally introduced by Danny Miller,[2] which plays a prominent role in our own research in the next chapter on service innovation, and continues to be of interest in NPD. For example, in one study the focus was on co-development: in a sample of 171 manufacturing firms, it was found that a firm's EO was associated with increases in joint innovation, although the effect declines with higher levels of uncertainty. However, the authors also report that as the focal firm absorbs partners' knowledge, joint innovation does increase joint product innovation.[3]

Sustainable new products

Sustainability research drives much of our own NPD work ethic,[4] and we are not alone. In the auto industry, stakeholders are exerting pressure to follow sustainable strategies and practices. The advantage the auto industry has is high economies of scale, which will allow profitable green operations.[5] Recently, the US EPA failed to succumb to lobbying pressure from the auto industry and did not soften the CAFÉ 54.5 mpg target for 2025, but this may change with a new administration.

Value co-creation (VCC) in NPD features prominently in literature currently, perhaps because of the lack of:

> ...understanding of its conceptual boundaries and empirical constituents. Our search of the diverse scholarly literature on VCC identified 149 papers, from which we extract the two primary conceptual VCC dimensions of co-production and value-in-use. Though the combination of these two distinct dimensions is theoretically necessary to describe VCC, 79% of the studies in our dataset consider only one or the other. Such underlying theoretical ambiguity may explain conflicting results in earlier studies....[6]

It seems unlikely that any further progress in understanding NPD will be made without casting a wider theoretical net beyond the marketing function. At a very minimum, R&D has to be included, whether formalized or practiced. Not surprisingly, one study found that for R&D alliances using longitudinal data in the IT industry:

> ...knowledge acquisition is on average positively associated with firms' numbers of new products. However, I also find that knowledge acquisition is substantially more beneficial for new product development both when firms and their partners are active in similar technology domains and when they operate in distinct product markets.[7]

Another example of this research stream is the recent contribution by Grimpe et al. The authors studied 866 cross-industry German firms and found that pursuit of a dual strategy, investing in both innovative marketing and R&D simultaneously, leads to degraded performance.[8] Further, Gmelin and Seuring conducted five in-depth case studies of the auto industry and found that sustainability is rare in the NPD process in these firms even when R&D is focused on sustainability projects.[9]

Dangelico et al. studied 189 Italian manufacturing firms and found that two ordinary sustainability-oriented capabilities (resource building and configuration) were the only factors directly linked to market performance.[10] External resource integration was also important in that it enhances green innovation capability. Hofman et al. also studied configuration and found contractual (configuration) coordination is important in achieving high performance in R&D projects, but this needs to be complemented with safeguarding functions in some contexts.[11]

Networks

Networks may be just as important as ownership. For example, in one study, it was found that networks provide resources needed for any number of tasks required to move ideas from R&D to commercialization, such as customer education, distribution, marketing, and the like.[12]

Strategic orientation continues to appear in literature. Mu et al. (2017) found that strategic orientation alone was insufficient to predict NPD performance and that networking capability and ability, market orientation, and EO need to be added to the causal model, especially these last three factors, which all need to be high to ensure NPD success.[13] Informal networks can also impact success. Sosa et al. (2015) report that task interdependence has a significant impact on team integration, moderated by third parties.[14]

This line of work is bolstered by continued interest in the "strength of ties" construct, which often is far reaching in its models of NPD. For example, O'Connor's framework examined:

> ...the formation of tie strength between first-time alliance [and] suggest[s] that the required "degree and type" of inter-organizational learning is contingent on the project characteristics (degree of innovation; "radical versus incremental," and the mode of development; "modular versus integrated"). This relationship is moderated by the partners' technical skills (complementary versus similar).[15]

We have extended this work on weak ties to include internal networks in R&D. We studied 6 out of 19 R&D departments and a total of 390 engineers in 49 project groups (69% response rate). These respondents had an average age of 38 years. We found that "...for high-performing project groups, boundary-spanning technical advice tends to compensate for a lack of internal group heterogeneity and vice versa." The implications of this study reinforce the need to simultaneously study internal and external crowdsourcing, which is introduced next.[16]

Crowdsourcing

Crowdsourcing has emerged as a central tool in the arsenal of NPD, and examples abound of the open innovation (OI) paradigm.[17] One example is a study that professionals and users can provide effective ideas to solve consumer goods market issues for baby products. However, the source of the idea will impact novelty versus feasibility. Users ideas are more novel and provide greater customer benefit but not as feasible.[18] The case examples of this effect are illuminating. Take for example the case of Barilla's effort at crowdsourcing (this is a case available from Harvard, but also published in *Business Horizons* Vol. 57, 2014, 425–434). This case of the world's largest pasta company does very well with MBAs, and I have used it with groups in class, as they present and discuss various questions, especially trying to ascertain why Barilla did not follow through on one of the most visionary suggestions of establishing a theme park. It turns out that Barilla has since made some important strategic shifts well beyond their MIW (Mill I Wish) crowdsourcing effort with customers in this case. Barilla has opened restaurants in New York City and has made a commitment to healthy food products. There are a number of teaching cases like this that illustrate the trade-offs of crowdsourcing as illustrated in emerging research. Further, there is research that supports the idea that crowdsourcing will convert local to distant search, but novel ideas are less likely to be adopted because they are not as familiar to the firm.[19]

Perhaps one of the most compelling lines of research investigates the pre- and post-crowdsourcing experience and whether or not participant satisfaction discourages future engagement. Pinto and dos Santos (2018) found that participants in crowdsourcing place greater importance on intrinsic motivational factors (learning, fun, and satisfaction) than extrinsic factors (acknowledgment).[20] Piyathasanan et al. (2018) found that customer loyalty decreased after a contest and announcement of winners, but their "epistemic value perception did not change over time."[21] The implication of this finding is that when participants received feedback, even when feedback was unexpectedly disappointing, epistemic, or self-fulfilling, aroused curiosity, fulfilled knowledge, and improved skills.

User innovation has enjoyed a renewed interest as enthusiasm for OI increases. Another example is Cui and Wu (2016)[22] who focused on:

> …three forms of customer involvement in innovation: customer involvement as an information source (CIS), customer involvement as co-developers (CIC), and customer involvement as innovators (CIN)…. Using primary data from multiple industries, we test a set of drivers along these three dimensions and find that the three forms of customer involvement are driven by different factors.[23]

Other research using meta-analysis has found that customer involvement in NPD has an impact on outcomes depending upon the context and finds that the timing of customers in the NPD will have different impacts on outcomes. For example, when customers are involved in ideation, it has a positive impact on product financial performance including acceleration of time to market. However, when customers are involved in the later stages of NPD, like development, it has the opposite effect and slows time to market. Further, customers have a greater impact on product performance in technologically turbulent contexts, in emerging countries, in low-technology industries, and for business customers and small firms.[24]

Another recent study by Cui and Wu (2017) attempted to find out how customer involvement impacts the NPD process. Drawing on a random sample of 264 respondents in the Product Development Management Association (PDMA) database, they found that there are two types of customer involvement with more or less direct involvement in the NPD process. Customers can be information sources (lower involvement) or co-developers (closer to the von Hippel notion of a lead user). They found that the information-providing customers are more beneficial to new product outcomes when the firm is taking an experimental approach to development. The co-development model works better when the firm is not experimenting or allowing little room for experimentation. The implications of these findings are that the two types of customer involvement can substitute for each other and are contingent on the learning approach taken by firms.[25]

Coopetition has emerged as an alternative to customer involvement in a number of industries. Bouncken et al. (2018) studied 1,049 NPD alliances in the German medical and machinery sectors and found that coopetition benefits incremental innovation in the pre-launch and launch phases of NPD, but radical innovation benefits only in the launch phase.[26] This reinforces findings reviewed in Chapter 3 and later in this chapter as well. Competitors don't always play fair,[27] and firms often rate "informal" competition as more important than formal competition. Panico (2017) found when firms perceive greater synergetic benefits, they invest more to create value, but they also compete more intensely in order to capture additional value.[28] This suggests that the way firms structure their alliances to create trust and value avoids wasting resources in competition.

Maria Stock et al. (2017) utilized the boundary theory to examine data from 135 managers and 415 subordinates and found that there was a positive interactive effect of innovation-oriented strategy and transformational leadership, but the combined effect does not hold. They also found an inverted U-shaped relationship between co-development and the companies' new product frequency, which suggests that "more is better" is not the case in co-development.[29]

Virtual teams, especially of engineers spread across many time zones, continue to occupy much of the literature on NPD, apparently because not all firms, especially small-to-medium enterprises (SMEs), have discovered the advantages of this "dislocated" method of idea generation and implementation. A recent example follows:

> Virtual research and development (R&D) teams in SMEs can offer a solution to speed up time to market of new product development (NPD). The results suggest that the process construct is strongly correlated to the effectiveness of virtual teams. Therefore, NPD managers in virtual R&D teams should concentrate on the process of new product development rather than simply equipping the teams with the latest technology or employing highly qualified experts.[30]

Another recent study on virtual teams found that information and communication technology (ICT) seems to be a key driver for integration of NPD teams. Higher quality, better service, and superior customer responsiveness results.[31]

Methods and tools to enhance NPD

Methods and tools to improve NPD performance continue to be touted in literature, including time and cost reduction and lean approaches to improving the process,[32] with no obvious end in sight. One wonders, with the general consensus in literature that radical new technology projects take longer, whether this is just nibbling at the margins of the challenge. Functional integration within the firm, as well as across external organizational boundaries, continues to be important in journals and at the stage of the development process. Examples include consideration of the role of finance in addition to the more typical interfaces like R&D and marketing. Hempelmann[33] studied:

> ...389 project team leaders and top management team members from companies in the United States, Australia, New Zealand, Germany, and Austria. The findings suggest that the integration of finance in cross-functional teams positively impacts project performance.... The results indicate that the R&D-finance interface is most critical at the early stage of a project, while the marketing-finance interface is most important at the late stage, and that the integration between R&D and finance is especially useful in the development of less innovative products.[34]

Blohm et al. (2018) provide guidelines to firms hosting crowdsourcing platforms, using 19 case studies. They found that integrating crowdsourcing with strategy is a necessary starting point echoed in much of the other literature cited here.[35] The next step is to build up from scalable structures, once proof of concept is established. The final action, once at full scale, is to monitor satisfaction using the addition of "direct feedback" from contributors (qualitative). Not surprisingly, this is the direction in which much of the current research on crowdsourcing is moving.

Much of the new literature on NPD and supply-chain impacts on NPD involve digital and other emerging technologies like additive manufacturing (3D printing). Digital manufacturing is an important development in several fields such as operations management and management information systems.[36] Seeking a balance between quantitative and qualitative means of obtaining data and feedback appears to emerge as a critical applied research topic in this stream of studies. For example, Nada Sanders and Morgan Swink have begun an important study on digital supply chain, and their initial observations are quite revelatory. It may be that just a few companies have established strategic commitments to digital manufacturing in their supply chain policies, but this may be quite rare in practice.[37]

Service innovation

Although the topic of service versus product innovation is taken up in the next chapter, it is worth noting here that NPD and new service development (NSD) are quite different in current theory and practice. For years, we have lived in a developing world that assumes new products and new services are more or less the same. Bankers, software companies, hospitals, insurance companies, universities, etc., took models like Stage-Gate™ and tweaked these methods to make them fit their service development realities.

One of the purposes here is to set the record straight: services are different, period. The intention is to show, with the aid of the best sources, experiences, and cases, how to take careful account of the differences that make every successful new offering unique. New services are taken up in Chapter 6.

New products: new-to-the-world and not so new

One of the principles introduced in Chapter 3 was that radical innovation is rare, different, and takes a long time when compared to incremental innovation. It is important to also assert that the process needed to introduce a successful new product with radical technological features is quite different than all other kinds of innovation (e.g., architectural, modular, and disruptive). Yes, radical innovation is sometimes called discontinuous, but recall from Chapter 4 that is it not disruptive technology.

Now, on to the point: radical innovation is rare, and radically new products are becoming scarce. Further, in the US there were 30,000 new products introduced in 2003, but only 5% were big winners.[38] Below are some statistics from the Academy of Marketing Science to demonstrate this conclusion.

The most recent data available on proportion of products new to the world is included in the 2012 PMDA survey. First, the reported success rate is stable:

> The success rate of NPD continued to be stable: 58% in 1990, 59% in 1995, and 59% in 2004. However, the percentage of sales and profits from new products declined: 28% for sales and 28.3% for profits in 2004 compared with 32.4% and 30.6% in 1995 and 32.6% and 33.2% in 1990.[39]

One explanation for this decline is that there continues to be fewer products introduced that are new-to-the-world.

Support for this conclusion is found in the results of a Deloitte survey[40] of board membership priorities: "… only 35% of [board members] respond that they had radical innovation as a bullet point on their board agenda, leaving 65% without a formalized item for discussion or action at meetings." Additionally, the same survey found that 78% of board members had no separate division or department devoted to radical change.[41] Ironically, we have no current data to quote on the proportion of products or services new to the world. In the Chen et al. survey of supply chain innovation (mostly new process) a comparable percentage of new-to-the-world examples was 5%.[42]

So what are we to make of these distinctions between radical and incremental product improvement? Early work sets the stage for understanding the implications of this distinction, which remains quite salient. The July 2017 special issue of the *Journal of Product Innovation Management* was devoted to organizing for radical innovation. In the editorial introducing the issue the editors say radical innovation is fraught with risk but brings extensive economic rewards, and that most problems stem from the inadequate organizational arrangements to support radical innovation processes.[43] This is the essence of synchronous innovation for weak appropriation conditions, which is a major theme of Chapter 7, as well as new products typical of strong appropriation regimes.

The open innovation paradox

There are enough case example exceptions to the general trends towards "open" everything to begin to ask serious applied research questions about what theory actually operates on the grand scale for innovators. The paradox is well documented in the literature—sharing with outsiders leaves the firm vulnerable to technological spillovers—regarding unintended sharing of intellectual property.[44] There are ways around the paradox. Take the case history of Välinge, the Swedish firm that conducts R&D, produces new flooring prototypes, and then contracts out manufacturing:

> Välinge Innovation AB operates as a research and development, and IP company in flooring, furniture, and surface industries. The company develops and patents new product concepts related to flooring, furniture, and surfaces; and commercializes those technologies through licensing and production. Its IP portfolio includes ACTIO2, a flooring additive that improves indoor air quality, and contributes to a cleaner and healthier floor surface; mechanical locking systems for various types of flooring; digital printing solutions; The Ammonite Creadigit, a single pass digital printer for demanding board printing; furniture technology; LVT 3D-Core, a technology for luxury vinyl tiles...[45]

What is suggested by this case example is that OI is only for incremental innovation, and it resolves the Arrow paradox of openness: why share information with outsiders and risk technological spillovers?

We have preliminary findings from a study of 75 US power train projects underway in auto suppliers and assemblers that also suggests a way of boundary management to partially reconcile the OI paradox.[46] What we have found so far is that firms that target powerful competitors are significantly more likely to achieve new product success, but success is inversely, and significantly, related to the novelty of technology incorporated in these projects. Further, targeting is inversely, and significantly related to the use of internal networks to source ideas and information for these same projects. These preliminary findings suggest that there is a boundary maintained by these firms to resolve the OI paradox—firms protect their advanced and novel technologies internally, and target competitors with incremental technology projects leading to new product launches.

What endures: understanding new product development

Many people believe there is a trade-off between speed to market, quality, and product performance. The work published by Cohen et al. (1996) might be the best place to visit the issue of what endures in NPD.[47]

Professor Cohen and his colleagues have developed a model that has much to say about the additive multistage model of the new product development process. Some of the most profound conclusions are:

- Concentrate efforts on the most productive stages of the new product development process—this may vary by firm—and outsource non-core strengths. Don't allocate efforts evenly across all the stages of the NPD process.
- There is little or no point in developing an *ambitious* new product if the competitive performance is either very low or very high.
- Concentrating on time-to-market alone and minimizing this time period tends to lead to incremental product improvement and does not maximize profits. Product performance must also be taken into account.
- New products with superior performance effectively act as an entry barrier—both timewise and performancewise—for competitors.
- Replacing existing products always delays the time-to-market and performance target for the new product vis-a-vis introducing the first generation of new products.
- The optimal strategy is to use faster speed of improvement to develop a better product rather than to develop a product faster.

The last result contradicts much of the common wisdom that it is better to use incremental product improvement over significant product improvement when competing.

Our own work supports these conclusions. In our recent survey of the new products and the development process efforts for US durable goods manufacturing, we asked representatives of 126 NPD teams if they had a program in place to upgrade the NPD process. In nearly 90% of these cases, managers answered yes to this question.[48]

What was the focus of these programs to improve the NPD process? We expected time to market to be the most important issue and to dominate these survey reports, given the popular and professional publications of the day. This was not the case: In 47 (39%) of the valid response cases of NPD, quality was the most important focus of the program development effort. True, time to market was second, with 44 (36%) of the cases, but it was not first, and it did not dominate responses. Quality and time to market accounted for 91 (75%) of the valid responses. [Recall that this includes 13 (11%) of the respondents who said they had no new program to upgrade the NPD process. Five cases were missing responses to this question.]

We concluded that a balanced strategy of NPD effort improvement was the key to success in durable goods manufacturing. Further, we found that an integrated approach to NPD—well beyond the minimal notion of simultaneous engineering teams—is required and significantly supports product market and customer knowledge development efforts. These NPD process improvement efforts can significantly enhance the odds of new product success. For example, "balanced" sourcing of ideas (i.e., giving equal weight to R&D and marketing in new product idea generation and refinement) can improve the odds of new product commercial success by 30%.[49]

This raises the issue of what the role of marketing should be in NPD. Our recent findings suggest the following. The relationship between marketing and R&D in the new product development process is central to successful commercialization and in learning how to improve this process faster than competitors. The history of formal investigation of this integration challenge is quite substantial, perhaps starting with the published work of William Souder.[50] The marketing-operations integration success was more dependent on project novelty than process, per se. Most studies underestimate the complexity of NPD.[51] There has been a resurgence in interest in boundary spanning as part of the new product and NSD process, most likely because of the increasing use of virtual teams in digital environments.[52]

We studied a sample of 75 US automotive R&D projects (assemblers and suppliers) engaged in jointly developed R&D projects initiated as a response to an increasingly stringent regulatory environment, and reported our pilot findings.[53] These R&D projects represented a multi-year research program and embody the aggregation of significant new powertrain technologies in response to changing regulatory requirements for fuel economy and emissions. We obtained a 33% response rate, which is quite good given the proprietary nature of the subject.

Only two of the project ideas were sourced from marketing and 12 from customers, but these two sources were significantly correlated ($r = 0.376$, $p = 0.002$, $n = 67$). Marketing ideation was inversely correlated with the stage of the project ($r = -0.272$, $p = 0.032$, $n = 62$), which indicates that the more recent-stage new projects were market driven. Marketing ideation was inversely related to novelty of the project ($r = 0.349$, $p = 0.004$, $n = 67$), which supports the market pull, technology-push hypothesis. Market sourcing ideas were inversely correlated with market performance of projects in the last few years ($r = -0.270$, $p = 0.04$, $n = 58$), which suggests that market information can be an important motivator for radical product technology inception.

Customer ideation was inversely correlated with combining existing capabilities for the project ($r = -0.229$, $p = 0.066$, $n = 65$) and novelty of the technology incorporated in the project ($r = -0.207$, $p = 0.093$, $n = 67$). Customer ideation was directly associated with technical services ($r = 0.264$, $p = 0.031$, $n = 67$) and use of external consultants ($r = 0.264$, $p = 0.031$, $p = 67$), which supports the boundary-spanning hypothesis. Customer ideation was inversely correlated with use of technology centers for internal networking ($r = -0.363$, $p = 0.019$, $n = 58$) as was marketing ideation ($r = -293$, $p = 0.025$, $n = 58$).

These findings, suggest a limited, but important role for marketing and customers in discontinuous technology projects in this industry. Feedback from warranty work and learning on projects that incorporate new technology might align internal and external boundary spanning in the NPD process. Market information can be an important motivator for radical product technology inception. Continuous improvement of existing product lines provides the resources needed for breakthroughs.[54]

Our first study of food packaging innovation was really the beginning of this research stream. Firms often adopt different structures for incremental innovation initiatives than for radical innovation processes.[55] Since then, ambidextrous organization literature has burgeoned,[56] with most firms (2/3) using simultaneous or structural means of focusing on short- and long-term innovation projects.

Much of our work on idea sourcing got started with a comparative study we did comparing US and German firms.[57] The results are presented in Table 5.1. What we found was that product and service firms are quite different in how they source ideas, with general management being very important in services

TABLE 5.1 Significant positive (+) and negative (−) correlates of idea source (Role within the firm) and overall commercial success

	Comparative Study			*Total = 254 firms*
	1990–1992 US[a]	*2004 (US)*	*2004 (GER)*	*Service 2005*
Role Inside the Firm	*(n = 126)*	*(n = 47)*	*(n = 39)*	*(n = 42)*
R&D staff		+	+	
First level technical supervision	+			
R&D middle management			+	
VP of R&D			+	
General management	−			+
Marketing/ distribution/sales	+	+	+	
Production				
Engineering		+	+	
Finance	−			
Technical services				
Other (e.g., purchasing)	−			

Source: Reproduced with permission, Ettlie, J. E., and Elsenbach, J. Res. Technol. Manage., 50, 59–66, 2007.

a   Not shown is the there was a significant, negative correlation between using a government source for the new product idea and new product success. That is, if the government was the source of the idea for the new product, it was significantly more likely to fail.

but not manufacturing, regardless of country of origin. We tested and replicated this finding later in our service-manufacturing comparative study. Quite unexpectedly, general-manager ideas are not likely to lead to successful new product in US manufacturing.[58] German firms find ideas in general management likely because SMEs are prevalent in the EU. Marketing, and to a lesser extent, engineering and R&D staff, are common sources of ideas in companies from both countries.

Updating the staged and phased approach to NPD

Perhaps the most important development in improving the NPD process has been the aggressive experimentation with virtual engineering and design that many global companies have experienced in the last five years. One of the things our current research has verified is that the vaulted stage-gate process, popularized by Professor Robert Cooper and others, has changed significantly since first introduced.[59]

Many a fan and proponent of the stage-gate or phase-gate process used to guide the new product and NSD process has argued that it has promoted speed-up, better quality, greater discipline, and overall better performance for all concerned.[60] Rarely has the question of the impact of stage-gate on innovation in NPD been raised or investigated.[61]

We surveyed 72 automotive engineering managers involved in supervision of the NPD process.[62] All the major companies were represented in the sample, including the largest assemblers like GM, Ford, DCX, Honda, Toyota, Subaru, Nissan, and Fiat/Alpha Romeo, as well as the large first-tier suppliers, like Delphi, JCI, Visteon, Lear, Magna, Bosch, Siemens, and many others, representing a total of 60 firms (company membership and results were not correlated).

First, we were able to replicate earlier findings from the PDMA's benchmarking survey in our distribution of stage-gate usage (e.g., NPD success rate after product introduction−=60%)[63] About half (48.6%) of respondents say their companies used a traditional stage-gate process. About 20% of respondents said they had no formal or informal stage-gate process. Nearly 30% of respondents said they used a modified stage-gate process. How were these 30%-ers different? In order to investigate this question, we correlated stage-gate responses (modified scored 4, etc.) with other constructs and measures in the survey. We found the following significant relationships:

1. Use of virtual teams ($r = 0.334$, $p = 0.005$, $n = 70$).
2. Adoption of collaborative and virtual NPD software supporting tools, like CAD-neutral technology ($r = 0.27$, $p = 0.048$, $n = 54$).
3. Formalized strategies in place specifically designed to guide the NPD process ($r = 0.331$, $p = 0.005$, $n = 70$).
4. Structured processes used to guide the NPD process ($r = 0.319$, $p = 0.008$, $n = 69$).

Given the apparent emerging importance of modified stage-gate in the NPD process, we began to look more closely at how companies report changing this reasonably well-accepted means of promoting NPD. Here is what we found:

1. All 21 respondents who said their companies used modified stage-gate explained how they did this.
2. The frequency distribution of types of modifications (See Table 5.2 for raw data) indicates a hierarchy of reasons for breaking the discipline of stage-gate, and some explanation will be required, given the nature of these responses. The most common way of modifying the stage-gate process is allowing backtracking (cases bolded in Table 5.2). In some instances, gates can swing both ways, depending upon circumstances. Nine of the 21 respondents said this.
3. The second most common reason given for modifying the stage-gate process was that program or project management dictates often overrule stage-gate, including guidelines for continuous improvement. One of the eight respondents in this category said "continuous improvement specific to our process." Another said "modified depending upon resources required, market...perceived opportunity." A third said "internal program management process."
4. Finally, we found in our earlier pilot study interviews and follow-up visits to nearly a dozen of these firms that collaborative engineering tools are

TABLE 5.2 Significant correlates of new product success

1. **Customer perception of product advantage (0.363)**
   Product Advantage. Product Advantage refers to the customer's perception of product superiority with respect to quality, cost-benefit ratio, or function relative to competitors.
2. **Protocol (product and marketing requirements) (0.341)**
   Protocol. Protocol refers to the firm's knowledge and understanding of specific marketing and technical aspects prior to product development, for example: (1) the target market; (2) customer needs, wants, and preferences; (3) the product concept; and (4) product specification and requirements. This factor includes "origin of idea measures as well."
3. **Proficiency in marketing activities (0.337)**
   Proficiency of Market-Related Activities. This factor specifies proficiency of marketing research, customer tests of prototypes or samples, test markets/trial selling, service, advertising, distribution, and market launch.
4. **Strategy for the project (0.324)**
   Strategy. This factor indicates the strategic impetus for the development of a project (e.g., defensive, reactive, proactive, imitative). Measures of product positioning strategy are included, as are measures of "fit" between the new product and corporate strategy.

Source: Adapted from Montoya-Weiss, M., & Calantone, R., *J. Prod. Innov. Manag.*, 11, 397–417, 1994.

allowing substantial improvement of the stage-gate. One manufacturer of diesel engines said that virtual teaming software has almost eliminated the need for program reviews thus preventing delays on projects by implementing "any-time, anywhere" program review processes. Managers typically do not delegate sign-off on design reviews in this industry, and delays often occur under the old methodologies when team members miss face-to-face meetings. Mini-reviews have streamlined the process significantly in this industry, making promises of 50% reduced time to launch a reality since this was an initial aspiration over a decade ago.

Predicting new product success

Mitzi Montoya-Weiss and Roger Calantone have published a meta-analysis (systematic statistical review of the literature) on new product performance.[64] For statistically inclined readers, their table, summarizing the statistical results of the meta-analysis, is reproduced below in Table 5.3.

In Table 5.2, the four top factors that predict new product commercial success are summarized for use in rating any new product idea, once it reaches the prototype stage.

These are not the only factors that are associated with new product success, but they are the most important. Study Table 5.3 for a comparison of these factors with the others evaluated. Note that speed to market was not very important. Montoya-Weiss and Calantone say that this could be because not many studies have rigorously investigated speed. Materials presented earlier suggest that speed is the only important factor under relatively rare circumstances. In some industries, like high-technology products markets where product life cycles are short, speed is essential. Occasionally, a firm encounters unusual circumstances, for example, when a competitor is about to enter your product or geographic space.[65]

The results of application of these four predictors of NPD commercial success have been adapted and used in workshops, graduate classes, and dozens of times in executive programs on NPD in many countries (US, Germany, Hungary, etc.). The outcomes of these exercises have replicated the effects of applying these four factors to predict the outcomes of a new product launch nearly 95% of the time (Table 5.4). The purpose of this line of research is twofold. First, can a reported summary of findings from meta-analysis be converted to a classroom or executive education seminar to further test and utilize finding from such summary work? Second, to what extent does culture influences these effects? The findings are clear and consistent in follow-up applications of the method is that experiences in four MBA classes in Portugal nearly perfectly replicated the earlier results.[66] That is, at least Western culturally embedded firms don't really impact outcomes of the exercise, but the technical (or not) background of participants does impact results: engineers and scientists tend to be more conservative than non-technical participants.

TABLE 5.3 Correlations of strategic, process, market, and organizational factors with new product success

Factor	Number of Studies	Percent of Total[a]	Number of Measures	Average Measures/ Study	r	IrI	Range	
Strategic factors:								
Technological synergy	6	50	18	3.0	0.218	0.273	−0.332	0.446
Product advantage	5	42	22	4.4	0.311	0.363	−0.426	0.518
Marketing synergy	5	42	24	4.8	0.137	0.303	−0.312	0.479
Company resources	3	25	4	1.3	0.297	0.297	0.191	0.446
Strategy	1	8	9	9.0	0.324	0.324	0.190	0.510
Development process factors:								
Protocol	7	58	27	3.9	0.293	0.341	−0.471	0.599
Prof. technical activities	7	58	27	3.9	0.256	0.282	−0.352	0.415
Prof. marketing activities	5	42	20	4.0	0.308	0.337	−0.0297	0.517
Prof. pre-develop. activities	5	42	14	2.8	0.240	0.288	−0.331	0.370
Top management support/skill	2	17	12	6.0	0.232	0.260	−0.169	0.380
Financial/business analysis	1	8	4	4.0	0.182	0.267	−0.170	0.330
Speed to market	1	8	1	1.0	0.177	0.177	0.177	
Costs	0	0	0	0	0	0	N/A	
Market environment factors:								
Market potential	4	33	18	4.5	0.179	0.244	−0.260	0.453
Environment	2	17	4	2.0	0.293	0.293	0.180	0.380
Market competitiveness	0	0	0	0	0	0	N/A	
Organizational factors:								
Internal/external relations	3	25	15	5.0	0.305	0.305	0.145	0.604
Organizational factors	3	25	16	5.3	0.304	0.304	0.080	0.500

Source: Reproduced with permission, Montoya-Weiss, M., and Calantone, R., *J. Prod. Innov. Manag.,* 11, 397–417.

a Twelve studies were included in this analysis.

TABLE 5.4 Portuguese graduate business class averages resulting from an exercise to predict new

	New Product Success			
	E.M.B.A.	M.B.A.	E.M.B.A.	M.B.A.
	July 2005	June 2005	June 2005	July 2003
	(Mixed)	(Mixed)	(Technical)	(Technical)
Mean %	70%	70%	65%	64%
Number of students	(n = 15)	(n = 22)	(n = 25)	(n = 23)
Means (%)		70%		64.5%

Source: Ettlie, J. E., J. Prod. Innov. Manag., 24, 180–183, 2007.

In a classroom setting in October 2018, we replicated the Acuson case exercise, and MBA students predicted the Sequoia's probability of success to be median value of 67.25% while the instructor (Dr. Ettlie) independently predicted 70%. In class, March 4, 2019, the MBA students predicted a median value of 72% for the commercial success of the Sequoia, and the instructor (Dr. Ettlie) independently predicted 72%, going out on a high note for the academic year.

Marketing and managers involved in NPD teams nearly always predict a new product example (Acuson Sequoia) to be successful 70% of the time, while engineers and other technically trained professionals with the same information say the probability of success of the launch case is either 64% or 65%, which replicated results from 2002.[67]

In 2016, I used this four-factor predictive model and the Acuson Sequoia case in my annual executive seminar in Holland in a 14-student, MIS, technically heavy class, and I predicted an average of 67%, similar to the results in Portugal. The actual results were the following: mean resulting prediction of product success (defined as a multiple-return on investment in a reasonable period of time) was 66.85% with a mean and a mode of 70%, which means it's not perfect, but consistently good as a predictor. Discipline and function matter, but country (at least Western countries) matters little. It is important to note that when I first started using this exercise in 1998 and compared US, Czech, and Hungarian students, there was a similar pattern. I didn't "prepare" the class with the year-after-year reported average success rate of launched new products of 60%. Twenty years later, this exercise, which fosters better understanding of the discipline collaboration needed for NPD success, is still effective as an exercise.

In the summer 2019 core course for MBAs on new products and new services, we ran the exercise on the Harvard Case of Curled Metal Inc.—Engineered Products Division (9-709-434, rev. March 14, 2014) with the following consistent results. The class rated the probability of success of the cushion pad product at median = 70%, and mean = 68.4%, and while the instructor (Dr. Ettlie) wrote down before the scores were tallied an estimate of 69%. The exercise is a gem. It even seems to transcend occupational and educational background in the more recent applications—as long as the group knows the average success rate after introduction is 60%.

Notes

1 Cassia, L., De Massis, A., & Pizzurno, E. (2011). An exploratory investigation on NPD in small family businesses from Northern Italy. *International Journal of Business, Management and Social Sciences, 2*(2), 1–14.
2 Miller, D. (1984). A longitudinal study of the corporate life cycle. *Management Science, 30*(10), 1161-1183.
3 Bouncken, R. B., Plüschke, B. D., & Pesch, R. et al. (2016). Entrepreneurial orientation in vertical alliances: Joint product innovation and learning from allies. *Review of Managerial Science,* 10, 381.
4 Rothenberg, S., & Ettlie, J. E. (2011). Strategies to cope with regulatory uncertainty in the auto industry. *California Management Review, 54*(1), 126–144.
5 Gouda, S. K., Jonnalagedda, S., & Saranga, H. (2016). Design for the environment: Impact of regulatory policies on product development. *European Journal of Operational Research, 248*(2), 558–570.
6 Ranjan, K. R., & Read, S. (2016). Value co-creation: Concept and measurement. *Journal of the Academy of Marketing Science, 44*(3), 290–315.
7 Frankort, H. T. (2016). When does knowledge acquisition in R&D alliances increase new product development? The moderating roles of technological relatedness and product-market competition. *Research Policy, 45*(1), 291–302.
8 Grimpe, C., Sofka, W., Bhargava, M., & Chatterjee, R. (2017). R&D, marketing innovation, and new product performance: A mixed methods study. *Journal of Product Innovation Management, 34*(3), 360–383.
9 Gmelin, H., & Seuring, S. (2018). Sustainability and new product development: Five exploratory case studies in the automotive industry. In M. Brandenburg, G. J. Hahn, & T. Rebs (Eds.), *Social and environmental dimensions of organizations and supply chains* (pp. 211–232). Cham, Switzerland: Springer.
10 Dangelico, R. M., Pujari, D., & Pontrandolfo, P. (2017). Green product innovation in manufacturing firms: A sustainability-oriented dynamic capability perspective. *Business Strategy and the Environment, 26*(4), 490–506.
11 Hofman, E., Faems, D., & Schleimer, S. C. (2017). Governing collaborative new product development: Toward a configurational perspective on the role of contracts. *Journal of Product Innovation Management, 34*(6), 739–756.
12 Aarikka-Stenroos, L., & Sandberg, B. (2012). From new-product development to commercialization through networks. *Journal of Business Research, 65*(2), 198–206.
13 Mu, J., Thomas, E., Peng, G., & Di Benedetto, A. (2017). Strategic orientation and new product development performance: The role of networking capability and networking ability. *Industrial Marketing Management, 64,* 187–201.
14 Sosa, M. E., Gargiulo, M., & Rowles, C. (2015). Can informal communication networks disrupt coordination in new product development projects? *Organization Science, 26*(4), 1059–1078.
15 Badir, Y. F., & O'Connor, G. C. (2015). The formation of tie strength in a strategic alliance's first new product development project: The influence of project and partners' characteristics. *Journal of Product Innovation Management, 32*(1), 154–169.
16 Wilson, D. O., & Ettlie, J. E. (2019). Boundary spanning, group heterogeneity and engineering project performance. *International Journal of Innovation and Technology Management, 16*(1), 1–36.
17 Tucci, C. L., Afuah, A., & Viscusi, G. (2018). *Creating and capturing value through crowdsourcing,* Oxford, UK: Oxford University Press.

18 Poetz, M. K., & Schreier, M. (2012). The value of crowdsourcing: Can users really compete with professionals in generating new product ideas? *Journal of Product Innovation Management, 29*(2), 245–256.

19 Piezunka, H., & Dahlander, L. (2015). Distant search, narrow attention: How crowding alters organizations' filtering of suggestions in crowdsourcing. *Academy of Management Journal, 58*(3), 856–880.

20 Pinto, L. F. S., & dos Santos, C. D. (2018). Motivations of crowdsourcing contributors. *Innovation & Management Review, 15*(1), 58–72.

21 Piyathasanan, B., Mathies, C., Patterson, P. G., & de Ruyter, K. (2018). Continued value creation in crowdsourcing from creative process engagement. *Journal of Services Marketing, 32*(1), 19–33.

22 Cui, A. S., & Wu, F. (2016). Utilizing customer knowledge in innovation: Antecedents and impact of customer involvement on new product performance. *Journal of the Academy of Marketing Science, 44*(4), 516–538.

23 Ibid., p. 516.

24 Chang, W., & Taylor, S. (2016). The effectiveness of customer participation in new product development: A meta-analysis. *Journal of Marketing, 80*(1), 47–64.

25 Cui, A. S., & Wu, F. (2017). The impact of customer involvement on new product development: Contingent and substitutive effects. *Journal of Product Innovation Management, 34*(1), 60–80.

26 Bouncken, R. B., Fredrich, V., Ritala, P., & Kraus, S. (2018). Coopetition in new product development alliances: Advantages and tensions for incremental and radical innovation. *British Journal of Management, 29*(3), 391–410.

27 McCann, B. T., & Bahl, M. (2017). The influence of competition from informal firms on new product development. *Strategic Management Journal, 38*(7), 1518–1535.

28 Panico, C. (2017). Strategic interaction in alliances. *Strategic Management Journal, 38*(8), 1646–1667.

29 Maria Stock, R., Zacharias, N. A., & Schnellbaecher, A. (2017). How do strategy and leadership styles jointly affect co-development and its innovation outcomes? *Journal of Product Innovation Management, 34*(2), 201–222.

30 Ebrahim, N. A. (2015). Virtual R&D teams: A new model for product development. *International Journal of Innovation, 3*(2), 1–27.

31 Lohikoski, P., Kujala, J., Härkönen, J., Haapasalo, H., & Muhos, M. (2015). Enhancing communication practices in virtual new product development projects. *International Journal of Innovation in the Digital Economy, 6*(4), 16–36.

32 Kane, G. C., Palmer, D., Phillips, A. N., Kiron, D., & Buckley, N. (2016). Aligning the organization for its digital future. *MIT Sloan Management Review, 58*(1); and Parker, H., & Brey, Z. (2015). Collaboration costs and new product development performance. *Journal of Business Research, 68*(7), 1653–1656; and Tyagi, S., Choudhary, A., Cai, X., & Yang, K. (2015). Value stream mapping to reduce the lead-time of a product development process. *International Journal of Production Economics, 160*, 202–212; and Karlsson, C., & Ahlström, P. (1996). The difficult path to lean product development. *Journal of Product Innovation Management, 13*(4), 283–295.

33 Hempelmann, F., & Engelen, A. (2015). Integration of finance with marketing and R & D in new product development: The role of project stage. *Journal of Product Innovation Management, 32*(4), 636–654.

34 Ibid., p. 636.

35 Blohm, I., Zogaj, S., Bretschneider, U., & Leimeister, J. M. (2018). How to manage crowdsourcing platforms effectively? *California Management Review, 60*(2), 122–149.

36 Nambisan, S., Lyytinen, K., Majchrzak, A., & Song, M. (2017). Digital innovation management: Reinventing innovation management research in a digital world. *Mis Quarterly, 41*(1).

37 Sanders, N., and Swink, M. (2019). Digital supply chain transformation: Visualizing the possibilities. *Supply Chain Management Review, 1*, 30–41.

38 Phil Lempert is The Supermarket Guru®, http://www.supermarketguru.com/page. cfm/485. Note that even though 5% might be big winners, about 60% of new products actually are successful once introduced (return a multiple of the investment) and this number has been stable for many years (cf. Crawford, M., *New Product Management*, 5th edition, 1997, Homewood, IL: Irwin). From Ettlie (2007). *Managing Innovation*, 2nd edition, London, Routledge, p. 528.

39 Markham, S. K., & Lee, H. (2013). Product development and management association's 2012 comparative performance assessment study. *Journal of Product Innovation Management, 30*(3), 408–429.

40 Kane et al. (2016).

41 Ibid.

42 Chen, D., Preston, D., & Swink, M. (2015). How the use of big data analytics affects value creation in supply chain management. *Journal of Management Information Systems, 4*(32), 4–39.

43 Colombo, M. G., von Krogh, G., Rossi-Lamastra, C., & Stephan, P. E. (2017). Organizing for radical innovation: Exploring novel insights. *Journal of Product Innovation Management, 34*(4), 394–405.

44 Nerlove, M., & Arrow, K. J. (1962). Optimal advertising policy under dynamic conditions. *Economica, 29*(114), 129–142. doi:10.2307/2551549.

45 Retrieved from https://www.bloomberg.com/research/stocks/private/snapshot. asp?privcapid=7185278.

46 Gianiodis, P. T., Ettlie, J. E., & Murthy, R. (2019). External networks and targeted competition: Resolving boundary issues in open innovation. Working paper, July, Rochester, NY: Rochester Institute of Technology.

47 Cohen, M. A., Eliashberg, J., & Ho, T. H. (1996). Erratum. New product development: The performance and time-to-market tradeoff. *Management Science, 42*(12), 1753.

48 Ettlie, J. E., & Elsenbach, J. M. (2007). Modified Stage-Gate® regimes in new product development. *Journal of Product Innovation Management, 24*(1), 20–33.

49 See Ettlie, J. E. (1997). Integrated design and new product success. *Journal of Operations Management, 15*(1), 33–55, for findings on balanced development. Revisit Tom Allen and his associates work on technological gatekeepers concerning communication patterns in R&D (1978).

50 Souder, W. E. (1988). Managing relations between R&D and marketing in new product development projects. *Journal of Product Innovation Management: An international publication of the product development & management association, 5*(1), 6–19; and Moenaert, R. K., & Souder, W. E. (1990). An analysis of the use of extra-functional information by R&D and marketing personnel: Review and model. *Journal of Product Innovation Management: An international publication of the product development & management association, 7*(3), 213–229.

51 Slater, S. F., Mohr, J. J., & Sengupta, S. (2014). Radical product innovation capability: Literature review, synthesis, and illustrative research propositions. *Journal of Product Innovation Management, 31*, 552–566.

52 Ettlie and Elsenbach (2007).

53 Ibid., Rothenberg and Ettlie (2011). In an earlier study we found that "Using survey data from 72 auto company managers and their suppliers, the proposed model in which IT support for NPD influences the success of interfirm NPD partnerships through the mediating role of interfirm NPD partnership dynamic capabilities in high- and low-technology contexts was generally supported." Ettlie, J. E., & Pavlou, P. A. (2006). Technology-based new product development partnerships. *Decision Sciences, 37*(2), 117–147.

54 Ettlie, J. E., "Idea generation in NPD." Working paper, 2016.

55 Ettlie, J. E., Bridges, W. P., & O'Keefe, R. D. (1984). Organization strategy and structural differences for radical versus incremental innovation. *Management Science, 30*(6): 682–695.

56 O'Reilly III, C. A., & Tushman, M. L. (2013). Organizational ambidexterity: Past, present, and future. *Academy of Management Perspectives, 27*(4), 324–338.
57 Ettlie, J. E., & Elsenbach, J. (2007). The changing role of R&D gatekeepers. *Research-Technology Management, 50*(5), 59–66.
58 Ettlie, J. E., & Rosenthal, S. R. (2011). Service vs. manufacturing innovation. *Journal of Product Innovation Management, 28*(2), 285ff.
59 Cooper, R. G., & Kleinschmidt, E. J. (1993). Stage-gate systems for new product success. *Marketing Management, 1*(4), 20–29.
60 Although this was adapted from Cooper's work (1990) it appeared as reproduced here in Jeffery B. Schmidt, "Managerial commitment can be detrimental as well as beneficial, according to award-winning paper." *PDMA Visions, 27*(4), 22–23.
61 Griffin, A. (1997). PDMA research on new product development practices: Updating trends and benchmarking best practices. *Journal of Product Innovation Management: An International Publication of The Product Development & Management Association, 14*(6), 429–458.
62 Ettlie, J. E. (2007). Modified stage-gate regimes in new product development. *Journal of Product Innovation Management, 24*, 20–33.
63 Ibid. p. 429., Griffin, A., & Hauser, J. (1996). Integrating R&D and marketing: A review and analysis of the literature. *Journal of Product Innovation Management, 13*(3), 191–215.
64 Montoya-Weiss, M., & Calantone, R. (1994). Determinants of new product performance: A reviews and meta-analysis. *Journal of Product Innovation Management, 11*, 397–417.
65 Montoya-Weiss and Calantone (1994).
66 Ettlie, J. E. (2007). Perspective: Empirical generalization and the role of culture in new product development. *Journal of Product Innovation Management, 24*(2), 180–183.
67 Ettlie (2007).

6

NEW SERVICES

What's new?

We begin the chapter on service innovation with the outstanding difference between services and manufacturing: how do you measure services and service innovation? Brouwer and Kleinknecht[1] say that traditional measures of innovation like R&D spending, patents, licensing, etc., simply don't apply to services. In the Netherlands, R&D expenditures amount to only about one-quarter of the total investments in innovation, including capital expenditures on fixed assets, which amount to about half of all innovation-related budgets. This measurement difficulty may account for the mixed results reported on outcomes of new service introduction.[2]

Two review articles have attempted to sort through the maze of definitions and typologies of service innovation with an eye toward helping the development of useful theory in a field in its infancy. In the first article,[3] the authors review 1,301 academic articles on service innovation and use a three-category perspective to sort the 84 definitions: assimilation—or knowledge of product innovations for all offerings, 11 definitions; demarcation—or service is unique, 38 definitions; and synthesis—service perspective holds for all offerings, 35 definitions. They also conclude that the definition of service is changing. Specifically, the dominance of the synthesis perspective appears to be overstated, given the recent emphasis of articles on assimilation, which product offerings feature.[4]

In the second article, the authors review 1,046 academic articles and identify four unique service innovation categories: (1) degree of change, (2) type of change, (3) newness, and (4) means of provision. They observe that these categories tend to ignore customer value and financial performance.[5]

In a special issue of the *Journal of Service Research*, the editors make the leap that service design (human-centered) and service innovation need to be understood together in an effort to integrate the variety of perspectives on new services, including both the technological and non-technological dimensions of service innovation. They attend to the service-logic perspective that focuses on what they do (e.g., change customer thinking), not on new features.[6] One can hardly ignore the explosive trend toward digital services.[7] In this same vein, typologies still are published at this early stage of development of the service innovation field. One study focused on co-creation and archetypes of service innovation and concluded that four types of archetypes emerge: process based, output based, experiential based, and systemic based.[8]

User or customer involvement in new service development (NSD) is often the reason service firms are founded. My father started his machine tool maintenance and remanufacturing business in 1948 because of a request from a customer and by observing other entrepreneurs do the same. Magnusson et al. (2003)[9] examine the assumption of user involvement in successful NSD and find that this assumption is not always valid. In an experiment comparing the inputs of different groups and ideation, the more creative ideas are not always producible. User communities, crowdsourcing, and open innovation (OI) are generally trending subjects in current literature trends.[10] Big data has now emerged to be a part of this information technology tradition on service innovation.[11] Mobile data sources like iPhones facilitate big data processes.[12]

Partnering is often very important in NSD[13] since there typically is no formal budget for R&D in services. More recently, these issues have been bundled under the umbrella of the OI construct.[14] These OI examples include 3D printing platforms.[15] Co-creation is challenging, let alone fostering front-line employee involvement in NSD.[16]

A challenge service innovators face is the tendency to concentrate on customers' needs, which tend to drive most NSD toward incremental improvements on current offerings. In our own work, we find that continual beta testing of new ideas to satisfy customers tends to eliminate laboratory work (alpha testing) or breakthroughs,[17] which is presented later. Other researchers have found additional profound differences between service innovation and new products. For example, Nijssen et al. (2006)[18] write the following:

> We argue that R&D strength is more important for new product than service development, while a company's willingness to cannibalize organizational routines and prior investments is more important in the case of new service than new product development. The model and hypotheses are tested using data from 217 service-based and 105 product-based companies in The Netherlands.[19]

Current evidence suggests that strategy is crucial. Grawe et al. (2009) found that, "Although the relationship between cost orientation and service innovation is not supported, the relationships between customer orientation and competitor orientation and service innovation are supported. Additionally, the relationship between service innovation and market performance is supported."[20]

Application of the lead user or user-innovation construct began to appear in the literature of services about a decade ago.[21] Magnusson et al. (2003)[22] studied telecom services in an experiment and found:

> During periods of 12 days, three different groups were assigned the task of generating ideas for end user telecom services. One group consisted of professional designers, whereas the other two consisted of ordinary users. The users in one of the groups coped with idea creation by themselves, whereas the other group consulted a service design expert at two controlled meetings who provided feedback regarding technical feasibility. Involving users makes the ideas more original, holding a higher perceived user value, but the users' ideas are less producible on average.[23]

Another study further elaborates this relationship of co-development with customers. Gustafsson et al. (2012)[24] surveyed 334 managers focused on how customer co-creation was instrumental in NSD. The resulting of 207 were documented, including 77 radical innovations. Findings indicated the following:

> ...three of the four dimensions of customer co-creation (frequency, direction, and content) have a positive and equally significant effect on product success when developing incremental innovations. For radical innovations, frequency has a positive effect and content has a negative significant effect on product success.[25]

Lead users tend to be rare, especially in NSD. We found only 1 case in 9 of NSD by manufacturing firms.[26] Belz and Baumbach (2010) report that:

> [l]ead users are rare subjects, which are difficult to detect, [and] empirical results of our explorative study of the online community utopia show that 9 out of 40 of the most active online community members possess lead user attributes (22.5%).[27]

Capabilities continue to be of interest to most researchers, regardless of innovation research stream. Van Riel et al. (2004)[28] used 251 innovation projects in Europe, the US, and Japan and report that the success of innovation was directly related to how well-informed and knowledgeable decision-makers are, although calculated risk-takers often decide with less information than peers. They also report that market orientation contributes to success through organizational climate favorable to information sharing, power, and intelligence gathering with respect to customers and technology. The effects of competitor orientation are important as we report in our study of external and internal networks.[29]

Many of these studies focus on one industry. Blazevic and Lievens (2004) found "...that the level of project learning contributes to the corporate reputation of the financial institution [and] learning during project innovation enhances the cost and the competitive position of the innovating bank."[30] A survey study of 1,000 travelers in the hospitality industry found ... that service innovation does matter when guests are selecting a hotel, with type of lodging having the largest impact on a customer's hotel choice. In addition, service innovation is found to have a larger influence on choices when guests are staying at economy hotels rather than mid-range to up-scale hotels [and] leisure travelers were found to be more influenced by innovative amenities such as childcare programs and in-room kitchenettes than business travelers:[31]

> Several of the more recent studies compare products and services, as covered later in this chapter. Nijssen et al. (2006)[32] used data from 217 service-based and 105 product-based companies in the Netherlands and found that "... R&D strength is more important for new product than service development, while a company's willingness to cannibalize organizational routines and prior investments is more important in the case of new service than new product development." Comparative studies are relatively rare as well. Alam (2006)[33] used a sample in the US of 274 northeastern large financial service firms and an Australian sampling frame consisting of 262 firms situated in the southeast region of Australia and found, "...firms in both the countries use different new service strategies to compete in the industry and emphasize different sets of development stages in developing new services."[34]

Service blueprinting continues as a dominant technique for applying research in the field. However, Bitner et al. (2008)[35] observe:

> [A] 2007 article [on] Business Week's top twenty-five most innovative companies includes a number of service businesses (e.g., Google, Walt Disney, Wal-Mart, Starbucks, Target, Amazon and E-Bay), [and] the number of innovators is not nearly reflective of the size of the service sector [and adoption of service blueprinting is rare]. A recent comprehensive review of the academic literature on product innovation also reveals little explicit coverage of research on service innovation.

Service-dominant logic (SDL)[36] is another emerging framework to organize service innovation efforts but also has limited citation in the literature. An exception is the study reported by Ordanini and Parasuraman (2011).[37] Using data from a sample of luxury hotels, they found:

> (a) ...collaborating with customers fosters innovation volume but not radicalness (and vice versa for collaborating with business partners); (b) a firm's customer orientation—both directly and in interaction with innovative orientation—contributes to innovation radicalness; (c) collaborating with contact employees enhances both innovation volume and radicalness; (d) the use of knowledge integration mechanisms contributes to innovation radicalness (but not volume); and (e) both innovation outcomes have significant but somewhat different effects on the two performance measures.[38]

The MIS perspective on SDL appears in Lusch and Nambisan (2015),[39] and digital technology generally in Barrett et al. (2015).[40]

Networks continue to be important in services and in innovation ecosystems generally. Agarwal and Selen (2009)[41] argue that partnering on networks requires substantial internal capabilities, similar to Chesbrough's contentions in his book[42] on open service innovation. Some limited empirical findings substantiate this theory (Eisingerich et al. 2009).[43] This contention is supported in other studies as well.[44] Other research on open service innovation continues to appear. Mina et al. (2014)[45] contend that OI practices promote the adoption of services in manufacturing firms, as well as informal knowledge-exchange activities.

Strategy concerning partners and service innovation continue as critical topics in the literature. Grawe et al. (2009)[46] surveyed the supply-chain manager and found, counter to predictions, that the "…relationship between cost orientation and service innovation is not supported [but] the relationships between customer orientation and competitor orientation and service innovation are supported [as well as] the relationship between service innovation and market performance [as predicted]."[47] Strategy and business model innovation appear to be part of this trend.[48]

We know firms co-develop new products with suppliers, but what about services? One study investigated that exact question.[49] The authors studied 157 IT firms in Taiwan and report that "… co-production positively influences service innovation to a degree that depends on the collaborative partner's compatibility and history of business relations, affective <emotional> commitment, and expertise. Moreover, the business's innovation orientation enhances (moderates) the relationship between co-production and service innovation."[50]

Particularly relevant to the second half of this chapter is research on manufacturing firms moving into services. Santamaría et al. (2012)[51] studied Spanish firms and found:

> …that almost 20 percent of the firms in the sample have introduced such services in the recent past and that important differences exist between service and product (goods) innovations, with service innovations being particularly related to human resource development and closer links to customers. This suggests that service innovation by manufacturers has much in common with the innovation patterns detected in service sector firms. Intriguing differences across manufacturing sectors are also noted, with the lowest- and highest-tech sectors reporting more service innovations than the medium-tech sector.[52]

SDL, or the shifting from physical attributes of goods to value derived and experiences of customers, continues to be a topic of interest, and more recent research has challenged the overarching nature of this concept with enhancements. SDL, originally introduced by Vargo and Lusch (2004),[53] replaces the economic model of goods with intangible resources and co-creation of value.

Osborne (2018)[54] questions if SDL applies to public services and if they are capable of co-production and value co-creation. Osborne argues that public service logic might ultimately prevail due to the unique context and nature of public services. For example, "repeat business" might be a sign of failure for public services. Vargo et al. (2008)[55] argue that service science requires focusing on the use (integration and application of resources in a specific context) not the exchange (output captured by price) as an alternative to SDL.

Servitization is the attempt of product companies to increase revenue potential. Industry literature often documents the journey companies make to achieve this end.[56] Hollebeek and Andreassen (2018)[57] argue that resource integration is the key to service-based logic for service innovation. They propose a "hamburger" model of service innovation with actors representing the lower bun, antecedents/development/implement of service innovation in the middle, and outcomes as the top bun.

What endures?

Remaining true to the leitmotif of this volume, which is what endures from 40 years of research in the innovation studies field, we start with two early studies of service innovation. Both of these projects utilized primary data from the US transportation sector—multiple cases from each of the six modes of transport (rail, barge, trucking, air, shipping, and pipelines) using in-depth, multi-respondent interviews. The primary focus of the first report was attributes of the innovation being developed or considered for adoption.[58] We considered both primary (e.g., cost) and secondary attributes (e.g., complexity) of an innovation, after Downs and Mohr (1976),[59] with the interstage adoption period taken as dependent. We found:

> [T]he single best predictor of the amount of time required to progress from one stage of the decision-making process to the next was the cost of the innovation ($R^2 = 0.23$, $p < 0.01$), and a total of four valid predictors (*cost*, *complexity*, of the innovation, organizational *risk-taking climate*, and *union* reaction) account for about 42% of the variance (R^2) in the innovation and adoption time period….secondary innovation attributes act as intervening variables for the influence of *climate*, *union* reaction, and government *regulation* and *intervention* on the innovation and adoption time period.[60]

Perhaps even more compelling in the results were the findings we didn't predict from extant theory at the time, and considering we published this paper nearly 40 years ago, these results are still relevant today. Organization climate supporting calculated risk-taking was correlated with other constructs: (1) the relative advantage necessary for consideration and adoption will be lower than for more conservative firms, but this lower required relative advantage will also stimulate RD&E spending; (2) innovations considered for adoption were likely

to have fewer concrete performance criteria; and (3) innovations under development or adoption consideration were likely to be viewed as less complex, but
more time will be required to reduce this complexity through learning. In summary, a calculated risk-taking climate tends to lower the threshold for entertaining adoption of a particular technology but also tends to be correlated with an
increase in RD&E spending.

These results may explain why innovation attributes may no longer appear
in mainstream literature. First, the distinction between primary (e.g., cost) and
secondary (e.g., relative advantage) attributes doesn't seem to matter—perhaps
all attributes are subject to perception, even cost. Second, other factors seem to
matter as much, maybe even more, in the ultimate outcomes, like how much
effort and time is required to effectively assimilate a new technology and capture benefits in what amounts to weak appropriation conditions. One might
even hypothesize that all service innovations—to the extent that they cannot be
protected with contracts or patents—constitute weak appropriation conditions.
We also found that the:

> ...risk-taking climate of an organization alone will not have an impact
> on the perceived compatibility of the innovations considered for adoption
> nor the relative ease of testing or trying innovations on a limited basis, even
> though these two innovation attributes vary significantly and directly. One
> possible explanation for this result is that during the trial period, the innova-
> tion is modified to make it more compatible with organization constraints.[61]

It seems clear that the relative importance of a risk-taking climate may be limited in
the strength of its impact on outcomes in spite of its pervasive early stage influence
in the service innovation adoption process.

In the next study, which is a secondary analysis of these same transportation
innovation cases using the Abernathy–Utterback model of evolution of the productive segment, findings resulted in better understanding of a different theoretical
perspective in the early development stages of the innovation management field.[62]
Using a sample of 34 transportation innovations, the results were as follows:

1. Transportation firms in Stage I of the evolution of the productive segment
   are more likely to adopt service innovations, while firms in Stage III are
   more likely to adopt innovations designed to improve the process ($p < 0.05$).
2. No statistically significant results were found to support the hypothesis that
   Stage I transportation firms originate more innovations than Stage III firms,
   although the results were in the predicted direction ($0.10 < p < 0.15$).
3. Stage I transportation firms are more likely to adopt or consider for adoption
   lower-cost innovations than Stage III firms ($p < 0.05$), which is contrary to
   the hypothesized direction of this relationship. It was also found that transportation firms tend to originate new service innovations but adopt new
   process innovations ($p < 0.05$), regardless of stage of development.[63]

Even in the early stages of testing this theory, it appeared to have great promise across both products and services, but there was also clearly room for theoretical development, which came later. One promising contribution on the developments is the relationship between service and products in R&D organizations has recently appeared by Hidalgo and Albors (2008).[64]

The debate on total quality management (TQM) versus innovation has raged in literature for many years. One the one hand, there is evidence that TQM applies only to repetitive work, not R&D. Thambusamy and Palvia (2018)[65] studied 202 US health-care provider organizations and found that "…service innovation and quality play significant roles in mediating the relationship between IT-enabled capabilities and healthcare provider performance."[66]

Mike Johnson and I completed two studies on quality and innovation. The summaries of these two studies appear next. The bottom line is a contingency approach to the relationship between quality and innovation. This is especially shown in the second study we published on things-gone-wrong (TGW) and things-gone-right (TGR). We found that there is a trade-off between efforts to benchmark product development practices and customer focus when using the house of quality (QFD). Benchmarking on how competitors, peers, or role models develop products facilitates process improvement but hinders customer focus. We also found that smaller firms using QFD tend to gain more from customer focus and process improvement than larger firms.[67]

In our second study, we sought to make the critical connection between innovation and quality generally. We measured the relative importance that customers placed on product reliability, or TGW, and customization, or TGR, across a range of industrial settings. We found that R&D intensity is related to how companies score on the relative measures of quality: (1) when technological intensity is relatively low or high, customers place greater value on customization; and (2) when technological intensity is more intermediate, product reliability and customization are more equally important. This suggests that there could be an important relationship between maturity of a product and the relationship between R&D and quality. The inspiration for these hypotheses was originally suggested by the Utterback–Abernathy model. The predictions are tested and supported using data from the American Customer Satisfaction Index (ACSI) survey.[68]

It seems clear in subsequent publications that there is a reasonable convergence in conceptualization and empirical evidence that incremental and radical distinctions in products and services are an important delimitation to understand outcomes of any innovation process. Myhren et al. (2018)[69] studied incremental and radical open service innovation using nested case studies and found that a firm can have several groups working on different service innovation projects of predictable archetypes (e.g., internal versus satellite groups) similar to the ambidextrous organization paradigm. Helkkula et al. (2018)[70] also introduced four archetypes of service innovation based on different literature streams and theories: output-based archetype (e.g., product innovation); process-based archetype (NSD, OM); experimental archetype (phenomenological); and systemic archetype (e.g., social systems).

Steve Rosenthal and I renewed our collaboration on manufacturing innovation by embarking on a four-year project to find out what the true differences were between service and product innovation. We started with a sample of new products and new services in major corporations provided by working managers in our executive courses. What we found for a relatively small sample of each type of innovation became the beginning of an NSF project on only manufacturing firms introducing new service innovations not directly related to their core business, like On-Star, GM's on-board service tracking and interactive technology.[71]

In the first study, we compared 38 new products and 29 new services in cross-classification analysis and found statistically significant differences between the two types of innovation.[72] For example:

> Manufacturing is more likely to report the need for new strategies and structures when products are new to the industry or new to the firm. However, services are more likely to convert novelty into success. Services are significantly more likely to have a short beta testing process and to exploit general manager (internally sourced) ideas for new offerings as an alternative to formal innovation structures. However, manufacturing and services exhibit a similar tendency to exploit customer (externally sourced) ideas for new offerings.[73]

In our second study, we followed nine major manufacturing firms in their quest to introduce new services. All were eventually successful offerings, although one was spun off as a separate firm and one turned out to be a lead user innovation with a major customer. We also conducted two in-depth pilot case studies to develop our interview protocols.[74] We found that manufacturing firms embark on:

> ...two primary strategies [to] launch significant new service innovations representing important diversification moves for the firm. Both require CEO/president sponsorship but are founded on different corporate cultures. The engineering culture path to commercialization tends to nurture concepts new to the firm, requires multi-functional strategy making, and does well with champions from operations that have deep knowledge of the conversion process in the respective industry context. The entrepreneurial orientation path to commercialization tends to nurture concepts new to the industry or new to the world paired with sole champions from R&D or engineering. Either strategy works well depending upon development culture and available resources.[75]

Although the US is a service economy, like most developed nations, most people would agree that the service and non-service economies are quite interconnected. These dependencies are complex and, in the main, not well understood. General statements like "products and services follow the same rules" might be true, but no one who has ever seen videos, visited an automotive assembly line, or stood next to a blast furnace in scalding heat would see any similarities.

My colleagues and I set out many years ago to find out what the fundamental differences and similarities are between services and products, with great attention to the process that generates successful and unsuccessful new ventures. Our first study investigating this question of similarities and differences between new product and NSD processes, in its unpublished form, won an award at a conference sponsored by IBM at Carnegie Mellon University. It was a fledgling first effort, and the actual paper underwent many revisions before it was published, but it was one of the first to make direct comparisons of this type. What we found is that:

> Service and manufacturing firms are different when it comes to innovation.... Manufacturing is more likely to report the need for new strategies and structures when products are new to the industry or new to the firm. Services, on the other hand, are more likely to convert novelty into success. Services are significantly more likely to have a short beta testing process...<but unlike manufacturing> services exploit general manager (internally sourced) ideas for new offerings as an alternative to formal innovation structures. The equalizer is this: manufacturing and services exhibit a similar tendency to exploit customer (externally sourced) ideas for new offerings.
>
> Services and manufacturing appear to show us how there are alternative ways to formalize the innovative process. Services have (or are forced to have) a unique way and opportunity to test customer concepts and engage general managers and professionals in the development process.[76]

There continues to be great interest in manufacturing services journeys. Most recently, Mennens et al. (2018)[77] investigated Dutch manufacturing SMEs. They found employee collaboration and search breadth have an important impact on a firm's absorptive capacity. Context is important to service innovation, and emerging patterns across different industries are part of emerging research trends.[78]

It should come as no surprise that most academic literature on services appears in marketing and operations management literature. The fundamental difference between NSD and new product development (NPD) is the former lacks R&D underpinning. Our service firms spent less than 1% on R&D but were able to leverage great outcomes from these comparatively meager investments. Now service R&D is catching on. One recent example is the CarMax story, which is worth reading and following.[79]

CarMax is the largest multi-market used car dealer in the US. It has a unique approach to using corporate social media management recruitment and contrasts it to the webmaster, which reflects the growth in time people are spending online socially. Social media management influences brand awareness and brand reputation as well. The internal emphasis on the open office is a means of achieving creative movement to solutions that would otherwise out of reach of the typical reseller of vehicles.[80]

When Steve Rosenthal and I decided to follow up our initial study with an NSF-sponsored study of manufacturing services, we insisted, based on case studies like Caterpillar Tractor's diversification in retail, that we'd only be interested in the kind of services that manufacturing performs in product support and truly represents a new category of market entrance. We found only 25% of our contacts were willing to participate in a long-term study of new services roll out, but many discussed their efforts off-record. The developing themes in these non-published reports are instructive. When customers ask for a service, and are willing to pay for it, it is extremely hard for a firm to turn them down.

Another emergent theme in these unpublished reports is how difficult it is to make a business case for a service when manufacturing is the core business of the firm. Often the service is an internal strength like the corporate logistics of Caterpillar. The logistics service business has taken on a whole different, independent business model and management as a result. Medical services are similar, but the liability of providing a non-regulated service in a regulated industry is often tricky for a firm to execute.

There is little doubt that service innovation and NSD will continue to dominate much of the future literature of innovation studies because the business case is now well established, as it always has been for the ease of starting a service firm with little or no capital. When my father started his machine-tool repair and remanufacturing business, we didn't even have a hot water heater in our house. Fortunately, my grandfather's garage, located near to the city center of Milwaukee, was warm winter and summer.

Notes

1 Brouwer, E., & Kleinknecht, A. (1997). Measuring the unmeasurable: A country's non-R&D expenditure on product and service innovation. *Research policy, 25*(8), 1235–1242.
2 Ordanini, A., Parasuraman, A., & Rubera, G. (2014). When the recipe is more important than the ingredients: A qualitative comparative analysis (QCA) of service innovation configurations. *Journal of Service Research, 17*(2), 134–149.
3 Wittel, L. et al. (2016). Defining service innovation: A review and synthesis. *Journal of Business Research, 69*(8), 2863–2872.
4 Ibid.
5 Snyder, H. et al. (2016). Identifying categories of service innovation: A review and synthesis of the Literature. *Journal of Business Research, 69*(7), 2401–2408.
6 Patricio, L. et al. (2017). Upframing service design and innovation for research impact. *Journal of Service Research, 21*(1), 3–16. doi:10.1177/1094670517746780.
7 Peters, C. et al. (2016). Emerging digital frontiers for service innovation. *Communications of the Association of Information Systems, 39*, 3–11. doi:10.17705/1CAIS.03908.
8 Helkkula, A. et al. (2018). Archetypes of service innovation: Implications for value co-creation. *Journal of Service Research, 23*(3), 284–301.
9 Magnusson, P. R., Matthing, J., & Kristensson, P. (2003). Managing user involvement in service innovation: Experiments with innovating end users. *Journal of Service Research, 6*(2), 111–124.
10 Di Gangi, P. M., Wasko, M. M., & Hooker, R. E. (2010). Getting customers' ideas to work for you: Learning from dell how to succeed with online user innovation

communities. *MIS Quarterly Executive, 9*(4), 4; and Balka, K., Raasch, C., & Herstatt, C. (2014). The effect of selective openness on value creation in user innovation communities. *Journal of Product Innovation Management, 31*(2), 392–407.

11 Agarwal, R., & Selen, W. (2009). Dynamic capability building in service value networks for achieving service innovation. *Decision Sciences, 40*(3), 431–475; and Mahr, D., & Lievens, A. (2012). Virtual lead user communities: Drivers of knowledge creation for innovation. *Research policy, 41*(1), 167–177.

12 Ye, H., & Kankanhalli, A. (2018). User service innovation on mobile phone platforms: Investigating impacts of lead userness, toolkit support, and design autonomy. *MIS Quarterly, 42*(1), 165–187. doi:10.25300/MISQ/2018/12361.

13 Eisingerich, A. B., Rubera, G., & Seifert, M. (2009). Managing service innovation and interorganizational relationships for firm performance: To commit or diversify? *Journal of Service Research, 11*(4), 344–356; and Chen, J. S., Tsou, H. T., & Ching, R. K. (2011). Co-production and its effects on service innovation. *Industrial Marketing Management, 40*(8), 1331–1346; and Gustafsson, A., Kristensson, P., & Witell, L. (2012). Customer co-creation in service innovation: A matter of communication? *Journal of Service Management, 23*(3), 311–327.

14 Mina, A. et al. (2014). Open service innovation and the firm's search for external knowledge. *Research Policy, 43*(5), 853–866. doi:10.1016/j.respol.2013.07.004, and Bogers, M., & West, J. (2012). Managing distributed innovation: Strategic utilization of open and user innovation. *Creativity and Innovation Management, 21*(1), 61–75.

15 Rayna, T., Striukova, L., & Darlington, J. (2015). Co-creation and user innovation: The role of online 3D printing platforms. *Journal of Engineering and Technology Management, 37*, 90–102.

16 Karlsson, J. (2018). *Frontline employees' role in service innovation and value creation.* Doctoral dissertation, Karlstads universitet.

17 Ettlie, J. E., & Rosenthal, S. R. (2011). Service versus manufacturing innovation. *Journal of Product Innovation Management Special Issue: Special Issue on Agent-Based Modeling of Innovation Diffusion, 28*(2), 285–299.

18 Nijssen, E. J., Hillebrand, B., Vermeulen, P. A., & Kemp, R. G. (2006). Exploring product and service innovation similarities and differences. *International Journal of Research in Marketing, 23*(3), 241–251.

19 Ibid., p. 241.

20 Grawe, S. J., Chen, H., & Daugherty, P. J. (2009). The relationship between strategic orientation, service innovation, and performance. *International Journal of Physical Distribution & Logistics Management, 39*(4), 282–300.

21 Eisenberg, I. (2011). Lead-user research for breakthrough innovation. *Research-Technology Management, 54*(1), 50–58; and Baldwin, C., & Von Hippel, E. (2011). Modeling a paradigm shift: From producer innovation to user and open collaborative innovation. *Organization Science, 22*(6), 1399–1417; and Marchi, G., Giachetti, C., & De Gennaro, P. (2011). Extending lead-user theory to online brand communities: The case of the community Ducati. *Technovation, 31*(8), 350–361; and Hienerth, C., and C. Lettl, 2011. Exploring how peer communities enable lead user innovations to become standard equipment in the industry: Community pull effects. *Journal of Product Innovation Management, 28*(s1), 175–195.

22 Magnusson, et al. (2003).

23 Ibid., p. 111.

24 Gustafsson et al. (2012).

25 Ibid.

26 Ettlie, J. E., & Rosenthal, S. R. (2012). Service innovation in manufacturing. *Journal of Service Management, 23*(3), 440–454.

27 Belz, F. M., & Baumbach, W. (2010). Netnography as a method of lead user identification. *Creativity and Innovation Management, 19*(3), 304–313.

28 Van Riel, A. C., Lemmink, J., & Ouwersloot, H. (2004). High-technology service innovation success: A decision-making perspective. *Journal of Product Innovation Management, 21*(5), 348–359.

29 Ibid.

30 Blazevic, V., & Lievens, A. (2004). Learning during the new financial service innovation process: Antecedents and performance effects. *Journal of Business Research, 57*(4), 374–391.

31 Victorino, L., Verma, R., Plaschka, G., & Dev, C. (2005). Service innovation and customer choices in the hospitality industry. *Managing Service Quality: An International Journal,* 15(6), 555–576.

32 Nijssen et al. (2006, p. 241).

33 Alam, I. (2006). Service innovation strategy and process: A cross-national comparative analysis. *International Marketing Review, 23*(3), 234–254.

34 Ibid.

35 Bitner, M. J., Ostrom, A. L., & Morgan, F. N. (2008). Service blueprinting: A practical technique for service innovation. *California Management Review, 50*(3), 66–94.

36 Spohrer, J., & Maglio, P. P. (2008). The emergence of service science: Toward systematic service innovations to accelerate co-creation of value. *Production and Operations Management, 17*(3), 238–246.

37 Ordanini, A., & Parasuraman, A. (2011). Service innovation viewed through a service-dominant logic lens: A conceptual framework and empirical analysis. *Journal of Service Research, 14*(1), 3–23.

38 Ibid., p. 3.

39 Lusch, R. F., & Nambisan, S. (2015). Service innovation: A service-dominant logic perspective. *MIS Quarterly, 39*(1), 155–175. doi:10.25300/MISQ/2015/39.1.07.

40 Barrett, M., Davidson, E., Prabhu, J., & Vargo, S. L. (2015). Service innovation in the digital age: Key contributions and future directions. *MIS Quarterly, 39*(1), 135–154.

41 Agarwal, R., & Selen, W. (2009). Dynamic capability building in service value networks for achieving service innovation. *Decision Sciences, 40*(3), 431–475.

42 Chesbrough, H. (2011). *Open Services Innovation.* Hoboken, NJ: Jossey-Bass.

43 Eisingerich et al. (2009).

44 Kindström, D., Kowalkowski, C., & Sandberg, E. (2013). Enabling service innovation: A dynamic capabilities approach. *Journal of Business Research, 66*(8), 1063–1073.

45 Mina, A., Bascavusoglu-Moreau, E., & Hughes, A. (2014). Open service innovation and the firm's search for external knowledge. *Research Policy, 43*(5), 853–866.

46 Grawe, S. J., Chen, H., & Daugherty, P. J. (2009). The relationship between strategic orientation, service innovation, and performance. *International Journal of Physical Distribution & Logistics Management, 39*(4), 282–300.

47 Ibid.

48 Maglio, P. P., & Spohrer, J. (2013). A service science perspective on business model innovation. *Industrial Marketing Management, 42*(5), 665–670.

49 Chen, J. S., Tsou, H. T., & Ching, R. K. (2011). Co-production and its effects on service innovation. *Industrial Marketing Management, 40*(8), 1331–1346.

50 Ibid., p. 1331.

51 Santamaría, L., Nieto, M. J., & Miles, I. (2012). Service innovation in manufacturing firms: Evidence from Spain. *Technovation, 32*(2), 144–155.

52 Ibid., p. 144.

53 Vargo, S., & Lusch, R. (2004). Evolving to a new dominant logic for marketing. *Journal of Marketing, 68*(1), 1–17.

54 Osborne, S. P. (2018). "From public service-dominant logic to public service logic: Are public service organizations capable of co-production and value co-creation?" *Public Management Review, 20*(2), 225–231.

55 Vargo, S. L., Maglio, P. P., & Akaka, M. A. (2008). On value and value co-creation: A service systems and service logic perspective. *European Management Journal, 26*(3), 145–152.

56 Lindhult, E., Chirumalla, K., Oghazi, P., & Parida, V. (2018). Value logics for service innovation: Practice-driven implications for service-dominant logic. *Service Business, 12*(3), 457–481.

57 Hollebeek, L. D., & Andreassen, T. W. (2018). The SD logic-informed "hamburger" model of service innovation and its implications for engagement and value. *Journal of Services Marketing, 32*(1), 1–7.

58 Ettlie, J. E., & Vellenga, D. B. (1979). The adoption time period for some transportation innovations. *Management Science, 25*(5), 429–443.

59 Downs, G. W., & Mohr, L. B. (1976). Conceptual issues in the study of innovation. *Administrative Science Quarterly, 21*(4), 700–714.

60 Ettlie and Vellenga (1979).

61 Ibid.

62 Ettlie, J. E. (1979). Evolution of the productive segment and transportation innovations. *Decision Sciences, 10*(3), 399–411.

63 Ibid.

64 Hidalgo, A., & Albors, J. (2008). "Innovation management techniques and tools: A review from theory and practice," *R&D Management, 38*(2), 113–127.

65 Thambusamy, R., & Palvia, P. (2018). US healthcare provider capabilities and performance: The mediating roles of service innovation and quality. *Information Systems Frontiers*, 1–21.

66 Ibid., p. 1.

67 Ettlie, J. E., & Johnson, M. D. (1994). Product development benchmarking versus customer focus in applications of quality function deployment. *Marketing Letters, 5*(2), 107–116. http://hdl.handle.net/2027.42/47150.

68 Johnson, M. D., & Ettlie, J. E. (2001). Technology, customization, and reliability. *Journal of Quality Management, 6*(2), 193–210. doi:10.1016/S1084-8568(01)00037-2.

69 Myhren, P., Witell, L., Gustafsson, A., & Gebauer, H. (2018). Incremental and radical open service innovation. *Journal of Services Marketing, 32*(2), 101–112.

70 Helkkula et al. (2018).

71 Ettlie and Rosenthal (2012).

72 Ettlie, J. E., & Rosenthal, S. R. (2011) Service versus product innovation. *Journal of Product Innovation Management, 28*(2), 285–299.

73 Ibid., p. 285.

74 Ibid.

75 Ettlie and Rosenthal (2012).

76 Ettlie and Rosenthal (2011).

77 Mennens, K., Van Gils, A., Odekerken-Schröder, G., & Letterie, W. (2018). Exploring antecedents of service innovation performance in manufacturing SMEs. *International Small Business Journal, 36*(5), 500–520.

78 Edvardsson et al. (2018). Examining how context Change foster service Innovation. *Journal of Service Management, 29*(5), 932–955.

79 Lal, R., & Kiron, D., "CarMax." Harvard Business School Case 505–080, June 2005.

80 Montalvo, R. E. (2011). Social media management. *International Journal of Management & Information Systems (IJMIS), 15*(3), 91–96. https://doi.org/10.19030/ijmis.v15i3.4645. Also see: © 2011 The Clute Institute Companies such as, Audi, E-Trade, and CarMax all used social media platforms that included Facebook, Twitter, and You Tube in support of their Super Bowl advertising (Steinberg & Schultz, 2011). ... Futurist, 45(2), 29–34. 5.

7

PROCESS INNOVATION

What's new?

Most of us have probably not heard of Eckart Frankenberger, who is the chief industrial architect at Airbus SE and responsible for leading the design of a new modular assembly process for the A320 in Hamburg. Eckcart says, "The philosophy of this hanger was to make it as flexible as possible and thereby more efficient," and this is enabled by "open spaces, robots, and mobile assembly platforms operated by remote control."[1] In other words, manufacturing scale has been surpassed by manufacturing scope[2] of operations in this assembly operation, which is at the heart of this chapter.

Consider an alternative case: Boeing's current dilemma captured by the front-page headlines in the *Sunday New York Times*: "Boeing Dreamline Plant Accused of Safety Lapses; Claims of Sloppy Work on the Popular Jet—Whistle-Blowers Cite Retribution,"[3] based on a review of "hundreds of pages of internal emails, corporate documents, etc." All of this was precipitated by the accelerated production schedule for the Boeing 787, which was more than 2 years late in launch. This is the most devastating news, on top of the issues apparently causing the grounding of the new 737 Max, which was implicated in two fatal crashes.

Digital manufacturing is a current version of this enabling technology to achieve scope-driven operations. Firms have been serious about manufacturing strategies including digital for at least 20 years. First and foremost, digital manufacturing is not just 3D printing or additive manufacturing.[4] The promise of digital manufacturing is the complete integration of the value-added chain for existing and new product offerings.[5] Digital integration represents the next stage of an evolution from computer-integrated manufacturing, enterprise resource planning (ERP), customer requirements management (CRM), and global integrated supply chains, for which considerable theory and research exist. It should come as no surprise the term "digital manufacturing" is slowly replacing terms like: advanced manufacturing technology (AMT), integrated manufacturing, and process innovation. These themes are covered separately below. The prediction of this chapter is that digital manufacturing will follow patterns already established in this evolutionary cycle and that synchronous innovation (SI) extrapolation of the mirroring hypothesis will predict the variance of successful adoption and implementation of these ecosystems.

Digital manufacturing represents the next step-function in manufacturing integration evolution,[6] especially as it incorporates open innovation, but this is by no means a foregone conclusion when it comes to value capture. At a recent operations management professional meeting in which I was in attendance, a vice president of a very large firm presented an in-depth case history of digital-supply-chain integration into manufacturing. At the end of the presentation, this senior manager was asked two questions. First, what was his firm doing about cybersecurity in their digital journey? The astounding answer was (paraphrased): no one is interested in our supply chain and manufacturing data. The second question was an observation that R&D had not been mentioned in his presentation (this firm spends 15% or more of revenues on R&D). His answer was (paraphrased): if you get things right with digital and can show that it works, then everyone else in the firm will come along with your plan. What plan was that? Leave R&D out of digital manufacturing? Urbinati et al.[7] argue that digital transformation is essential to enable innovation, but if our speaker quoted above is typical, and there is a silo between R&D and operations coupled with supply chains, then there continue to be significant challenges ahead. Others[8] raise concerns in the transition to digital and the commercial outcomes.

The theory-based, empirical evidence concerning the successful adoption of digital manufacturing is quite limited. Ardolino et al.[9] argue that the internet of things (IoT) is essential for digital services. It is argued in Chapter 10 that IoT is one of the challenges of the dark side of innovation that further complicates understanding of this technology even more.

Case studies abound. For example, Holmstrom and Partanen[10] use "... the theory of combinatorial technological evolution [to] examine the F-18 Super Hornet... to illustrate service supply chain for a complex product." However, supply chain alone is not truly an application of digital manufacturing because the customer wasn't part of the ecosystem. Urbinati et al. (2018) used nine case studies in different industries to suggest management actions needed to enable digital technologies, including reorganization of R&D and transition to open innovation.[11]

In a case study of the Italian food industry's transition to digital manufacturing, Savastano et al. (2018) observe that "only a limited number of companies have already made rapid advances by developing high digital capabilities necessary to obtain competitive advantage."[12] Most authors include additive manufacturing within digital transitions,[13] but there are a wide range of technologies such as holographic, IoT, beam interference, fused deposition, and many others.

Additive manufacturing in small-to-medium enterprises (SMEs) has become a separate and special topic, which echoes earlier generations of adoption of new process technology like ERP. Martinsuo and Luomarant[14] find that depending upon the position in the supply chain, design firms experience different challenges than manufacturing suppliers making capital investment decisions.

It is rarely recognized that digital manufacturing is an evolutionary step from material requirement planning (MRP), ERP, product data management (PDM), and CRM systems already in place in many firms worldwide. This transition has been variously called Industry 4.0,[15] and many authors show how AMT and its link to R&D have enabled decentralization of innovation connecting to subsidiaries. Most authors agree that Industry 4.0 and digitization apply across economic sectors and many industries. There continues to be interest in accounting for AMT[16] and factors that influence implementation success. Kumar et al. found:

> The redesign of the production system and organization strategy is directly related to the AMT implementation. The notable finding is that the AMT implementation has no direct impact on the redesign of human resources, but it has mediated impact on the production system.[17]

The issue of organization innovations enabling successful adoption of process innovation is taken up in the next section at the end of this chapter with the introduction of SI.

Rare exceptions to case studies are observations like those in Lee et al. (2011),[18] which show how digital manufacturing capitalizes on existing integrated systems like ERP. They say that digital manufacturing can be used as a means of data integration between PDM and ERP.[19] Other authors have been early to predict this trend and this view of digital manufacturing.[20]

Several authors are continuing to study *process innovation* at the meta-level of analysis. In a recent case study, French ski-lift operators demonstrated how investments in process technology led to important improvements in productivity.[21] Nguyen and Harrison found significant customer leverage with process innovation and performance among 650 global manufacturing firms and 10 countries grouped by "developed" (e.g., USA, Korea, and Australia), "emerging" (e.g., Hungary), and "developing" (e.g., Croatia).[22]

More recently, cloud-based computing has topped digital manufacturing. Wu, Rosen, Wang, and Schaefer[23] extend the digital cloud-based system whereby "… consumers are enabled to configure, select, and utilize customized product realization resources and services ranging from computer-aided engineering software to reconfigurable manufacturing systems." The authors contend that the remaining challenges to cloud-based digital manufacturing are "definitions, key characteristics, computing architectures, communication and collaboration processes, crowdsourcing processes, information and communication infra-structure, programming models, data storage, and new business models." They also question, as we have above, if this is really anything new or radical. The contention of this chapter is that digital manufacturing is not about the technologies, but the beneficial adoption strategies, and an incremental step in SI.

Green manufacturing and supply chains continue to dominate a subset of relevant literature. However, the topic deserves a book in and of itself. Another important topic is the impact of digital manufacturing on employment. Dale Rogers is a pioneer in reverse logic and has contributed significantly to the research stream of reverse logistics. Most recently he introduced, with collaborators, a logistics index, which attempts to forecast economic trends from logistics decisions.[24]

Employment and digital transformation continue to be in the news and in the streams of applied research.[25] Given the wide-spread human capital shortages, the conclusion in literature is that this is not an issue of robots or AI taking over human jobs, but rather which jobs are best suited to robots and which to human intervention?[26]

What endures: the challenge of synchronous innovation

One has only to look at the research papers published after our original work appeared on simultaneous adoption of technological and organizational (sometimes called administrative) innovation to begin to understand the challenge of SI. Effective leveraging of corporate culture to create the unique capture of benefits from the adoption of new technology is often confused with organizational change. There are even courses on organizational change in graduate curricula, which do not help to clarify the difference between the two rubrics of change and innovation. Change involves implementing known solutions to problems and challenges. Innovation involves implementing new solutions: new-to-the-firm, new-to-the-industry, or new-to-the-world. This confusion is enabled by the typical process by which firms end up in the sweet spot of SI as outlined below:

> *Stage 1*: Planners underestimate the degree of difference between current technology in place and the stretch required to effectively implement the new technology: new skills, new complementary assets, new supporting technology, especially new organizational policies and structures, etc. They are often convinced, with the help of suppliers, that the gap between current capabilities and what will be required to master the new technology can be closed with training. This specific lack of understanding of what the future skill requirements will be, as well as what attendant structures are needed to support new capabilities including training and development is taken up below as a separate issue because it is important to grasp. Suffice it to say that the amount and type of training and development are not well understood early on in the process. Typically, training offered by suppliers is not an administrative innovation as most firms do it and often train the wrong people.

Stage 2: For those firms that can rise above the denial of what constitutes the adoption of new technology, there is hope. The first step of Stage 2 is to scale back the attempted technology in terms complexity and dynamism, or divide the project into phases and extend the period of implementation significantly. It is true that most large adoption projects would probably never be attempted if the actual time required to get it right was known from the beginning. Scope creep can be a good thing if exploited as a mutual learning experience between suppliers and adopters.

Stage 3: Stage 3 is the most difficult from the perspective of managing of the innovation process. Economists like David Teece rarely deal with firms facing weak appropriation conditions. Because it is investment folly to think that gains can be made on your competitors by investing in technology that you have no rights to and which can easily be purchased or otherwise acquired by your competitors. Invest in R&D that can be protected by strong intellectual property; don't "invest" in technology that is not protected. Some firms do try to protect adopted technology by contracting for exclusive rights to one supplier but they quickly find that just capturing a supplier's capacity is a more efficient strategy, even if it has a limited time horizon. Purchasing a supplier can even lead to more significant problems like the merger of two technology firms.

What happens next in Stage 3 of successful adoption makes this subject extremely worthwhile and why a deep understanding of SI is the hallmark of all competitive innovating firms. Stage 3 involves the development of organizational innovations: new strategies, policies, practices, and structures that exploit the unique cultural strengths of any firm that make it great. The thesis of this book, which is based on over 40 years of research, is that you can't have strong appropriation without weak appropriation. No one firm or entity can develop and protect all the technology it needs to be innovative. Therefore, both are important, and strong appropriation alone, even with complementary assets, is insufficient for sustained corporate growth and success.

Now we come to the critical challenge of Stage 3: what organizational innovations to set in motion to capture the benefits of adopted technology? There are several detailed examples of AMT in production and ERP in information technology (the "four factor" model), and office technology.[27] Beyond these context-dependent examples, a general theory of SI does not yet exist. However, there are some indications of what such a theory might look like, and this "mirroring hypothesis" is taken up later.

In addition to asking what innovation strategy and structure best exploits corporate culture and then acting on the answers with administrative experiments, it is essential to understand that trying to use benchmarking or other "externally" oriented methods of idea generation for organizational innovation typically doesn't work. Next we take up the misguided approach to SI, which is assuming that training is the answer to all challenges.

Training is not organizational innovation

A challenge on the journey to SI is the idea that organizational or administrative innovations will leverage the unique culture of the division or firm in question. While it is not necessary to be an expert in organizational culture to engage in this stage of the process, as most firm members understand the way things are done in their workplace, it is a difficult hurdle because of the variation associated with past remedies that have worked to solve problems. Training and development are a near-perfect example of this struggle because it is obvious that new skills will be required with new technologies. The way in which training and/or development is designed and applied is typically not innovative or even appropriate for successful adoption of new technology. Several examples from manufacturing and information systems follow.

There are many detailed accounts of how training is applied in cases of adoption of new manufacturing technology that demonstrate how training can be inappropriate, ineffective, and ultimately impede performance. The cases also delineate how training can rarely be considered an organizational or administrative innovation. Earlier accounts include our study of training for robotic system adoption in manufacturing.[28] At the time we did this research, the US was in what appeared to be a perilous competition with Japanese firms for the heart and soul of manufacturing. Two framing studies cited in our article set the stage for our study of 203 companies adopting robotic systems in the US, including a study by the National Commission for Employment Policy. The National Commission reported data from a 16-plant study showing little or no formal training was conducted in-house, leaving this to trade schools or the military, and that when a new machine was purchased, a few engineering staff received training from vendors. The engineers then *informally* trained workers.[29]

Another study by our colleagues at Boston University, Meg Graham and Steve Rosenthal, of eight US flexible manufacturing systems, found that foremen are usually the last to be trained, if trained at all.[30] One of the robotics companies we worked with at the University of Michigan was kind enough to provide the data from 203 installations of their systems for a secondary analysis, which reinforced the conclusions from these earlier studies. We focused on the question of how supplier training is utilized by these companies with, what seemed at the time, to be startling conclusions.

We found that the data included information on more than 4,500 trainees in 203 firms or divisions that purchased robots between 1981 and 1986. Only 23 (11%) of these installations included operator training. 50 firms (25%) included supervisors in training. By comparison, skilled trades were trained in 126 (62%) of these cases and engineers in 138 (68%) of the cases. Supplier representatives told us that the latter two groups get advanced training including programming in addition to the basics for operators or supervisors.[31]

Does it matter which occupational groups are trained? The simple answer is yes, in regards to "troubled robot" reports from the field from customers who could not solve problems with the system on their own. The supplier kept records of troubled robots from 1984 to 1986. There was a total of 23 troubled robot reports, which demonstrated chronic installation problems. We had data on four job titles, and three showed statistically significant differences for whether or not at least one member of the job title had been trained. Operators were least likely to be trained in troubled robot cases, and the difference was statistically significant ($p = 0.017$). In the same cases, skilled trades ($p = 0.047$) and engineers ($p = 0.005$) were more likely to be trained. The results for supervisors are not significant, since they were trained in 11 cases and not trained in 12 cases, a virtual tie.[32]

In later studies,[33] we found operators had job description changes and broadening skills and responsibilities in 50% of the cases for adoption of flexible and computer-integrated manufacturing systems, which is consistent with these robot system findings. Training alone will not qualify as an organizational innovation, even when it is accomplished, and when it is especially needed. It is typical for robotic system suppliers to only budget for vendor training or rely on training from local trade schools, which is often subsidized by the state where the plant is located.

In our study of ERP adoption, which included 60 original cases and 20 validating cases of adoption of enterprise systems in the US,[34] we found a similar pattern as reported in adoption of AMT. Adopters of these complex IT systems typically underestimated the amount and type of training and development needed. The classroom training model implemented in advance of release of an ERP module simply does not work to capture the best opportunities for learning how to use these systems. Simulations, on-demand training, and phased implementation are more likely to work, and border on being innovative approaches to utilizing the best a supplier has to offer. Typically, these ERP systems have a third party coordinating the installation phase of the project and adding value with other suggestions, for example, how to restructure the firm for implementation.

In our study of adoption of virtual engineering technology in the auto industry,[35] we found that successful firms launched these projects with "shadow IT" organizations, dedicated to R&D and engineering, and they insisted on using on-demand training for engineers. Highly skilled engineers are in constant demand for services and simply will not be released by their managers for training. Intervention is only tolerated when problems are encountered by engineers, and they need assistance in virtual engineering acquisition.

In summary, training, as it is typically delivered by suppliers of new technology systems, does not qualify as an organizational or administrative innovation. Even when it is supplied, it is often not delivered in a manner that promotes high, differentiated usage of a technology available to competitors. Unique training delivery, tailored to the needs of a particular adopting unit of a firm, in conjunction with other innovative interventions, is needed to meet the requirement of SI. More recent literature confirms these trends and is discussed next.

In one recent case study of training for new technology, it was reported that training effectiveness was influenced by supervisor support in a culture characterized by continuous learning, as well as emphasis on intrinsic motivation and multi-skilling. That is, training alone is insufficient to promote success in a new technology setting, as evidenced by comparing before and after trainee knowledge.[36] Another study of computerization found that both training and education are required for success and that allowance for an initial period of adjustment and slowdown is to be expected.[37]

In a study of 16 hospitals "...implementing an innovative technology for cardiac surgery," Edmondson et al. (2001) found that "successful implementers used enrollment to motivate the team, designed preparatory practice sessions and early trials to create psychological safety and encourage new behaviors, and promoted shared meaning and process improvement through reflective practices."[38] Finally, in a field study of 316 participants the focus was on:

> ...the effect of mood on employee motivation and intentions toward using a specific computer technology at two points in time: immediately after training and 6 weeks after training. Actual usage behavior was assessed for 12 weeks after training. Each individual was assigned to one of three mood treatments: positive, negative, or control. Results indicated that there were only short-term boosts in intrinsic motivation and intention to use the technology among individuals in the positive mood intervention. However, a long-term lowering of intrinsic motivation and intention was observed among those in the negative mood condition.[39]

Theories of synchronous innovation

The theory of SI was originally advanced in a conference paper[40] and then later documented in a book with case illustrations.[41] See Figure 7.1.

The essence of this theory is that adoption (not development) of incremental innovation requires modest adaptation in organizational strategy and structure, and adoption of radical technological innovation requires significant new policy and organizational structure implementation. This produces a "sweet spot" of adaptation. It is consistent with the differentiated economic model of weak (adopted and adapted) versus strong (R&D) investments in the innovation process.

In a creative replication of our original study of SI in manufacturing, Georgantzas and Shapiro[42] sought to investigate:

> ...what theoretical forms might best describe the relationships among administrative innovation [they focused on]. Thirty-five plant managers' perceptions of the relationships underlying synchronous innovation provide data...[that]show how administrative and technological innovation

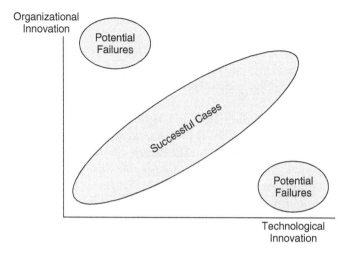

FIGURE 7.1 Successful management of the new adopted technology (Reproduced with permission Ettlie, J.E., *Managing Innovation*, 2nd ed., Routledge, London, UK, 325, 2007.)[43]

dimensions interact with, intervene among or moderate the contributions of each other on organizational performance, rendering their independent effects negligible without synchronous innovation. These results were essentially replicated for software reuse by Ravichandran, who found that "synergies exist between administrative and technological dimensions of reusability which are more important in explaining variance in systems delivery performance than these dimensions individually."[44]

More generally, Mol and Birkinshaw[45] found that management innovation is directly related to firm performance like productivity growth.[46] These findings were further elaborated in theory development of evolving interorganizational development of management innovation by the same authors.[47]

In a study of supply-chain reconfiguration and information technology, Lee et al.[48] found that:

A Hong Kong-based apparel manufacturer, TAL Apparel Limited, has used IT strategically to gain competitive advantage in the cut-throat global apparel industry. We show how the company has developed a sophisticated information management system to manage the supply chain of its major retailer customers, while at the same time providing backward integration into its own production and material sourcing networks, [and to achieve] sustainable competitive advantage through process integration and synchronization.[49]

Although supply chain innovation research is still quite rare, it is becoming more prevalent in literature.[50]

It also appears that the adoption of administrative (or management or organizational, as the terms are typically used interchangeably) innovation can precede adoption of technical innovation. For example, Damanpour studied the:

> ...adoption of administrative and technical innovations over time and its impact on organizational performance was studied. A confirmatory analysis of the data from 85 public libraries showed that, over consecutive time periods, changes in the social structure, portrayed by the adoption of administrative innovations, lead to changes in the technical system, portrayed by the adoption of technical innovations.[51]

Perhaps the most promising line of theory development is the advent of the "mirroring" hypothesis,[52] which "...predicts that organizational ties within a project, firm, or group of firms (e.g., communication, collocation, employment) will correspond to the technical patterns of dependency in the relevant work being performed."[53] In a complex system, the technical architecture and division of labor will "mirror" each other, as the network structure of the technical system will correspond to the labor structure. We are not concerned with the origins or derivation of the mirroring hypothesis here, but only how (1) the theory applies to the innovation process, and (2) how it maps or doesn't map onto the SI construct. These two issues of focus are taken up next. It is argued that the "partial" mirroring, which results in "technologically dynamic industries" and then further results in "strategic mirror breaking," has the greatest potential use and concordance with SI developments to date. Mirroring shows that collaboration across firm boundaries has the greatest application in weak appropriation conditions that require the importation of technology across a firm boundary, typically external to the firm's or unit's environment. This does not preclude the possibility of corporate technology sharing, which most multi-divisional firms find so challenging.[54] This aspect of the mirroring hypothesis, which requires "higher-than-normal levels of communication and coordination between actors...,"[55] is consistent with findings in the adoption of AMT where integration on four dimensions predicts different metric performance[56] and is quite independent of any consideration of modular separation of tasks central to much of the mirroring hypothesis paradigm. However, relational contracts might apply, as we also report evidence of the need for Union-Management technology agreements in organized workplaces of manufacturing industries.[57]

Subsequent work on supply-chain innovation also confirms the summary finding reported by Colfer and Baldwin that "all cases of successful across-firm collaboration in our sample were characterized by compatible motivation." DeCampos[58] found that it is not the gaps in understanding of collaborative requirements between supplier and buyer of new technology in powertrains, but understanding these gaps, which suggests that strong or joint motivation to succeed in the innovation process is an important predictor of outcomes. Further, we also have published evidence that technology can be used to facilitate cross-boundary integration, such as the example of virtual engineering in new product development (NPD). So, we concur in the general conclusion by Colfer and Baldwin that "Across all cases of successful across-firm collaboration, we found that the mechanisms used by collaborating groups to share design information fell into two classes: (1) those that were analogues of traditional organizational ties; and (2) those that departed from a genuine departure from tradition," including "broadband electronic" communication. Ironically, our findings show increases in efficiency quite independent of novelty of the design departures.[59]

Colfer and Baldwin[60] find that of the three categories of organizational groups in their sample of studies on mirroring, open collaboration projects provided the least support for the general hypothesis. Whether virtual engineering falls into the digital tools subcategory of open collaboration or the "mirror breaking" segment of cross-firm boundary crossing is not clear, but much of weak approbation assumption that underpins SI actually spans both categories. Therefore, one cannot escape the conclusion that the mirroring hypothesis informs some but not all of the contexts in need of theoretical underpinning in the SI construct. Of the three categories of open collaboration that the authors cover in their review of cases, which include assembly of transient groups, technical systems with high modularity, and core-periphery technical and organizational structures that might not be mirrored, the first and third categories are most likely areas to explore theoretical development.

Transient groups often operate across different time zones, making even digital collaboration difficult because work often continues after engagement in real time. And there is little or no data on core-periphery structures in a given project, which means there is possibly overlap in task and technology and there is speculation that "...core members...may frequently find themselves working in the technical core even if they do not know exactly where it is."[61] The authors admit a limitation that "when technical systems are changing rapidly and becoming more complex, deviations from the logic of strict mirroring will be beneficial for both firms and groups of firms (ecosystems)."[62]

What is missing in the mirroring hypothesis discussions to date is the pairing of innovation in the two corresponding domains of technical and organizational systems. The emerging central issue of the SI construct is the ideation of organizational (management or administrative) innovations needed to capture value from adoption of new technologies typically available to competitors.

What would a continued theory development effort look like, given this review? We have entered the digital world, which means some, albeit not important, upgrades on the mirroring hypothesis. In application of the mirroring hypothesis to the adoption of innovation context in a digital world, we already are informed by findings cited earlier. One of the most relevant contexts is the virtual engineering for R&D and NPD. Capability enhancement and new structures emerge as the key to understanding the transition process. The general trend toward more decentralized decision-making and new structural forms of the information technology function in the firm have appeared.[63] The redefinition of boundaries in open innovation constructs applying competitive dynamics concepts also seems to be consistent with the treatment of mirroring in open collaborative projects of Cofler and Baldwin.[64] In the former study, centers of excellence have emerged as an important structural adaptation, and this may be an important example of "breaking the mirror" unless confined to just internal R&D project management. If these centers emerge to manage across firm boundaries, this could be a verifiable exception to the mirroring hypothesis, requiring the appending of new theory like dynamic capabilities and competition.

Configuration theory and research[65] could potentially lend insight into the SI construct as well, and this approach is evaluated next:

> Theory posits that organizing marketing activities in ways that fit the implementation requirements of a business's strategy enhances performance. However, conceptual and methodological problems make it difficult to empirically assess this proposition in the holistic way that it is theoretically framed. Drawing on configuration theory approaches in management, the authors address these problems by assessing marketing organization fit with business strategy as the degree to which a business's marketing organization differs from that of an empirically derived ideal profile that achieves superior performance by arranging marketing activities in a way that enables the implementation of a given strategy type. The authors suggest that marketing organization fit with strategic type is associated with marketing effectiveness in prospector, defender, and analyzer strategic types and with marketing efficiency in prospector and defender strategic types. The study demonstrates the utility of profile deviation approaches for strategic marketing theory development and testing.[66]

There is some evidence that strategic planning is more useful for early-stage development firms versus late-stage firms, and that the link between strategy and performance is moderated by resources.[67] However, much of the research and theory under the umbrella of the configuration hypothesis does not focus sharply on innovation, per se, but organizational change. One of the recent examples of the configuration research stream illustrates this conclusion:

> This paper contributes to the understanding of the executive team dynamic managerial capabilities by developing theory about the interplay between the firm's dominant logic and dynamic managerial capabilities (including managerial human capital, social capital, and cognition). We underscore the criticality of the two key CEO-level functions: configuration and orchestration of senior executive team dynamic capabilities. We develop theory on how these functions create and sculpt the management team's absorptive capacity, which in turn shapes the team's adaptive capacity. We present theory about the distributed nature of efforts for organizational

renewal where a CEO's dynamic managerial capabilities in concert with senior executive managerial capabilities will drive top management's ability to revitalize the firm's dominant logic and to achieve evolutionary fit.[68]

A study of supply chains links contingency theory and configuration:

> By placing organizational culture within the competing value framework (CVF), this study establishes a conceptual model for the relationships between organizational culture and SCI. The study uses both a contingency approach and a configuration approach to examine these proposed relationships using data collected from 317 manufacturers across ten countries. The contingency results indicate that both development and group culture are positively related to all three dimensions of SCI. However, rational culture is positively related only to internal integration, and hierarchical culture is negatively related to both internal and customer integration. The configuration approach identifies four profiles of organizational culture: the Hierarchical, Flexible, Flatness and Across-the-Board profiles. The Flatness profile shows the highest levels of development, group, and rational cultures and the lowest level of hierarchical culture. The Flatness profile also achieves the highest levels of internal, customer, and supplier integration.[69]

The convergence of this supply chain study and our work on adoption of AMT is unlikely to be a coincidence, so what remains to be done is to make the theoretical connection between culture, contingency, configuration, and innovation. In spite of the potential for this path of theory development, nothing has appeared to emerge to date to fill this gap.[70] Literature on organization design has been tangential to this type of research question.[71] There have been some preliminary studies in the area of knowledge generation and management that might show the way:

> Studies the relationship between egocentric collaboration networks and knowledge creation at the individual level. For egocentric networks we focus on the characteristics of tie strength and tie configuration, and knowledge creation is assessed by the number of citations. Using a panel of 1,042 American scientists in five disciplines and fixed effects models, we found an inverted U-shaped relationship between network average tie strength and citation impact, because an increase in tie strength on the one hand facilitates the collaborative knowledge creation process and on the other hand decreases cognitive diversity. In addition, when the network average tie strength is high, a more skewed network performs better because it still has a "healthy" mixture of weak and strong ties and a balance between exploration and exploitation. Furthermore, the tie strength skewness moderates the effect of network average tie strength: both the initial positive effect and the later negative effect of an increase in tie strength are smaller in a more skewed network than in a less skewed one.[72]

Another promising avenue of research going forward is the configuration of (health care) networks:

> The study has a multiple case study design and covers 22 health care networks. Using a configuration view, combinations of network governance and other network characteristics were studied on the level of the network. Based on interview and questionnaire data, network characteristics were identified and patterns in the data looked for. Neither a dominant (or optimal) governance structure or mechanism nor a perfect fit among governance and other characteristics were revealed, but a number of characteristics that need further study might be related to effective networks such as the role of governmental agencies, legitimacy, and relational, hierarchical, and contractual governance mechanisms as complementary factors. Although the results emphasize the situational character of network governance and effectiveness, they give practitioners in the health care sector indications of which factors might be more or less crucial for network effectiveness.[73]

The findings of several studies suggest the presence of an "ideal" NPD network profile (in terms of goal complementarity, resource complementarity, fairness trust, reliability trust, and network position strength). The more a company's NPD network profile differs from this ideal profile, the lower the innovation performance. In addition, the results of the study indicate that the NPD network profiles of successful and less successful SMEs in the medical devices sector significantly differ in terms of "goal complementarity," while this is less the case for trust and resource complementarity labeled distinctive by previous research. Results show that a relatively closed networking approach, which is characterized by result orientation and professionalism, is related to high-innovation performance. SMEs in the medical devices are advised to distinguish themselves from competitors in terms of innovation performance focus on goal complementarity and pay greater attention to partners.[74]

Information technology literature has examples that might show the way:

> Strategic alignment is a theory-based state that is considered as crucial for organizations in order to realize performance gains from information technology (IT) investments and deployments. Within the domain of purchasing and supply chain management there has been a growing interest on how purchasing strategy can be effectively aligned with IT and what conditions facilitate a view taken by configuration theory approach. Sometimes purchasing alignment is dependent upon patterns of multiple contingencies. In a sample of 172 international companies the authors <find there are several alternatives ways to achieve alignment>. For companies following an operational excellence strategic orientation, a high contract binding scheme or a small firm size facilitates purchasing alignment.

There were enabling elements for product leadership companies include a decentralized purchasing structure, a broad supplier base, and a large firm size. Purchasing alignment for companies is supported by a centralized purchasing structure, loose contract binding, and a large supplier base.[75]

In another study, using 1978–2009 data in the bioethanol industry, the authors find support for our predictions that transaction hazards, decomposed as either enduring or transient over the stages of industry evolution, are positively associated with the choice to internalize value chain activities. Pre-entry experience in an activity increases the likelihood of its internalization and reduces the effect of enduring transaction hazards on the internalization choice. It is necessary to distinguish between firm- and founder-level pre-entry capabilities (that is, the capabilities of firms versus those of founders). Diversifying entrants with firm-level integrative capabilities are more likely to internalize value chain activities than start-ups, and this effect persists over the industry's life cycle. Pre-entry experience with an activity and the "likelihood of internalizing it, is also stronger for diversifying entrants."[76]

There have been attempts in service innovation literature to link to configuration theory. The empirical evidence about the impact of innovativeness on new service adoption seems inconclusive. Perhaps service innovation has been studied using new product frameworks that do not fully capture the complexity of new service assessments by customers. An alternative, holistic framework suggests that new service adoption does not depend on individual service attributes, but on specific configurations of such attributes.

The first full empirical support of SI appeared in Ettlie and Reza[77] and has since been replicated in several large sample studies[78] and extensions theoretically, especially by Morgan Swink and his colleagues.[79] In the latter study of 224 manufacturing plants, the authors found that design-manufacturing integration plays a complementary role to advanced manufacturing usage, for quality, flexibility, and delivery, but not for new product flexibility.

Assessing benefits of advanced manufacturing technologies: the role of context

Organizations adopt various programmable machinery called advanced manufacturing technologies, such as flexible manufacturing systems, computer-aided manufacturing, and computer numerically controlled machines, to organize the production or manufacturing process for improved production quality, efficiency, and flexibility. AMT offers two seemingly paradoxical benefits: flexible product customization and cost-efficiency. AMT can improve workflow, information-sharing across functions, and managerial control, which can, in turn, enhance employees' abilities to diagnose and solve problems effectively and efficiently.[80] Yet, research shows mixed results regarding the outcomes of AMT; while some organizations report gains in flexibility or productivity or both, many report AMT failure. About 50%–75% of implementations fail in terms of quality, flexibility, and reliability.[81]

Small found that the more complex the AMT portfolio, the more departments were involved in the justification and installation stage of adoption.[82] Regardless of the portfolio, more departments tended to be involved in early justification rather than later installation. Finance and general management tended to drop involvement when installation begins. Marketing involvement tended to be low regardless of portfolio complexity. MIS/IT involvement was higher for the more complex portfolios of AMT adoption, as would be expected. Small also focused on the justification process for advanced manufacturing and design technologies, with a survey of 82 plants. He found that larger firms (sales and employees) and firms using a combined justification approach (strategic and economic) adopted the more complex technology portfolios. The most popular measures of performance of these new systems was payback (58.7%) and ROI (53.3%) with cost-benefit analysis used third most often (44% of respondents). Small found no statistically significant relationship between type of performance measure and complexity of the adopted portfolio. However, complex portfolio adopters were significantly more likely to use discounted cash flow (DCF) justification and significantly more likely to use multiple justification techniques.[83] One implication of these results is that complex justification techniques probably need to be simplified so non-financial managers can use them routinely.

While there are many factors that determine the success of AMT implementation, amongst the ones often cited by researchers and often ignored by managers involve issues related to organization strategy, design or structure, culture, and human resource management (HRM) practices. Researchers have consistently documented the need for changes in organization strategy, structure, and HRM practices to complement AMTs. Indeed, Jaikumar and Bohn stated early on that the problem is not with the technology itself but *how* it is implemented.[84] Below, we discuss in turn the findings and implications related to organization strategy, organizational structure, organization culture, and HRM practices.

Organization strategy

Small found that the more complex the AMT portfolio, the more likely strategic benefits were measured. The majority of the 82 plants he studied (82.3%) reported evaluation intentions for operations and technical performance. Only 38% said they were going to evaluate strategic benefits. This seems rather unusual since 75% of these plants use both strategic and operational justification in general, but for AMT these numbers drop to 33% and 62%, respectively.[85]

Operational improvements under the SI approach have been reported to be rather impressive and significant. For example, throughput time reduction of 50% with AMT is typical.[86] For large, integrated system adoption, like ERP systems, general management appears to have a much bigger role in directly influencing outcomes. In a study of 80 ERP systems, Ettlie et al. (2005) found that general managers needed to demonstrate support for ERP adoption by actually modeling the behavior they wanted others in the firm to emulate. They had to actually use the ERP system rather than just command its use.[87]

Perhaps one of the most intriguing recent contributions is the notion that product and process innovation are intimately related, which is clearly a strategic issue in need of more research. What the authors propose is a number of empirically derived upgrades to the SI model, including the types of integration choices needed. This line of research is one promising path forward.[88]

Organization structure

While it is clear that AMT implementation inherently requires changes in organizational structure, there has been some debate over the type of organizational structure best suited to achieve both flexibility and productivity benefits. Some researchers have argued that AMT results in a more mechanistic organization structure emphasizing control and coordination, while others have argued for a more organic structure emphasizing flexibility and empowerment. In an attempt to resolve this controversy, Dean and colleagues, in a seminal study, found that AMT implementation requires aspects of seemingly contradictory organic and mechanistic forms of organization design. Specifically, they found support for decentralization and formalization, with the former being a characteristic of an organic form and the latter of a mechanistic form. They explain the findings in view of key AMT characteristics—their integrative capacity and capital-intensive nature. Integrative capacity allows for better workflow, information-sharing, and communication across functions, enabling employees at the lower levels to make decisions independently. Centralized decision-making will prevent organizations from achieving flexibility benefits.

AMTs' special ability to integrate across functions can also increase interdependence and, therefore, the need for control and coordination.[89] Formalization can provide guidance on acceptable form and boundaries for employee behavior and actions. It can also help minimize the risk that may come with decentralized decision-making, given that AMTs are often expensive, requiring large capital investments. Taken together, it seems that AMTs' characteristics such as their integrative capacity and capital-intensive nature pose challenges that may be managed if paradoxical organization structural elements like formalization and decentralization coexist.

Organization culture

A debate somewhat similar to the one about the nature of the relationship between organization structure and AMT has gone on about the relationship between organization culture and AMT benefits. Organization culture is often defined broadly as a collection of values, beliefs, and norms shared by its members and reflected in organizational practices and goals.[90] As organization structure and culture are intertwined, with one shaping the other, research suggests a paradoxical culture embracing seemingly competing values—being flexible and being control-oriented, suited for achieving AMT benefits. In an earlier study, McDermott and Stock found that flexibility-oriented values emphasizing creativity, spontaneity, empowerment, and internal focus on maintenance and improvement of existing organizations were significantly related to managers' satisfaction with AMT implementation.[91] Organizational culture indirectly influences AMT plant performance as managerial satisfaction can be an important factor in encouraging managers to use AMT in a way that would help realize organization goals.[92] It is also important to note that managerial satisfaction was found to be significantly correlated with more tangible AMT benefits, such as productivity and flexibility. They also found control values emphasizing stability and order, along with external focus on market, competition, and adaptation with the external environment, were significantly related to increases in growth and market share following AMT implementation.

Recently, Khazanchi, Lewis, and Boyer,[93] in an attempt to further clarify the relationship between culture and plant performance following AMT implementation, found flexibility-oriented values as proximal and control-oriented values as predictors of AMT plant performance. They suggest that control values with supporting practices can help alleviate fear of losing control associated with flexibility-oriented values and practices. For example, established routines and clearly specified AMT objectives can facilitate trust in employees' spontaneous decision-making and creative problem-solving necessary to realize AMT's flexibility benefits.[94] Taken together, organization culture that embodies paradoxical values of flexibility and control-orientation are reinforced through complementary—practices that provide clearly established goals, as well as discretion, to employees is critical in achieving AMT benefits.

Human research management practices

As discussed above, AMT adoption changes the work environment by stream-lining the workflow and distributing information across functions, resulting in changes in task structure in most plants. In essence, AMT adoption alters the nature of factory jobs from being job based where employees performed a fixed set of tasks, duties, and functions, to skill based where employees engage in a range of activities with greater discretion and empowerment. AMT adoption requires employees to utilize all the available information, engage in independent decision-making, and participate in creative problem-solving. Employees' knowledge about their own job or function may not be sufficient; knowledge about other functions may be equally, if not more, important to handle problems related to other functions. HRM practices should be designed to support the nature of jobs, as well as accommodate new orientation toward employees where they are selected, trained, evaluated, and compensated for skills, cross-functional experience, and knowledge.

Earlier research, as well as a more recent study, examined the relationship between AMT implementation and HRM practices including staffing, training, performance appraisal, and compensation. Their research suggests that HRM practices, training in particular, should be changed to meet new job requirements and human capital needs. Snell and Dean[95] and Snell, Lepak, Dean, and Youndt[96] found that organizations should invest particularly in training programs that would help employees gain conceptual knowledge about other functions. Training should focus on employees acquiring new problem-solving skills that are critical in the changed work environment following AMT implementation. Both job rotation and on-the-job training can serve this purpose. Similarly, performance appraisal and compensation systems should be used to encourage and support learning and empowerment by evaluating and rewarding creative problem-solving and practices.

In summary, AMT implementation requires changes in the work environment in terms of the organizational strategy, structure, culture, and HRM practices in order to realize AMT benefits, such as productivity and flexibility. AMT plants often require competing values and practices, emphasizing both flexibility and control, which increases the possibility of confusion and conflict. It is vital that structure, culture, and HRM practices are aligned and fit one another. Any mismatch between the three is likely to result in mixed messages to employees and dysfunctional conflict. Organization structure, culture, and HRM practices should not only complement AMT implementation, but also be congruent with one another. This is the essence of the SI model. More work is needed in this area, and what remains is to develop a theory of SI that applies to all industries.

Conclusion

What emerges in this chapter on innovation and operations is nothing less than a general paradigm for successful capture of benefits from both adoption of process-enhancing innovation and weak appropriation conditions of all types. Although the details may vary by technology type and degree of departure from existing practice, the key is found in understanding the nuances of administrative innovations needed to support unique absorption of the full potential of the adopted changes.

The most typical mistake most adopting units make is in underestimating how much change is actually represented by the adopted process improvement—usually a radical technology is at hand, and it often takes time to appreciate how much change is precipitated by the new requirements. In the learning process, the typical reaction is to back off on the extent of adoption or simplify the actual new process technology installed in order to find a more reasonable pace of change. This may or may not lead directly to discovery of the organizational innovations that will be required to capture the benefits of the adopted innovation. Unionized production plants and operations like the dock workers in Long Beach, California[97] often take years to understand the process of establishing a union-management technology agreement or modifying an existing technology agreement in order to go forward in the implementation process and achieve a successful transition to the new process technology platform.

This tendency of finding a better way to learn an accelerated change is not limited to production operations, nor is it restricted to just hourly employees. It is often middle and top management, as well as technical staff, that ultimately will be required to make the greatest changes and adapt to absorb the new technology potential. The adoption of computer-aided drafting, design, engineering, and virtual development networks typically requires a complete change in strategy and structure of organizations.[98]

Organizations that anticipate the need for change in both process technology and supporting innovations in procedures like business processes are well ahead of the game and are much better prepared to learn faster than competitors. The learning process often requires abandonment of the original ideals for the project, but, in the end, benefits will be uniquely captured that are difficult for competitors to emulate because they cannot easily duplicate the conditions that led to this learning process. Therein lies the secret to the successful adoption of any challenging new process-enhancing technology.

Synchronous innovation in a digital manufacturing world

If one looks closely at the evolution of manufacturing core technologies (or as Bill Abernathy and Jim Utterback called it, the productive segment) 40 years ago and now, there is a natural progression toward integration to achieve control of processes. This refers not just to the four walls of the factory but the entire value-added chain—suppliers to you and logistics to your customers. As the evolution progressed from standalone computer-aided manufacturing to integrated enterprise systems, one can easily see that digital manufacturing is an incremental step in this evolution, not a radical leap across a chasm.

Therefore, is it quite reasonable to see how slight modifications of the SI model would be useful in predicting the outcomes of adoption of digital manufacturing. First, there is little chance that a firm can leapfrog to digital manufacturing without mastering ERP and CRM. Second, it is still a matter of integration, which is rarely accomplished in most firms. The challenge is to find ways of implementing good strategies for integration. In our article for the *California Management Review*, we predicted that there would be two necessary types of integration going forward for success. This integration model is reproduced in Table 7.1.[99]

First, the model suggests there are two important types of integration needed for success in manufacturing: (1) platform integration, which is intergenerational shifts in technology, such as from internal combustion to electric power trains; and (2) functional integration, including marketing and R&D and manufacturing and information technology. Depending upon the degree of market uncertainty, our data suggest there are preferred ways of achieving these two types of integration. This is where the theory and empirical research needs to go to

TABLE 7.1 Functional versus platform integration in the global automotive industry

	Platform integration	*Functional integration*
Market uncertainty	• Existing technologies • Existing markets • Short term response	• Discontinuous Innovation • New markets (especially emerging) • Longer term response
Non-market uncertainty	• Political (i.e. lobbying) on incremental social change • Incremental environmental performance improvements	• Expecting radical social demands for environmental performance • Greater focus on technologies for large environmental performance improvements.

Source: Rothenberg, S., and Ettlie, J.E., *Calif. Manage. Rev.*, 54, 126–144, copyright 2011. Reprinted by Permission of SAGE Publications; Ibid., p. 133.

inform the next step in evolution of the productive segment including digital manufacturing, and it is very likely to add the greatest value to our fund of knowledge. The integration of product, process, and service innovation appears to be the next major challenge to address in the research stream on synchronous innovation.[100]

Notes

1 Kessenides, D., & Rocks, D. (2019). Future of work: A ballet of airbus jets. *Bloomberg-Business Week*, April 20, 2019, 44–45.
2 Ettlie, J. E., & Penner-Hahn, J. (1994). Flexibility ratios and manufacturing strategy. *Management Science, 40*(11), 1444–1454.
3 Kitroeff, N., & Gelles, D. (2019). Boeing dreamliner plant accused of safety lapses. *New York Times*, April 21, 2019, 1–22.
4 Chen, D., Heyer, S., Ibbotson, S., Salonitis, K., Steingrímsson, J. G., & Thiede, S. (2015). Direct digital manufacturing: Definition, evolution, and sustainability implications. *Journal of Cleaner Production, 107*, 615–625.
5 Ardito, L., Petruzzelli, A. M., Panniello, U., & Garavelli, A. C. (2019). Towards industry 4.0: Mapping digital technologies for supply chain management-marketing integration. *Business Process Management Journal, 25*(2), 323–346.
6 Chryssolouris, G., Mavrikios, D., Papakostas, N., Mourtzis, D., Michalos, G., & Georgoulias, K. (2009). Digital manufacturing: History, perspectives, and outlook. *Proceedings of the Institution of Mechanical Engineers, Part B: Journal of Engineering Manufacture, 223*(5), 451–462.
7 Urbinati, A., Chiaroni, D., Chiesa, V., & Frattini, F. (2018). The role of digital technologies in open innovation processes: An exploratory multiple case study analysis. *R&D Management*.

8 Özüdoğru, A. G., Ergün, E., & Ammari, D., & Görener, A. (2018). How industry 4.0 changes business: A commercial perspective. *International Journal of Commerce and Finance, 4*(1), 84.

9 Ardolino, M., Rapaccini, M., Saccani, N., Gaiardelli, P., Crespi, G., & Ruggeri, C. (2018). The role of digital technologies for the service transformation of industrial companies. *International Journal of Production Research, 56*(6), 2116–2132.

10 Holmström, J., & Partanen, J. (2014). Digital manufacturing-driven transformations of service supply chains for complex products. *Supply Chain Management: An International Journal, 19*(4), 421–430.

11 Ibid., p. 421.

12 Savastano, M., Amendola, C., & D'Ascenzo, F. (2018). How digital transformation is reshaping the manufacturing industry value chain: The new digital manufacturing ecosystem applied to a case study from the food industry. In *Network, Smart and Open* (pp. 127–142). Cham, Switzerland: Springer.

13 Khorram Niaki, M., & Nonino, F. (2017). Additive manufacturing management: A review and future research agenda. *International Journal of Production Research, 55*(5), 1419–1439.

14 Martinsuo, M., & Luomaranta, T. (2018). Adopting additive manufacturing in SMEs: Exploring the challenges and solutions. *Journal of Manufacturing Technology Management, 29*(6), 937–957.

15 Szalavetz, A. (2018). Industry 4.0 and capability development in manufacturing subsidiaries. *Technological Forecasting and Social Change, 145*, 384–395.

16 Rasit, Z. A., & Ismail, K. (2017). Incorporating contingency Theory in understanding factors influencing target costing adoption. *Advanced Science Letters, 23*(8), 7804–7808.

17 Kumar, R., Singh, H., & Chandel, R. (2018). Exploring the key success factors of advanced manufacturing technology implementation in Indian manufacturing industry. *Journal of Manufacturing Technology Management, 29*(1), 25–40.

18 Lee, C., Leem, C. S., & Hwang, I. (2011). PDM and ERP integration methodology using digital manufacturing to support global manufacturing. *The International Journal of Advanced Manufacturing Technology, 53*(1–4), 399–409.

19 Ibid.

20 Freedman, S. (1999). An overview of fully integrated digital manufacturing technology. In *WSC'99. 1999 Winter Simulation Conference Proceedings. 'Simulation-A Bridge to the Future' (Cat. No. 99CH37038)* (Vol. 1, pp. 281–285). IEEE; Brown, R. G. (2000). Driving digital manufacturing to reality. In *2000 Winter Simulation Conference Proceedings (Cat. No. 00CH37165)* (Vol. 1, pp. 224–228). IEEE; Kim, H., Lee, J. K., Park, J. H., Park, B. J., & Jang, D. S. (2002). Applying digital manufacturing technology to ship production and the maritime environment. *Integrated Manufacturing Systems, 13*(5), 295–305; and Westkämper, E. (2007). Digital manufacturing in the global Era. In P. F. Cunha & P. G. Maropoulos (Eds.) *Digital Enterprise Technology* (pp. 3–14). Boston, MA: Springer.

21 Corne, A., & Goncalves, O. (2018). Is innovation a productive leverage for the ski lift companies? *Innovations,* 1, 173–197.

22 Nguyen, H., & Harrison, N. (2019). Leveraging customer knowledge to enhance process innovation: Moderating effects from market dynamics. *Business Process Management Journal, 25*(2), 307–322.

23 Wu, D., Rosen, D. W., Wang, L., & Schaefer, D. (2015). Cloud-based design and manufacturing: A new paradigm in digital manufacturing and design innovation. *Computer-Aided Design,* 59, 1–14.

24 Dale Rogers, presentation at Rochester Institute of Technology, and Wang, J. J., Chen, H., Rogers, D. S., Ellram, L. M., & Grawe, S. J. (2017). A bibliometric analysis of reverse logistics research (1992–2015) and opportunities for future research. *International Journal of Physical Distribution & Logistics Management, 47*(8), 666–687.

25 González-Ramos, M. I., Donate, M. J., & Guadamillas, F. (2018). An empirical study on the link between corporate social responsibility and innovation in environmentally sensitive industries. *European Journal of International Management, 12*(4), 402–422.

26 McClure, P. K. (2018). "You're fired," says the Robot: The rise of automation in the workplace, technophobes, and fears of unemployment. *Social Science Computer Review, 36*(2), 139–156. A Chiacchio, F., Petropoulos, G., & Pichler, D. (2018). *The impact of industrial robots on EU employment and wages: A local labour market approach.* Brussels, Belgium: Bruegel.

27 Gattiker, U. E., Gutek, B. A., Berger, D. E. (1988). Office technology and employee attitudes. *Social Science Computer Review, 6*(3), 327–340.

28 Ettlie, J. E., Vossler, M. L., & Klein, J. A. (1988). Robotics training. *Training & Development Journal, 42*(3), 54–57.

29 Ibid.

30 Graham, M. B., & Rosenthal, S. R. (1986). Flexible manufacturing systems require flexible people. *Human Systems Management, 6*(3), 211–222.

31 Ettlie et al. (1988). An interesting footnote to this study is that after we completed the project, a VP from the robotics supplier showed up at our door and demanded we return the data and that it had been released to us in error. Of course, it was too late for that.

32 Ettlie et al. (1988).

33 Ettlie, J. E., & Reza, E. (1992). Organizational integration and process innovation. *Academy of Management Journal, 34*(4), 1992, 795–827.

34 Ettlie, J. E., Perotti, V., Cotteleer, M., & Joseph, D. (2005). Strategic predictors of successful enterprise system deployment. *International Journal of Operations and Production Management, 25*, 953–1153.

35 Ettlie, J., & Pavlou, P. (2006). Technology-based new product development partnerships. *Decision Sciences, 37*, 117–147.

36 Kontoghiorghes, C. (2001). Factors affecting training effectiveness in the context of the introduction of new technology—a US case study. *International Journal of Training and Development, 5*(4), 248–260.

37 Helpman, E., & Rangel, A. (1999). Adjusting to a new technology: Experience and training. *Journal of Economic Growth, 4*(4), 359–383.

38 Edmondson, A. C., Bohmer, R. M., & Pisano, G. P. (2001). Disrupted routines: Team learning and new technology implementation in hospitals. *Administrative Science Quarterly, 46*(4), 685–716.

39 Venkatesh, V., & Speier, C. (1999). Computer technology training in the workplace: A longitudinal investigation of the effect of mood. *Organizational Behavior and Human Decision Processes, 79*(1), 1–28.

40 Ettlie, J. E., Academy of Management Annual Meeting, 1986.

41 Ettlie, J. E. (1988). *Taking charge of manufacturing.* San Francisco, CA: Jossey-Bass.

42 Georgantzas, N. C., & Shapiro, H. J. (1993). Viable theoretical forms of synchronous production innovation. *Journal of Operations Management, 11*(2), 161–183, and Ravichandran, T. (1999). Software reusability as synchronous innovation: A test of four theoretical models. *European Journal of Information Systems, 8*(3), 183–199.

43 Ibid.

44 Georgantzas and Shapiro (1993, p. 161).

45 Mol, M. J., & Birkinshaw, J. (2009). The sources of management innovation: When firms introduce new management practices. *Journal of Business Research, 62*(12), 1269–1280.

46 Ibid.

47 Birkinshaw, J., Hamel, G., & Mol, M. J. (2008). Management innovation. *Academy of Management Review, 33*(4), 825–845.

48 Lee, H., Farhoomand, A., & Ho, P. (2004). Innovation through supply chain reconfiguration. *MIS Quarterly Executive, 3*(3), 131–142.

49 Ibid., p. 131.

50 Ettlie and Pavlou (2006).

51 Damanpour, F., Szabat, K. A., & Evan, W. M. (1989). The relationship between types of innovation and organizational performance. *Journal of Management Studies, 26*(6), 587–602. Quoted from the abstract.

52 Colfer, L. J., & Baldwin, C. Y. (2016). The mirroring hypothesis: Theory, evidence, and exceptions. *Industrial and Corporate Change, 25*(5), 709–738.

53 Colfer and Baldwin (2016, p. 709).

54 Rubenstein, A. H. (1989). *Managing technology in the decentralized firm.* New York: Wiley-Interscience.

55 Colfer and Baldwin (2016, p. 709).

56 Ettlie and Reza (1992).

57 Ibid.

58 DeCampos, H. A., Ettlie, J. E., & Melynk, S. A. (2017). *Supply chain interoperability: The latent capacity to integrate resources, processes and behavior across firm boundaries in pursuit of innovation performance,* working paper, Detroit, Michigan: Wayne State University.

59 Ettlie and Reza (1992).

60 Colfer and Baldwin (2016, p. 709).

61 Ibid., p. 733.

62 Ibid., p. 734.

63 Ettlie, J. E., Tucci, C., & Gianiodis, P. T. (2017). Trust, integrated information technology and new product success. *European Journal of Innovation Management, 20*(3), 406–427.

64 Colfer and Baldwin (2016, p. 734).

65 Dess, G. G., Newport, S., & Rasheed, A. M. (1993). Configuration research in strategic management: Key issues and suggestions. *Journal of Management, 19*(4), 775–795.

66 Vorhies, D. W., & Morgan, N. A. (2003). A configuration theory assessment of marketing organization fit with business strategy and its relationship with marketing performance. *Journal of Marketing, 67*(1), 100–115.

67 Sarason, Y., & Tegarden, L. F. (2003). The erosion of the competitive advantage of strategic planning: A configuration theory and resource-based view. *Journal of Business and Management, 9*(1), 1.

68 Kor, Y. Y., & Mesko, A. (2013). Dynamic managerial capabilities: Configuration and orchestration of top executives' capabilities and the firm's dominant logic. *Strategic Management Journal, 34*(2), 233–244.

69 Cao, Z., Huo, B., Li, Y., & Zhao, X. (2015). The impact of organizational culture on supply chain integration: A contingency and configuration approach. *Supply Chain Management: An International Journal, 20*(1), 24–41.

70 Ibid.

71 Van de Ven, A. H., Ganco, M., & Hinings, C. R. (2013). Returning to the frontier of contingency theory of organizational and institutional designs. *The Academy of Management Annals, 7*(1), 393–440.

72 Gulati, R., Puranam, P., & Tushman, M. (2012). Meta-organization design: Rethinking design in interorganizational and community contexts. *Strategic Management Journal, 33*(6), 571–586.

73 Willem, A., & Gemmel, P. (2013). Do governance choices matter in health care networks?: An exploratory configuration study of health care networks. *BMC Health Services Research, 13*(1), 229.

74 Pullen, A. J., de Weerd-Nederhof, P. C., Groen, A. J., & Fisscher, O. A. (2012). Open innovation in practice: Goal complementarity and closed NPD networks to explain differences in innovation performance for SMEs in the medical devices sector. *Journal of Product Innovation Management, 29*(6), 917–934.

75 Mikalef, P., Pateli, A., Batenburg, R. S., & Wetering, R. V. D. (2015). Purchasing alignment under multiple contingencies: A configuration theory approach. *Industrial Management & Data Systems, 115*(4), 625–645.

76 Qian, L., Agarwal, R., & Hoetker, G. (2012). Configuration of value chain activities: The effect of pre-entry capabilities, transaction hazards, and industry evolution on decisions to internalize. *Organization Science, 23*(5), 1330–1349.

77 Ettlie and Reza (1992).

78 Gittleman, M., Horrigan, M., & Joyce, M. (1998). "Flexible" workplace practices: Evidence from a nationally representative survey. *ILR Review, 52*(1), 99–115. Brandyberry, A., Rai, A., & White, G. P. (1999). Intermediate performance impacts of advanced manufacturing technology systems: An empirical investigation. *Decision Sciences, 30*(4), 993–1020; Pagell, M., Handfield, R. B., & Barber, A. E. (2000). Effects of operational employee skills on advanced manufacturing technology performance. *Production and Operations Management, 9*(3), 222–238; Carroll, B. (1999). Motorola makes the most of teamworking. *Human Resource Management International Digest, 7*(5), 9–11; Zammuto, R. F., & O'Connor, E. J. (1992). Gaining advanced manufacturing technologies' benefits: The roles of organization design and culture. *Academy of Management Review, 17*(4), 701–728; and Chung, C. A. (1996). Human issues influencing the successful implementation of advanced manufacturing technology. *Journal of Engineering and Technology Management, 13*(3–4), 283–299. Schroeder, D. M., & Congden, S. W. (2000). Aligning competitive strategies, manufacturing technology, and shop floor skills. *Production and Inventory Management Journal, 41*(4), 40.

79 Swink, M., & Nair, A. (2007). Capturing the competitive advantages of AMT: Design–manufacturing integration as a complementary asset. *Journal of Operations Management, 25*(3), 736–754.

80 Ettlie and Reza (1992).

81 Lewis, M. W., & Boyer, K. K. (2002). Factors impacting AMT implementation: An integrative and controlled study. *Journal of Engineering and Technology Management, 19*(2), 111–130.

82 Small, M. H. (2007). Planning, justifying and installing advanced manufacturing technology: A managerial framework. *Journal of Manufacturing Technology Management, 18*(5), 513–537.

83 Ibid.

84 Jaikumar, R., & Bohn, R. E. (1992). A dynamic approach to operations management: An alternative to static optimization. *International Journal of Production Economics, 27*(3), 265–282.

85 Small, M. H. (2006). Justifying investment in advanced manufacturing technology: A portfolio analysis. *Industrial Management & Data Systems, 106*(4), 485–508.

86 Ettlie and Reza (1992).

87 Ettlie et al. (2005).

88 Hullova, D., Simms, C. D., Trott, P., & Laczko, P. (2019). Critical capabilities for effective management of complementarity between product and process innovation: Cases from the food and drink industry. *Research Policy, 48*(1), 339–354.

89 Dean Jr, J. W., Yoon, S. J., & Susman, G. I. (1992). Advanced manufacturing technology and organization structure: Empowerment or subordination? *Organization Science, 3*(2), 203–229.

90 Hofstede, G., Neuijen, B., Ohayv, D. D., & Sanders, G. (1990). Measuring organizational cultures: A qualitative and quantitative study across twenty cases. *Administrative Science Quarterly, 35*(2), 286–316.

91 McDermott, C. M., & Stock, G. N. (1999). Organizational culture and advanced manufacturing technology implementation. *Journal of Operations Management, 17*(5), 521–533.

92 Ibid.

93 Khazanchi, S., Lewis, M. W., & Boyer, K. K. (2007). Innovation-supportive culture: The impact of organizational values on process innovation. *Journal of Operations Management, 25*(4), 871–884.

94 Ibid.

95 Snell, S. A., & Dean Jr, J. W. (1992). Integrated manufacturing and human resource management: A human capital perspective. *Academy of Management Journal, 35*(3), 467–504.

96 Snell, S. A., Lepak, D. P., Dean, Jr, J. W., & Youndt, M. A. (2000). Selection and training for integrated manufacturing: The moderating effects of job characteristics. *Journal of Management Studies, 37*(3), 445–466.

97 See the end of Chapter 8.

98 Ettlie and Pavlou (2006).

99 Rothenberg, S., & Ettlie, J. E. (2011). Strategies to cope with regulatory uncertainty in the auto industry. *California Management Review, 54*(1), 126–144.

100 Ibid.

8

INFORMATION TECHNOLOGY

In this chapter, the focus is laser-sharp on adoption of information technology (IT) from outside the firm or business unit. It is not about development of software or software/hardware systems or outsourcing versus insourcing IT. In many ways, most prominent example of weak appropriation models of the innovation process is information technology. IT is most often adopted by organizations, even those that have an IT department and a chief information officer (CIO). The reason is simple: most companies are not in the IT business, so suppliers are out there that can solve problems cheaply and more effectively than most in-house IT departments. At the end of this chapter, the West Coast Dockworkers case is used to demonstrate the development of product offerings versus the other common practice of adoption of enterprise software.

What's new?

Our work adoption of virtual teams continues to appear as a topic in literature.[1] Han and Mithas[2] report that according to Gartner, "…IT outsourcing services reached U.S. $314.7 billion in 2011, and will increase with a 4.4% compound annual growth rate through 2015," and that on average, "…U.S. firms spend about 14% of their IT budget on IT outsourcing."[3] The primary reason for outsourcing IT is cost reduction. Another important reason for IT outsourcing is that suppliers have a production advantage.

CIO magazine does a survey every year of executives (in 2015, it was 571 respondents), and the challenge of managing the information function increases every year. Issues of the most concern are security and digital conversion or Cloud migration.[4] Integration has emerged as the top strategic challenge— satisfaction of customers requires IT to work with marketing. This challenge is at least as daunting as the adoption of enterprise resource planning (ERP) systems (which is covered later in this chapter). Not surprisingly, Cisco and others are bundling products and services, and this is already an established, increasing trend. Further, there is a trend to adopt and integrate robotic process automation (RPA) with IT service delivery.

Revisiting Han and Mithas[5] would seem appropriate since the study found that IT outsourcing has a significant negative correlation with a firms' non-IT operating costs and that firms benefit more in terms of reduction in non-IT operating costs when they also have higher levels of complementary investments in internal IT. One has to wonder if the finite resources available for innovation might degrade R&D ratios during critical IT adoption periods, as mentioned in the last chapter.

Some economic sectors are so unique that a pattern in adoption trends is hard to generalize. For example, Tutusaus et al. studied adoption of information and communication technologies (ICT) in the water-supply industry of Greece, and found more agreement among cases on barriers to adoption (e.g., scale and budget) than on consistent drivers (e.g., networks, entrepreneurship, autonomy, and competition).[6]

Green IT systems adoption is among the current consistent new topics in literature supporting sustainable practices.[7] Health care information system adoptions are central to the growth in extant literature. The majority (81%) of publications reviewed in the last five years evidenced improved medical outcomes from adoption of health care IT.[8] Industry studies abound including social work IT,[9] social welfare agencies,[10] blockchain, and other technologies adopted in logistics systems.[11]

The technology acceptance model (TAM) has been most recently used widely in education systems[12] and adoption management,[13] as well as meta-analysis specifically to predict teachers' adoption[14] of IT.[15] A recent study using TAM in adoption of mobile learning has extended the TAM with external variables, such as performance expectancy, self-efficacy, and satisfaction.[16] Experience moderates the intention to adopt mobile social network usage by extending the TAM model.[17] Ease of use and perceived usefulness were found to extend the TAM model in adoption of mobile banking and explained 78% of the variance in intention.[18] Adoption of big-data analytics using the TAM among 150 individual users included perceived usefulness and attitude as well as the characteristics of the big data system characteristics.[19] Meta-analyses of TAM have appeared and critical evaluations of the TAM model have appeared.[20]

Survey data on third-party logistics (3PL) providers reinforces and is in general agreement with these CIO trends. In a recent industry survey, it was reported that the three top challenges are labor shortages, competition, and IT improvements.[21]

What endures: synchronous innovation (SI) and information technology adoption

An example case that best illustrates the understanding and applications of the SI approach to adoption of new IT is the West Coast Dockworkers Lockout. This case is about the adoption of bar-coding technology in Long Beach.[22] In order to successfully adopt a new technology in a unionized organization or industry, a union-management technology agreement is the essential organizational innovation required. The dockworkers, their union, and the shipping lines still have not signed a new agreement about technology first installed with containerization in 1960.

The importance of a technology agreement was what we found in our first round of data collection in the plant modernization study.[23] This was replicated by Bobbie Turnianksy in her dissertation at Michigan.[24] As it turns out, having a technology agreement predicts successful adoption of advanced manufacturing technology, but the language in the agreement doesn't matter. No one can predict the details (like those covered in most union contracts) that will be needed to successfully adopt a truly new production method. Therefore, the language is obsolete as soon as the agreement is signed, but it gives the parties the motivation and trust to work together to solve any new challenge precipitated by the implementation unfolding. If joint action and gains sharing are part of the agreement, little else is needed to succeed under these circumstances.

The model we developed for successful adoption (i.e., on-time, on-budget) resulted from an empirical study of 80 ERP installations, and is summarized next.[25] The synchronous innovation sweet spot is very difficult to achieve in these situations due to the novelty, and especially the complexity of ERP systems, even when adopted with the help of a third-party consultant. Even with the limitations of this model (35% of the variance explained for on-time/on-budget), it has a nearly perfect track record in predicting outcomes in any new ERP case that appears (The summary of the findings appears in Box 8.1). Therefore, it is included here as an enduring result from this applied research stream.

This work on synchronous innovation has recently been extended by my colleague Chih Liu,[26] in his work on the mirror hypotheses. There are many more large-sample survey studies that have shown that adoption of new technology and new HR practices go hand-in-hand to produce desired outcomes.

BOX 8.1

SUCCESSFUL ADOPTION OF ENTERPRISE SYSTEMS[a]

John E. Ettlie, PhD

Executive Summary

We undertook and completed an empirical study of 80 US, Fortune 1000 companies on the strategic deployment of enterprise systems, most commonly known as enterprise resource planning (ERP) systems. We emphasized predicting strategic outcomes in this applied research project: performance to *time and budget* projections and performance in deployment of ERP *relative to competitors*. We were able to predict over 40% of the variance of the strategic performance on these enterprise systems.

We found deployment of these challenging enterprise systems were significantly more likely to be successful if the following conditions (four predictors) were met:

1. *Leadership*: We measured leadership specifically in the context of ERP deployment, and it included five critical behaviors or conditions.
   a. *General managers* across the board (with no exceptions) in each firm had to demonstrate with hands-on use of the ERP system in order to model the behaviors they wanted others in the company to emulate.[b] Giving strategic direction and support, and even leaving one senior manager out of this process decreased the odds of strategic success.
   b. *Quality and ERP* systems were linked and fully integrated.
   c. *General managers* (not middle managers) *managed third-party* (e.g., consultants) involvement in the ERP deployment.
   d. *Focus goals* in a way that is clear to the entire adopting firm with clarity of purpose, and no question what is the top priority of the adoption.
   e. *Focus deployment strategy* on goals related to satisfaction of customer needs, not cost reduction or some other performance factor.
2. *Acquisition Strategy*: Buy at least 80% off the shelf, even of in a suite of solutions using best of breed. Don't make (more than 20%) or buy tailored (more than 20%) systems.
3. *Business Process Engineering*: Make sure that (at least) one critical business process (none emerge as the key process in every case) is reengineered first or in parallel to ERP adoption and implementation.

Continued

BOX 8.1

SUCCESSFUL ADOPTION OF ENTERPRISE SYSTEMS[a]—*Continued*

4. *EDI History*: We find that companies that have a legacy of support for EDI systems are slower to adopt and successfully implement ERP. It is not that EDI is bad, quite the opposite. Some companies utilized this earlier generation of integrating IT that they are reluctant to move to new, more complex, and perceived as riskier technology.

Source: Managing Innovation, Ettlie (2007, pp. 350–351).

a   John E. Ettlie, Victor J. Perotti, Daniel A Joseph, Mark J. Cotteleer (2005). "Strategic predictors of successful enterprise system deployment." *International Journal of Operations & Production Management*, 25(10), 953–972, https://doi.org/10.1108/01443570510619473.

b   This construct is based, in part, on the social learning theory interpretation of leadership in new technology deployment under weak economic appropriation conditions (again, see, for example, Ettlie, J., (2000). *Managing technological innovation*. New York, Wiley, pp. 276–277).

West coast dockworkers lockout[27]

A West Coast dock slowdown on Friday degenerated over the weekend with waterfront employers locking out workers on Saturday.…At the heart of the dispute is employer management's plan to bring information technology to West Coast docks, thereby increasing efficiency and making better use of terminal space to handle projected doubling of cargo in the next 10 years.

When the dispute was finally settled after threat of government intervention, union reaction was swift and direct: Headlines: "West Coast Dockworkers: Victory in the Face of the Bush Doctrine: Union Compares Negotiations to a "Barbed Wire Straight Jacket."

In the movie *On the Waterfront* (1954), which takes place on the docks in New York Harbor, Marlon Brando mesmerized millions of moviegoers with those famous words to Rod Steiger in the backseat of a taxi: "You was my brother, Charlie, you should'a looked after me a little bit. You should'a taken care of me just a little bit.…I could'a had class. I could'a been a contender."[28] That scene created a powerful image of dockworkers as tough union loyalists, often violent men, doing backbreaking work, and eventually fighting corruption like Charlie's brother, played by Brando. When the technology fails in this movie, dockworkers get killed.

Has anything changed? Has technology made a difference? Should it? Can the recent West Coast dockworkers lockout provide a tentative answer to this question? How representative is this technology deployment situation compared to all factories, offices, and workplaces around the country and world?

Dockworkers and waterfront technology:
"An injury to one is an injury to all"

The International Longshore and Warehouse Union (ILWU) is regarded as one of the most cohesive unions in the world. For over 100 years, waterfront workers have struggled with employers to gain higher wages, increased worker safety, better working hours, and control at the point of production on the docks. The ILWU was not always the unified organization that it is today; it took a series of failures and losses for the workers to realize what it takes to create a powerful union.

Before the creation of the ILWU, dockworkers along the West Coast were affiliated with the International Longshoreman's Association (ILA).[29] One of the first large-scale waterfront strikes occurred in 1916, a time when wages had been stagnant for three decades at fifty cents an hour, and workers sought to replace the gang mode of work assignment with job rotation.[30] Influenced in part by the Industrial Workers of the World (IWW), longshoremen had begun to organize themselves with the goal of creating "one big union," achieved by militant tactics and solidarity amongst workers. The workers walked off the job on June 1, 1916, and after 127 days of bloody conflict, the strike ended with no gains for the union. However, workers recognized their ability to organize on a large geographic scale, setting the stage for future strikes.

This strike was followed by another large-scale strike in 1919, when the longshoremen took part in the Seattle General Strike. After 5 days, the strike collapsed with no material gains for the workers. Strikers lacked a clearly defined objective and a strategy for realizing workers' interests. Workers were left feeling powerless, and general unionism declined for more than a decade.

It was not until 1934 that workers realized the benefits of planned objectives and strong leadership. The union was rebuilt in 1933, with a greater understanding of the "principles of worker unity, internal democracy, and international solidarity advocated by the members of the militant IWW." In addition, they recognized that discrimination of any kind was not acceptable if the members were to achieve total unity. Two major issues had been at the core of workers' concerns over the year. The first was the "shape up" system of employment, where workers were required to carry registration books so they could be monitored by employers. The second issue was "speed up," where workers had to work fast enough to "meet the hook," meaning longshoremen had to work as quickly as the winch operators. Improvements in winch technology sped up the pace of the work. In addition, ship owners cut wages, driving the workers to strike.

In February 1934, a West Coast convention of the ILA was created to organize worker demands. Under the leadership of the convention and a strike committee, 12,500 West Coast longshoremen walked off the job on May 9, 1934. Later that month, they were joined by 4,500 sailors, marine fishermen, water tenders, cooks, and stewards. These groups allied together presented a formidable contender for the waterfront employers. Many minority workers that had previously worked as strikebreakers refused to scab, which was attributed to the longshoremen's developing policy against racial discrimination. The strike ended when the federal government intervened and the union agreed to arbitrate all strike issues. This strike and subsequent "quickie strikes" put the workers in power, improving working conditions and leading to a contract for increased wages and a 30-hour work week. With strong leadership, improved union organization, and widespread worker solidarity, longshoremen were finally able to gain power:

> Every contract over the past 40 years between the ILWU and shipping companies, which organized in 1971 to become the Pacific Maritime Association (PMA), has dealt with the issue of modernization and its impact on workers' jobs. In 1959, it became evident that new technology was needed to speed up cargo handling and ship turnaround time to offset rising costs. Employers had the right to make changes in operations, and the union hoped to retain some control over work at the point of production. The shipping industry and the ILWU worked together to produce the Modernization and Mechanization Agreement of 1960 (M&M). It gave the shipping companies more freedom over the introduction of new technology onto the docks in exchange for increased benefits for the workers. The conditions of the agreement included: The current workforce would not be laid off. If the unhindered introduction of new machinery and methods of work resulted in the loss of work opportunity so that the workforce had to be reduced, it would shrink from the top, with an innovative voluntary early retirement program instead of layoffs. If employers later needed to cut the workforce further, they could invoke a compulsory retirement provision with a higher pension benefit. Increased profits would be shared with the workers in the form of increased wages and benefits. Machines and labor-saving devices would be introduced wherever possible to lighten the burden of hard and hazardous work.

In 1966, the M&M agreement was extended under union pressure to include provisions that any net labor cost savings due to introduction of mechanical innovations or removal of contractual restrictions would be shared with the work force. Despite the attempts to improve relations between the union workers and the employers, a younger and militant generation of ILWU members was starting to question their level of jurisdiction in the late 1960s and early 1970s. Negotiations for the next five-year union contract began in late 1970, with the major focus for negotiations being containerization. The new contract was to start on July 1, 1971. In April of 1971, the union refused to handle containers in the Bay Area packed by anyone other than the ILWU. Subsequent negotiating sessions failed to resolve the issues of union jurisdiction, wage parity, and work rules, and as a result, 96.4% of ILWU members voted "yes" to strike. On July 1, 1971, the longest coast-wide longshoremen's strike in US history began. For the first time in 23 years, all 56 Pacific Coast ports were shut down.[31]

The US government intervened under the conditions of the Taft–Hartley Act and work resumed in most ports on October 6, 1971. Disagreements between the two groups continued, and the strike resumed in January of 1972. It was not until late February, after 134 days on strike, that the two sides reached an agreement. The settlement included improved language on container jurisdiction, dental benefits, five paid holidays, and a "Pay Guarantee Plan" that aided those workers whose work declined as an effect of introduction of new machinery.

Disputes continued through the 1990s on the issue of ILWU jurisdiction over introduction of non-union labor and use of new technologies, especially with the exponential growth of computerized technologies.[32]

The September 2002 lockout

The dockworkers' contract expired on June 30, 2002, but negotiations had been underway since May and continued after the contract lapsed. On one side was the PMA, representing shipping lines and stevedoring companies, and on the other side was the ILWU, representing 10,500 dockworkers at 29 Pacific ports, which handle about half of all US containerized cargo going in or out of the country, valued at approximately $300 billion per year. Closing the docks costs US business about a billion dollars a day. (*Wall Street Journal* and *LA Times*)

> At the heart of the dispute is employer management's plan to bring IT to West Coast docks, thereby increasing efficiency and making better use of terminal space to handle projected doubling of cargo in the next 10 years. But labor groups are seeking to protect high-paying union jobs.

What is the nature of this "information technology" referred to in this quote? Accounts appear to agree on the elements of the proposed changes, but these are not the only contract issues at stake:

1. Shippers offered a 17% wage hike over five years in May 2002, which was accepted by the union.
2. Computerized cargo tracking systems [bar-coding and electronic data interchange (EDI) systems]. This provision was accepted by the union in July 2002, and in turn [the ILWU] asked that only union clerks (currently entering movement of goods manually) be used in vessel planning (about 30% reduction in clerks jobs would result from the new technology introduction). The planning and configuration of containers is now done by computer operators, typically non-union, and often at remote sites. The shippers rejected this demand, since these jobs do not currently belong to the union and, further, shippers would not agree to bring new jobs into union that were created by new technologies. The real issue here is the conditions and terms under which any new technology would be introduced. The union wanted security of jobs and voice in subsequent technology changes on the docks.

3. Union officials contend that the PMA fails to recognize the importance of the fact that there has not been a port strike since 1971, and that the agreement will eventually eliminate 400 jobs of the 1,200 clerks on the West Coast (although no clerk will actually lose his/her job under contract guarantees). According to the *Journal of Commerce*, there has been a 30% increase in cargo handled at the docks last year, the greatest in history, and a consequent increase in accident rates, including the loss of lives of five longshoremen in 2002. The union has ordered work at a safe speed, and the PMA contends this is a slowdown. The hourly rate for dockworkers ranged from $27.68 to $33.48 ($80,000 to $158,000 per year, similar to a union plumber or electrician) before the lockout. Union officials fear that scanners are the next step on the way to fully automated cranes and dockside equipment, operated by remote control.[33]

The White House moves to prevent a strike

As early as May 2002, when negotiations were clearly breaking down, the White House made sure a working group was convened to monitor the proceedings comprised of people from the Departments of Commerce, Labor, Transportation, and Homeland Security.[34]

Department of Labor officials had been quite active in the negotiations and met twice with union officials in San Francisco and made phone calls almost every day on behalf of the Administration. It was made quite clear to the union that the Administration was prepared to take several actions to avert a strike, including invoking the Taft–Hartley Act (last used in 1978 during a coal miners' strike), which would force the delay of the strike for 80 days. Administration representatives correctly predicted that if the union did not see progress made toward accepting demands, they would begin slowdowns, and they wanted to avert this pattern. The union retorted that the government's intervention compromised their bargaining position and was part of a general trend to weaken unions.[35] It has also been reported both parties in the negotiation were influenced by Administration representatives. A sample of these reports follows:

1. Jim Miniace, who is the president of the PMA, contends that the Bush Administration has requested that he add better medical benefits to the latest contract offer.
2. ILWU President Jim Spinosa says he has been warned by Homeland Secretary Tom Ridge that any interruption of work on the docks represents a threat to national security. Labor department officials have hinted that a long-term strategy might be to break up the coast-wide bargaining unit into a port-by-port contract basis, so that cargo can be diverted when there is a strike. The use of Navy personnel to substitute for union workers appeared to be an extreme option only considered during time of war.

One has to wonder what the government's position would have been in this lockout before September 11, 2001. We'll never know, but the study of this lockout and its consequences might provide answers to much broader questions about unionized work and the adoption of new technology. After the lockout went into the 10th day, the Administration intervened to end the stalemate at the busiest ports in the US.

Before the lockout, the ILWU increasingly worked "by the book," which translates to a continued slowdown, but they were working without a contract, and five members had been killed in accidents during that past six months. In October, the ILWU accepted an offer from the Solicitor General of the Labor Department (Antonin Scalia) for a voluntary cooling-off period, which the PMA first accepted and then rescinded three hours later. President Bush was forced to invoke the Taft–Hartley Act, and the PMA filed a grievance in October 2002 because of a continued slowdown on the docks. The Attorney General filed two findings on the grievance: "there is a slowdown…(and) the employer is equally responsible for the slowdown as the workers."[36]

The new contract

Eventually, the two (or three depending on how you count) parties settled over the reasons for the lockout. The provisions for the settlement, according to the *Wall Street Journal*,[37] were as follows:

1. Pension benefits and arbitration procedures were the last thing to be settled and had been holding up the accord.
2. Implementing technology and maintaining health benefits had been previously agreed upon and were included in the final package.
3. "The tentative agreement gives management more freedom to introduce technology, particularly scanners and other electronic gear, to improve the flow of cargo through the West Coast maritime terminals.… ILWU… members become involved in tasks such as checking trucks into the terminals and providing instructions to equipment operators, often rekeying information already available in computers."
4. Rail and yard planning jobs are now open to the union, and the six-year contract doubles the normal contract period of three years. President Bush said, "This agreement is good for workers, good for employers, and it's good for America's economy."

According to two accounts, the final agreement came when union officials got concessions on pension demands and owners got arbitration procedures that would allow easier implementation of technology. The new agreement eliminates the need to reenter or rework data and promises a 50% productivity increase when the new technology is fully implemented. The agreement protects dockworkers whose tasks are replaced until they retire, and the union dropped the demand for minimum staffing of clerks. Neither side has made any extensive statements about the accord, but observers have said that the "tentative technology agreement represents a 'major piece' of reaching a new contract." Expanding pension benefits allows the union to share in the increased earnings brought by any new technology, including optical character recognition, TV cameras, or other technology for tracking and controlling cargo movement. All union-management technology agreements, whether covering local operations or at the national level, trade off flexibility for management in introducing new technology while giving unions what they typically want most: job security, health-care benefits, and increased safety measures but rarely higher wages. Union-management technology agreements have been found to be significantly and directly correlated, among other administrative innovations, which integrate the vertical hierarchy, with the ultimate success of new manufacturing technologies.[38] Further, whether or not a plant is unionized matters little to the success of new manufacturing technologies. Administrative innovations need to be incorporated along with adopted manufacturing technologies in order to achieve successful outcomes.[39] It is important to note that specific contract language of technology agreements doesn't typically predict success with the new technology when a unionized plant undergoes modernization with purchased technology. In sum, having a technology agreement matters as it promotes success, but technology agreement language does not predict success or failure.[40]

The challenges of adopting technology to enhance a business process

In economic terms, the real challenge of dockworker productivity, assembly-line quality, or any other work situation where technology comes into play is not just making the technology stable but capturing value from technology adopted from suppliers. The technology available to track cargo in ports is the same technology available to: UPS, Federal Express, United Airlines, US Lines, and the Santa Fe Railroad. Any competing mode of transportation has the same chances of success. Docks have a monopoly position in handling cargo, but any logistics system has many links in the chain. Also, ports do compete for goods. What factors predict the success of these new technology systems? Which docks and ports will be more successful with these new technologies? How does the M&M context impact this set of issues? These are the next set of questions that need to be answered to have a complete understanding of this complex technology management challenge.

Union reaction was swift with this forced settlement of the dispute:

West Coast Dockworkers: Victory in the Face of the Bush Doctrine Union Compares Negotiations to a "Barbed Wire Straight Jacket"[41]

San Francisco—Not since 1981, when President Ronald Reagan broke the air traffic controllers strike, have US labor relations gone through such a profound sea change as they did during recent west coast dockworkers contract negotiations. The Bush administration's overt, and behind-the-scenes, intervention on the side of management lead dockers to compare recent negotiations to bargaining in a "barbed wire straitjacket." Although union membership overwhelmingly ratified an agreement reached with the world's largest shipping companies, the circumstances overshadowing the talks were a clear warning shot to both the dockworkers and the rest of the US labor movement.[42]

"Given what we went through over the last six months, including the lockout of workers in every port, and then the invocation of the Taft-Hartley Act, we're glad we were able to reach an agreement at all," explained Steve Stallone, communications director for the International Longshore and Warehouse Union (ILWU). "So the fact that we were able to make progress on all three issues important to us was a big achievement."[43]

Debriefing this case: Fast Company ran a sponsored story for **Lineage**, on page 27 of the May 2019 issue, titled "Silicon Valley Meets Our Nation's Heartland." Linaege was No. 23 on Fast Company's Top 50 most innovative companies, specializing in controlled temperature storage and logistics featuring Lineage Cool Port Oakland, "…is the anchor of Northern California's temperature-controlled cargo transitioning through the Port of Oakland."

Notes

1 Kasemsap, K. (2016). Examining the roles of virtual team and information technology in global business. In C. Graham (Ed.), *Strategic Management and Leadership for Systems Development in Virtual Spaces*, (pp. 1–21). Hershey, PA: IGI Global.
2 Han, K., & Mithas, S. (2013). Information technology outsourcing and non-IT operating costs: An empirical investigation. *MIS Quarterly, 37*(1), 315–331.
3 Ibid., p. 315.
4 Muse, D. (January 2016). State of the CIO 2016: It's complicated. Retrieved from https://www.cio.com/article/3022833/state-of-the-cio-2016-its-complicated.html.
5 Han and Mithas (2013, p. 315).
6 Tutusaus, M., Schwartz, K., & Smit, S. (2018). The ambiguity of innovation drivers: The adoption of information and communication technologies by public water utilities. *Journal of Cleaner Production, 171,* S79–S85.
7 Bokolo, A. J., Majid, M. A., & Romli, A. (2018). A proposed model for green practice adoption and implementation in information technology based organizations. *Problemy Ekorozwoju, 13*(1), 95–112.
8 Kruse, C. S., & Beane, A. (2018). Health information technology continues to show positive effect on medical outcomes: Systematic review. *Journal of Medical Internet Research, 20*(2), e41.
9 Melville, N., Gurbaxani, V., & Kraemer, K. (2007). The productivity impact of information technology across competitive regimes: The role of concentration and dynamism. *Decision Support Systems, 43*(1), 229–242.
10 Gillingham, P., & Graham, T. (2017). Big data in social welfare: The development of a critical perspective on social work's latest "electronic turn." *Australian Social Work, 70*(2), 135–147.
11 Aggarwal, S., Gupta, A. R., Singh, D. P., Asthana, N., & Kumar, N. (2018). Application of Laplace transform for solving population growth and decay problems. *International Journal of Latest Technology in Engineering, Management & Applied Science, 7*(9), 141–145.

12 Wu, B., & Chen, X. (2017). Continuance intention to use MOOCs: Integrating the technology acceptance model (TAM) and task technology fit (TTF) model. *Computers in Human Behavior, 67,* 221–232.

13 Wang, K., Yu, J., Yu, Y., Qian, Y., Zeng, D., Guo, S., ... Wu, J. (2018). A survey on energy internet: Architecture, approach, and emerging technologies. *IEEE Systems Journal, 12*(3), 2403–2416.

14 Al-Emran, M., Mezhuyev, V., & Kamaludin, A. (2018). Technology acceptance model in M-learning context: A systematic review. *Computers & Education, 125,* 389–412.

15 Nagy, J. T. (2018). Evaluation of online video usage and learning satisfaction: An extension of the technology acceptance model. *The International Review of Research in Open and Distributed Learning, 19*(1), 161-185. doi:10.19173/irrodl.v19i1.2886, and Cantabella, M., López, B., Caballero, A., & Muñoz, A. (2018). Analysis and evaluation of lecturers' activity in learning management systems: Subjective and objective perceptions. *Interactive Learning Environments, 26*(7), 911–923.

16 Rospigliosi, P. A. (2019). The role of social media as a learning environment in the fully functioning university: Preparing for Generation Z, *24*(4), 429–431; and Nurakun Kyzy, Z., Ismailova, R., & Dündar, H. (2018). Learning management system implementation: A case study in the Kyrgyz Republic. *Interactive Learning Environments, 26*(8), 1010–1022.

17 Wingo, N. P., Ivankova, N. V., & Moss, J. A. (2017). Faculty perceptions about teaching online: Exploring the literature using the technology acceptance model as an organizing framework. *Online Learning, 21*(1), 15–35.

18 Mutahar, A. M., Daud, N. M., Ramayah, T., Isaac, O., & Aldholay, A. H. (2018). The effect of awareness and perceived risk on the technology acceptance model (TAM): Mobile banking in Yemen. *International Journal of Services and Standards, 12*(2), 180–204.

19 Rehouma, M. B., & Hofmann, S. (2018). Government employees' adoption of information technology: A literature review, 1–10. doi:10.1145/3209281.3209311.

20 Fosso Wamba, S. (2018). Social media use in the workspace: Applying an extension of the technology acceptance model across multiple countries. In Vol. 747, A. Rocha, H. Adeli, L. Reis & S. Costanzo (Eds.), *Trends and Advances in Information Systems and Technologies.* WorldCIST'18 2018. Advances in Intelligent Systems and Computing, Cham, Switzerland: Springer; Lim, W. M. (2018). Dialectic antidotes to critics of the technology acceptance model: Conceptual, methodological, and replication treatments for behavioural modelling in technology-mediated environments. *Australasian Journal of Information Systems, 22*; and Verma, P., & Sinha, N. (2018). Integrating perceived economic wellbeing to technology acceptance model: The case of mobile based agricultural extension service. *Technological Forecasting and Social Change, 126,* 207–216.

21 Langley, C. J. (2013). Third-party logistics study: The state of logistics outsourcing. Atlanta, GA: Capgemini Consulting.

22 CorpWatch: David Bacon, January 2, 2003, "West coast dockworkers: Victory in the face of the bush doctrine." www.corpwatch.org/issues/PID.jsp?articleid=5168.

23 Ettlie, J. E., & Reza, E. M., 1992. Organizational integration and process innovation. *Academy of Management Journal, 35*(4), 795–827.

24 Turniansky, R. R. (1986). The implementation of production technology: A study of technology agreements. PhD dissertation, Ann Arbor, MI: University of Michigan.

25 Ettlie, J. E., Perotti, V., Cotteleer, M., & Joseph, D. (2005). Strategic predictors of successful enterprise system deployment. *International Journal of Operations and Production Management, 25*(9/10), 953–1153.

26 Chih Liu, PhD Dissertation, University of Illinois, 2014, and personal communication, with permission.

27 Copyright © 2003, 2004, John E. Ettlie and Kristin E. Alexander, all rights reserved. No part of this case may be reproduced by any means mechanical or electronic without the written permission of the author. We would like to acknowledge the helpful comments of David Olson, Harry Bridges Chair Emeritus of Political Science, University of

Washington, and Professor Margaret Levi, Department of Political Science University of Washington. West Coast Dock Workers appeared as Case 7-2, in Ettlie, J. E., Managing Innovation, Elsevier/BH, Burlington, MA, 2007, pp. 356–373.

28 Kazan, E., Brando, M., Malden, K., Cobb, L. J., & Steiger, R. (1954). *On the waterfront.* Los Angeles, CA: Columbia Pictures.

29 The ILWU Story," http://www.ilwu.org/ilwu_story_frame1.htm.

30 Levi, M., & Olson, D. J. (March 2000). "STRIKES! past and present—And the battles in Seattle." Working Paper, http://depts.washington.edu/pcls/LeviOlsonwp2.pdf.

31 "Strike of 1971," http://www.pmanet.org/docs/index.cfm/id_subcat/92/id_content/2142586624.

32 Levi and Olson (2000).

33 Sources for these statistics include Seattle's NPR website on September 4, 2002, www.kuow.org/full_program_story.asap?NewsPage_Action=Find('ID,'3352'); Machalara, D., & Sook Kim, Q. (2002). Dock slowdown disrupts ports, raises fears on economic impact. *The Wall Street Journal,* A2; *Wausau Daily Herald,* November 25, 2002.

34 Jablon, R. (2002). *Longshore union's latest battle over modernization repeats history.* New York: Associated Press.

35 Nancy Cleeland. (2002). White house signals it will move to forestall west coast port strike; labor: Officials have warned of steps the government could take to avert a job action. Los Angeles Times. Retrieved from https://ezproxy.rit.edu/login?url=https://search.proquest.com/docview/421742049?accountid=108.

36 The third party might be considered the government or the West Coast Waterfront Coalition (WCWC) which is the business group of large retailers like Walmart, Home Depot, Target, the Gap, etc., or even the AFL-CIO which the ILWU rejoined in 1988 after being expelled in 1937 (World Socialist Web Site, International Committee of the Fourth International, ICFI), 30 August 2003.

37 Machalaba, D., & Sook Kim, Q. (2002). Dockworkers reach tentative accord on 6-year pact. *The Wall Street Journal,* A3, A10, and Machalaba, D., & Sook Kim, Q. (2002). West coast ports set tentative deal. *The Wall Street Journal.*

38 Ettlie, J. E., & Reza, E. M. (1992). Organizational integration and process innovation. *Academy of Management Journal, 35*(4), 795–827.

39 Ettlie, J. E. (2000). *Managing technological innovation.* New York: John Wiley & Sons, p. 258. Technology agreements and performance of new manufacturing technology are significantly and directly related. The only significant correlation between unionized shops (vs. nonunionized plants) and implementation of new production technology was size of the firm: larger companies with larger plants tend to be unionized. There were no significant correlations between union vs. no union and any performance measure advanced manufacturing technology (e.g., throughput improvement, quality improvement, up-time, utilization, inventory turns).

40 See, for example, Turniansky, R. R. (1986). The implementation of production technology: A study of technology agreements. PhD dissertation, Ann Arbor, MI: University of Michigan. The notion that the hierarchical structure of all organizations allows for "substrategies" among middle and lower level managers attenuates top management intentions and also allows "shopfloor politics" to enter into the implementation plan for new technology and often accounts for much of the variance in outcomes with these adopted innovations. See Thomas, R. J. (1994). *What machines can't do.* Berkeley, CA: University of California Press, esp. p. 22.

41 CorpWatch: David Bacon, January 2, 2003, West Coast Dockworkers: Victory in the Face of the Bush Doctrine. www.corpwatch.org/issues/PID.jsp?articleid=5168. & LA Times, August, 5, 2003.

42 Source, in part, from Personal communication from Professor Olson, D. (2003). *Political Science Department.* Seattle, WA: University of Washington, transmitted on September 6, 2003.

43 Sources throughout included the following: *LA Times,* August, 5, 2003. CorpWatch, Ob. Sid. And By David Bacon *Special to Corpwatch,* January 2, 2003.

9

CREATIVITY AND INNOVATION

What's new?

Creativity is the new innovation. In a recent visit to a well-known campus that hosts innovation conferences annually, the dean began by outlining their new college strategy: innovation is dead, long live creativity. In order to position the innovation agenda of their new mission, they had to derive something that is as novel as the mission, and innovation would no longer do. Creativity sounds newer and therefore became the marquee for the college. It doesn't matter that creativity is not the same as innovation and is far from the outcome plans of most firms. In this chapter, we come full circle back to one of the main themes of this book: creativity, innovation, and entrepreneurship are quite different concepts.

There appears to be some hope of integrating the contextual dimension of organizational ambidexterity and creativity, but the contributions to literature on this are still rather traditional in their methods and outcomes. One study found that typical on-the-job interventions pay off primarily in larger firms, with higher levels of R&D for manufacturing.[1]

We are suggesting a significant alternative to diurnal interventions to promote creativity and innovation by attending to the nocturnal interventions that are introduced below.

There continue to be studies showing a "labor friendly impact of R&D expenditures,"[2] unlike the controversy visited in Chapter 7 on the impact of robots, AI, and a plethora of other "dark" technologies.[3] What about the central issue that threads its way through all theory, research, and practice that is the theme of this chapter? That is the concern at hand: why is individual creativity and innovation so important? For academics, it is significant because behavioral patterns are at odds in the vast majority of organizational behavioral literature. At the organizational level, creativity and innovation have become the raison d'etre of corporate strategy of many firms.

Since creativity is a mature topic in many discipline-related research streams, much of the current mainstream literature is dominated by books. Some examples of this are *Creativity Now* by Jurgen Wolff and *Playfulness: Its Relationship to Imagination and Creativity* by J. Lieberman.[4] Both focus on interventions to improve individual creativity. The themes of this chapter go against this orthodoxy. First, creativity is not innovation. Second, all these books and papers generally focus on interventions into the conscious mind not on interventions into the unconscious mind. The latter is much more thought provoking and relates to what endures in this chapter.

Recent literature is not devoid of contributions on this matter, but they are rare. One exception is the article by N. Anderson, K. Potočnik, and J. Zhou.[5] The authors conceive of creativity and innovation as part of the same underlying process, but creativity focuses on ideation, and innovation focuses on idea implementation. In an earlier contribution and empirical study, Zhang and Bartol[6] wrote:

> In China, we found that, as anticipated, empowering leadership positively affected psychological empowerment, which in turn influenced both intrinsic motivation and creative process engagement. These latter two variables then had a positive influence on creativity. Empowerment role identity moderated the link between empowering leadership and psychological empowerment, whereas leader encouragement of creativity moderated the connection between psychological empowerment and creative process engagement.[7]

However, this is a case study of one firm in a country not known for creativity and especially not for breakthrough innovation.

Innovation, according to Roberts, is capitalization on new ideas, commercialization, or implementation of some new product, process, or service that improves people's lives. Bob O'Keefe and I developed a self-report measure of innovation intention for individuals and published our results in 1982.[8] The scale is still being used today, and most recently we have shown how it is related to a balanced thinking style.[9]

In an effort to better understand the multi-faceted phenomenon known as creativity, Rhodes[10] set out to find a universal definition. He believed of creativity that "when analyzed, as through a prism, the content of the definitions form four strands."[11] The four strands Rhodes refers to are person, product, process, and press. This framework for understanding creativity has become a "cornerstone" for previous and current research conducted by the International Center for Studies in Creativity at Buffalo State College—State University of New York.

Osborn[12] introduced the structure of creative problem solving (CPS) as a method for confronting challenging questions. The first CPS process has three distinct stages: Fact-Finding, Idea-Finding, and Solution-Finding. The concepts of deferred judgment and quantity yielding quality were also explored. Imaginative and judicial thinking were brought forth to demonstrate that people engage in both types of thinking. These fundamental beliefs set forth by Osborn have prompted followers to continue to research and develop the CPS process, which would evolve from three to five stages and include Problem-Finding and Acceptance-Finding.[13] The Problem-Finding stage was developed to discover the broad perspective of the situation, while the Acceptance-Finding stage allows individuals to consider how an idea or option will succeed or fail.

Isaksen and Treffinger[14] introduced a revision in the framework of CPS. This modification introduced the sixth stage, Mess-Finding, and renamed Fact-Finding stage as the Data-Finding stage. Prior versions of CPS described rules for divergent thinking;[15] Isaksen and Treffinger strengthened the concept of "dynamic balance."[16] They believed that "in CPS, we learn to use effective methods for generating and evaluating ideas, and we try to accomplish a reasonable balance between 'diverging' and 'converging.'…We talk about this as the 'dynamic balance' that makes CPS powerful and productive."[17] Isaksen, Dorval and Treffinger[18] further revised the CPS framework by describing it in three distinct components and six stages. The three components are understanding the problem, generating ideas, and planning for action.[19] The authors also introduced the step of Task Appraisal. Isaksen, Dorval and Treffinger argued that in order to use CPS effectively, it is necessary to understand the people who are involved and context and the task at hand.

Vehar, Miller and Firestien presented another revision of the CPS process.[20] This CPS version depicts the same three components and six stages described earlier; however, the language used to describe CPS was modified to become "easier to learn and use."[21] The language of the divergent and convergent guidelines was also changed, and a fifth convergent thinking rule was added.

Puccio, Murdock and Mance introduced the latest revision of the CPS process.[22] The structure of this version of CPS is described as follows: "[W]orking from the outside inward, [CPS is comprised] of three conceptual stages, six explicit process steps with six repetitions of divergence and convergence within each, and one executive step at the heart of the model to guide them all."[23]

The three conceptual stages are related to one's natural creative process. The stages are:

1. Clarification—to identify what needs to be resolved.
2. Transformation—the ability to generate ideas and develop them into feasible solutions.
3. Implementation—select the solutions with the most potential and produce a plan of action.

What endures

In this chapter, the preoccupation is with innovation—but for individuals, and not groups, not business units and or organizations. What Bob O'Keefe and I set out to do was to develop a predictive self-report instrument that would transcend occupations and contexts. An impossible dream, you say? As it turns out, we were successful, in part due to generous funding and blessed with time and energy to complete the project. The self-report protocol appears below in Box 9.1.

BOX 9.1

GAGING INNOVATIVE INTENTIONS

My Work Environment

Please indicate the extent to which each of the statements below is true of either your *actual* behavior or your *intentions* at work. That is, describe the way you are or the way you intend to be on the job. Use the following for your responses:

> 5—Almost always true
> 4—Often true
> 3—Not applicable
> 2—Seldom true
> 1—Almost never true

_____ 1. I openly discuss with my boss how to get ahead.

_____ 2. I try new ideas and approaches to problems.

_____ 3. I take things or situations apart to find out how they work.

_____ 4. I welcome uncertainty and unusual circumstances related to my tasks.

_____ 5. I negotiate my salary openly with my supervisor.

_____ 6. I can be counted on to find a new use for existing methods or equipment.

_____ 7. Among my colleagues and co-workers, I will be the first or nearly the first to try out a new idea or method

_____ 8. I take the opportunity to translate communications from other departments for my work group.

_____ 9. I demonstrate originality.

_____10. I will work on a problem that has caused others great difficulty.

_____11. I provide critical input toward a new solution.

_____12. I provide written evaluations of proposed ideas.

_____13. I develop contacts with experts outside my firm.

_____14. I use personal contacts to maneuver myself into choice work assignments.

_____15. I make time to pursue my own pet ideas or projects.

_____16. I set aside resources for the pursuit of a risky project.

_____17. I tolerate people who depart from organizational routine.

_____18. I speak out in staff meetings.

_____19. I work in teams to try to solve complex problems.

_____20. If my co-workers are asked, they will say I am a wit (good sense of humor).

Source: Ettlie, J.E., and O'Keefe, R.D., *J. Manag. Stud.*, 19, 163–182, 1982 and Reproduced with permission Ettlie, J. E., *Managing innovation: New technology.* Elsevier Science & Technology, 2007.

Scoring is in the Appendix, so you are not distracted should you choose to try the measure. We are amazed and gratified that the scale is still in use.

The development of this innovation intention and behavior scale had a broader context worth mentioning. Bob O'Keefe, Bill Bridges, and I were investigating the radical transition in food-packaging technology in the 1980s as the food industry was moving from rigid (e.g., tin cans) to flexible (e.g., boil in frozen plastic bag) technology. In the course of the early stages of the study and in background interviews, we found that not only were a few key technical and R&D people involved at the center of this transition, but they moved from firm to firm, from firms to government agencies, and then back again to private organizations. We wondered if there was a way to find out what made these people, who were not really entrepreneurs, engage in this risky food-packing business. Don't forget the food industry is regulated by the FDA and USDA. One fatal error and you would be out of business.

It took years and considerable cooperation from others, including our students at DePaul University (we are eternally grateful for their participation), to: develop, test, retest, and then validate the measure. The ultimate compromise turned out at the time to be a 20-item scale, which we continue to use even today. The questions are produced in the predecessor to this book,[24] and Box 9.1. Summaries of validation appear elsewhere, so there is no need to take up space here with that discussion.[1] Scoring appears in the Appendix.

Next up in this chapter, we concentrate on case histories that illustrate two types of individual innovation: start-ups and corporate innovators. A recent compilation of the latter type was published by three enterprising individuals Griffin, Price, and Vojak in their book *Serial Innovators*.[25] Here is a quote from the Amazon promotional material:

> In this pioneering study, authors Abbie Griffin, Raymond L. Price, and Bruce A. Vojak detail who these serial innovators are and how they develop novel products, ranging from salt-free seasonings to improved electronics in companies such as Alberto Culver, Hewlett-Packard, and & Gamble. Based on interviews with over 50 serial innovators and an even larger pool of their co-workers, managers and human resources teams, the authors reveal key insights about how to better understand, emulate, enable, support, and manage these unique and important individuals for long-term corporate success. Interestingly, the book finds that serial innovators are instrumental both in cases where firms are aware of clear market demands, and in scenarios when companies take risks on new investments, creating a consumer need.

In earlier chapters of this book, there are numerous examples of successful start-up innovators. Of course, the prominent example of Elon Musk has been mentioned several times. In our own work, we discovered that social learning theory is a good predictor of radical innovation in an industry that cherishes modernization: haute cuisine. Of all the competent models, radical restaurant chefs are vicariously learning from, it is the primary influence of parents that matters the most. Gianni Versace learned his trade at his mother's knee and became one of the most famous of all designers and a successful leader in haute couture.

The case histories of successful innovators like Jeff Bezos and Elon Musk are beset in most instances by a resistant context, widely vary, and often not helpful to nascent entrepreneurs. Steve Jobs is not one of these case examples because the success of Apple was due as much to Jon Ives and Tim Cook, as we have learned now[26] Another, unpublished example is my father, Joseph Ettlie. He never graduated from high school, but after serving in the Marines in the Central Pacific, he started and grew a machine tool and printing press remanufacturing business with 50 employees. I was one of them.

The smoking gun

This entire chapter has been devoted to convincing readers that for the unique focus of the individual and the creative and innovative process, Rokeach[27] was wrong. It is not the attitude toward the situation versus attitude toward the object that is a better predictor of the behavior; it's the other way around. To clarify: a situation matters little when it comes to creative individuals on the job. For example, creative employees often make repeat visits to their boss's office with iterations of an idea that begins as half formed and is shaped by interactions with others, often co-workers.

Now a study has finally appeared that not only shows this to be the best supporting evidence available validating this alternative view, it also includes crossing organizational boundaries. In two of my own related publications,[28] it was shown that C-level manager movement across the firm boundary (hire) precipitated radical process innovation adoption, and movement across an internal barrier (promotion to project or functional manager) promoted higher performance in advanced manufacturing systems.

The new evidence appeared as an upgraded conference paper authored by Bhaskarabhatla, Hegde and Peeters[29] in a 37-year panel study of patenting US inventor productivity. Quoting from the abstract:

> ...[We] find strong evidence for the persistence of inventory productivity...the inventors' human capital is 4–5 times more important than firm capabilities for explaining the variance in inventor productivity. We find high human capital inventors match with firms that have (a) other high human capital inventors, (b) superior financial performance, and (c) weak firm-specific invention capabilities. These findings provide evidence of the importance of human capital, and the tension between human capital and firm-specific capabilities in shaping innovation performance, QED.[30]

Diurnal versus nocturnal creativity enhancement

Our current preoccupation includes a quest to show that understanding and then intervention into the dream state is the next big thing in creativity and innovation enhancement. Our first, as yet unpublished, large sample results are very encouraging. What we found is not for publication yet, but is based on two studies of nearly 500 MBA and MS students over the past four years. If these results can be replicated and extended in experiments, we will have a strong argument that nocturnal interventions will ultimately surpass diurnal interventions to enhance creativity and innovation. The following is taken from the unpublished abstract:[31]

> Anecdotes proliferate about how dreams at night become reality during the day. Is there evidence of a general relationship between dreams and acquired behavioral predispositions—especially a direct link between dreams and innovation distinguished from creativity? This question is investigated using self-report data on the relationship between reliable measures of attitudes toward dreams, cognitive learning styles, and innovation intentions and behaviors. For a large sample of MBA and MS students, we found a significant and direct relationship between dreams and innovation. Further, we found this dream–innovation relationship to be significantly and positively moderated by cognitive thinking styles that tend toward linear thinking. This suggests a dream-recall-based, cognitively moderated predictor of innovation intentions and behaviors in the workplace. Implications for future studies are presented with suggestions for research on the ultimate role of nocturnal versus diurnal interventions to promote creativity and innovation.

This reminds me of the Bob Dylan song, "Series of Dreams."

Appendix: Scoring the Innovation Intentions Protocol. (Reproduced from Ettlie, J.E., *Managing Innovation*. 57–58, 2007.)

1. Step one in the scoring of your innovative potential is to add your total score for all 20 statements, according to the directions in Box 9.1.
2. Next, you can compare yourself to the norms established by our samples of evening MBA students and managers. A *total score of 70 is average.* Note that if you said "not applicable" to every question, your total score would have been 60. And if you had said "often true" to every question, your score would have been 80 the average is exactly halfway between these two response averages (or about 3 and 4 to every other question). A score *above 90 is truly remarkable,* and places you among the top 10 percent in our samples. If you scored at 90 or above, you have true innovative tendencies among the people in your job setting.

3. Our research also shows that some questions are better indicators than others of innovative intentions in organizations. In particular, question numbers 6 (new uses for existing methods); 7 (first to try new ideas); 12 (written evaluations of proposed ideas); 13 (develop contacts with experts outside the firm); and 18(comments at staff meetings) are the best five questions indicating innovative tendencies. Go back to your individual statement scores and see how you responded to these five questions as a second check on the reliability of this paper-and-pencil measure of individual innovative tendency. If you scored 5 ("almost always true") to these five questions, and scored more than 90 total points, it is an even stronger indicator of your (or anyone else's) innovation tendencies. But remember, it takes all kinds of people in all types of roles (mentors, champions, managers, funds providers, etc.) to make an innovative system work. There is a role for *everyone* in an innovative, successful organization.

4. Special note on Item 17: "I tolerate people who depart from organizational routine," is a red herring that was inadvertently entered on the protocol, which should have been "I take risks," and the latter can be substituted safely on the scale for use today. However, Item 17 can be used as a "faking" item to see if someone is just giving answers that we want to hear. If this item is marked, "Almost always true," *beware*. I want to thank the PhD student in Germany for pointing out this flaw in the protocol, whose name I can no longer retrieve. If you are reading this, please contact me for proper credit.

Notes

1 Revilla, E., & Rodríguez-Prado, B. (2018). Building ambidexterity through creativity mechanisms: Contextual drivers of innovation success. *Research Policy, 47*(9), 1611–1625. Also: Hughes, D. J., Lee, A., Tian, A. W., Newman, A., & Legood, A. (2018). Leadership, creativity, and innovation: A critical review and practical recommendations. *The Leadership Quarterly, 29*(5), 549–569.

2 Piva, M., & Vivarelli, M. (2018). Technological change and employment: Is Europe ready for the challenge? *Eurasian Business Review, 8*(1), 13–32.

3 Fort, T. C., Pierce, J. R., & Schott, P. K. (2018). New perspectives on the decline of us manufacturing employment. *Journal of Economic Perspectives, 32*(2), 47–72.

4 Wolff, J. (2009). *Creativity now.* Harlow, UK: Pearson Education and Liberman, J. N. (1977), *Playfulness: Its Relationship to Imagination and Creativity*, New York: Academic Press.

5 Anderson, N., Potočnik, K., & Zhou, J. (2014). Innovation and creativity in organizations: A state-of-the-science review, prospective commentary, and guiding framework. *Journal of Management, 40*(5), 1297–1333.

6 Zhang, X., & Bartol, K. M. (2010). Linking empowering leadership and employee creativity: The influence of psychological empowerment, intrinsic motivation, and creative process engagement. *Academy of Management Journal, 53*(1), 107–128.

7 Ibid., p. 107.

8 Ettlie, J. E., & O'Keefe, R. D. (1982). Innovative attitudes, values, and intentions in organizations. *Journal of Management Studies, 19*(2), 163–182.

9 Ettlie, J., S. Groves, K., M. Vance, C., & L. Hess, G. (2014). Cognitive style and innovation in organizations. *European Journal of Innovation Management, 17*(3), 311–326.

10 Rhodes, M. (1961). An analysis of creativity. *The Phi Delta Kappan, 42*(7), 305–310.
11 Ibid., p. 307.
12 Osborn, A. F. (1953). Applied imagination.
13 Noller, R. B., & Mauthe, E. (1977). *Scratching the surface of creative problem-solving: A bird's eye-view of CPS.* East Aurora, NY: DOK Publishers; Noller, R. B., Parnes, S. J., & Biondi, A. M. (1976). *Creative action book: Revised edition of creative behaviour workbook.* Charles Scriber's Sons'; Parnes, S. J. (1967). *Creative behavior guidebook.* New York: Scribner; and Parnes, S. J., Noller, R. B., & Biondi, A. M. (1977). *Guide to creative action.* MacMillan Publishing Company.
14 Isaksen, S. G., & Treffinger, D. J. (1985). *Creative problem solving: The basic course.* Buffalo, NY: Bearly Limited.
15 Noller and Mauthe (1977), Noller et al. (1976, 1977), Parnes (1967).
16 Isaksen and Treffinger (1985, p. 20).
17 Ibid., p. 25.
18 Isaksen, S. G., Dorval, B. K., & Treffinger, D. J. (1994). *Creative approaches to problem solving.* New York: American Management Association.
19 Isaksen et al. (1994, p. 60).
20 Vehar, J. R., Firestien, R. L., & Miller, B. (1999). Creativity unbound. *An introduction to creative problem solving (Innovation Systems Group).*
21 Ibid., p. 91.
22 Puccio, G. J., Mance, M., & Murdock, M. (2011). *Creative leadership: skills that drive change.* Thousand Oaks, CA: SAGE.
23 Ibid., p. 35.
24 Ettlie, J. E. (2007). *Managing innovation:* New technology, new products, and new services in a global economy. Amsterdam; Boston: Elsevier/Butterworth-Heinemann.
25 Vojak, B. A., Price, R. L., & Griffin, A. (2012). Serial innovators: How individuals create and deliver breakthrough innovations in mature firms. *Research-Technology Management, 55*(6), 42–48.
26 Kane, Y. I. (2014). *Haunted empire: Apple after Steve Jobs.* New York: Harper & Collins.
27 Rokeach, M., & Kliejunas, P. (1972). Behavior as a function of attitude-toward-object and attitude-toward-situation. *Journal of Personality and Social Psychology, 22*(2), 194–201.
28 Ettlie, J. E. (1980). Manpower flows and the innovation process. *Management Science, 26*(11), 1086–1095, and Ettlie, J. E. (1985). The impact of interorganizational manpower flows on the innovation process. *Management Science, 31*(9), 1055–1071. Also see: Ettlie, J. E. (1990). Intrafirm mobility and manufacturing modernization. *Journal of Engineering and Technology Management, 6,* 281–302.
29 Bhaskarabhatla, A., Hegde, D., & Peeters, T. (2017). Human Capital, Firm Capabilities, and Innovation. Tinbergen Institute Discussion Paper 2017-115/VII.
30 Ibid. (2017, abstract).
31 Ettlie, J. E., & Murthy, R. (2019). Dreams become you: Cognitive learning style, innovation and the dream state. Under review at the *Journal of Creative Behavior.* An Earlier version of this study was published as an abstract in the Proceedings of the Academy of Management Annual Meeting, August 2014.

10

THE DARK SIDE OF THE INNOVATION PROCESS

Easily ripped from the headlines is the emerging issue of the unintended, negative consequences of the innovation process—the dark side. The CEO and founder of Facebook, Mark Zuckerberg's testimony to the House Energy & Commerce Committee and the Joint Hearing of the Senate Judiciary and Commerce Committee could be one of the most recent and visible rationales for renewed interest in the dark side of the innovation process. Privacy is just one of many issues under the general category of unintended negative consequences.[1] At this writing, Facebook set aside $3–5 billon to settle claims that it misappropriated users' personal information.[2] This is what the chief technical officer (CTO) of Facebook, Mike Schroepfer, said in response to a question about the posting of a video showing the shootings in Christchurch, New Zealand: "It won't be fixed tomorrow. But I do not want to have this conversation again in six months from now."[3] It appears that "rogue images" are easier for AI to identify and remove than hate speech or false news.

Tesla was on the precipice of a giant leap forward with its electric-powered passenger vehicle when a fatal crash devastated this hope. According to the National Transportation Safety Board:

> On Friday, March 23, 2018, about 9:27 a.m., Pacific daylight time, a 2017 Tesla Model X P100D electric-powered passenger vehicle, occupied by a 38-year-old driver, was traveling south on US Highway 101 (US-101) in Mountain View, Santa Clara County, California. As the vehicle approached the US-101/State Highway (SH-85) interchange, it was traveling in the second lane from the left, which was a high-occupancy-vehicle (HOV) lane for continued travel on US-101. According to performance data downloaded from the vehicle, the driver was using the advanced driver assistance features traffic-aware cruise control and auto-steer lane-keeping assistance, which Tesla refers to as "autopilot."[4]

Obviously, this is not what Tesla intended for its autopilot technology.

What better way to illustrate the emerging importance of the unintended consequences of the innovation process than to review the case of the sharing economy and firms like Uber with its personal transportation on demand? While Uber claims that its service reduces drunk driving, only now does there appear to be evidence that this is true.[5] In any case, this supposedly positive effect often gets negated by Uber's almost daily harmful headlines of yet another transgression. Most recently, according to the *New York Times*, an autonomous Uber vehicle killed a pedestrian in Arizona even though there was a driver in the car. There is ongoing research on this issue.[6] Uber has come under sharp attack for a number of ethical concerns. Mobility services on demand have added significantly to a population of "contractors" that are actually unprotected and have no access to a socially accepted safety net, according to states like California and New Jersey. This becomes especially pertinent because companies like Lyft are opting to go to an initial public offering and have not made a profit; and when autonomous vehicles become viable, drivers will no longer be needed and safety concerns become more prominent.[7]

The Uber ethical issues extend well beyond whether drivers are contractors or employees and are common to a wider range of new "app" or "gig" economy offerings. For example, Uber drivers make less than minimum wage when all costs are accounted for. Ride-hailing services do not substitute for public transportation since the service is not accessible to all people, including those without credit cards. Uber drivers are not trained to deal with handicapped riders and cannot substitute adequately for emergency vehicles (Uber Health). Children under 18 cannot ride without a caregiver. Drivers and riders must use their own insurance, which would not cover most emergency situations. As of this writing, Uber reports the company wants to be on the right side of law by cooperating with authorities and has 70 members assigned to working with 300 agencies worldwide to thwart criminal activity.[8]

The more ride-hailing cars on the road, especially in cities, the greater the congestion. To the extent that software developers are at the core of "app" innovations, gender issues will persist. Company cultures, especially in Silicon Valley, which restrict access to hardware–software development jobs often keep women out of the app workforce. Uber and other app organizations raise the fundamental question of what the purpose is of innovation and advancement.[9] As of this writing, Uber's IPO stock offering may have actually caught up with the company's challenges: "Uber Technologies, Inc. skidded into the public markets Friday <May 10, 2019>, falling 7.6% below the ride-haling giant's already conservative offering price in a bleak debut for the nation's most valuable startup."[10]

Other firms have demonstrated similar behaviors, which incur societal costs missing from balance sheets. Airbnb routinely violates city hotel codes for rental rooms, and 15% of Twitter accounts are robots. Airbnb was recently "hit with a $20 million suit" in New York City for "circumventing state and local laws and

Airbnb's rules" and essentially running illegal hotel chains. What is more, Airbnb is also in battles with other cities, including Amsterdam, Paris, and Los Angeles— cities that have all passed laws restricting Airbnb rentals. In New York City, the largest Airbnb market, it is estimated that there are more than 100 Airbnb host accounts and 18 corporations used to run illegal hotel businesses. The city has issued a subpoena for information including 20,000 home-sharing listings in New York, and Airbnb has voluntarily taken down 5,000 commercial listings since 2015. An estimated one-third of listings for homes share websites of commercial operators, although Airbnb disputes that number.[11]

Although theory-based empirical research on related issues precedes such headline-grabbing events by many decades, now is the perfect time for the academic research streams underpinning the discourse on the positive and negative consequences of innovation to formally surface in the national policy debate. This will help to stimulate new research on this complicated subject. The policy issues refuse to go away. Take for example the rise and fall of the Office of Technology Assessment.[12]

There is extensive literature on creativity and its consequences[13] presented below, but extant research streams have been almost exclusively focused on positive creativity and have ignored the negative elements of these technological developments.

Literature review

Perhaps it all began with Danny Miller's now-forgotten model of Entrepreneurial Orientation.[14] He predicted there was a downside, maybe even a dark side, of innovation and that too much innovation may have unexpected negative outcomes. We consider this seminal contribution to innovation literature as a theoretical explanation for why there continues to be examples of unintentional damaging outcomes generated by the innovation process.

For individuals, the concern that creativity can be directed toward nefarious purposes and not to solving societal needs has surfaced in recent media.[15] There is even evidence that creativity and original thinkers are linked to dishonesty,[16] as well, as some dysfunctional traits such as "…moving against people."[17] In organizational behavior literature, attention has focused on the dark side of leadership like narcissism at the individual level.[18] This work has also included the group level of analysis.[19] For example, Gonzalez-Roma and Hernandez found that, "Whereas the numbers of innovations implemented had a positive direct effect on team performance, it had a negative indirect effect on team performance and aggregate job satisfaction…."[20] Collectively, this research suggests that because innovation processes are part of complex systems, they are subject to possible "bad behavior," which affects performance at all levels of the organization.

There is no consensus in literature on the likelihood and the extent to which the negative, unintended consequences are derived from creative and/or innovative processes. Plucker and Dakwa[21] reviewed the Cropely et al. edited volume on the dark side of creativity. They note that findings are mixed and that research has focused almost exclusively on positive outcomes of creativity, largely rejecting the "troubled artist" view of creativity.[22] For example, there is very little evidence to support a connection between creativity and substance abuse, although one study found a positive and direct connection between social rejection and greater artistic creativity.[23] Niepel, Mustafić, Greiff, and Roberts failed to find any connection between students' creativity assessments and any changes in subsequent ethical decision-making, even after controlling for reasoning skills.[24] Finally, Dahmen-Wassenberg et al. report that, "...facets of the bright side of personality (such as openness) seem to have a much stronger link to creativity than less desirable [dark side facets]."[25]

One of the contributions in this volume[26] is very useful for two important guiding assumptions. First, there is a difference between positive creativity, negative creativity (in intentions and outcomes), and unintended consequences of the creative process. It is the latter that we are interested in. James and Taylor give two examples of the unintended negative consequences of creativity: (1) Einstein didn't intend to assist in the development of nuclear weapons, and (2) the invention of the internal combustion engine was not intended to achieve air pollution.[27] These developments were derived from positive innovation expectations yet resulted in deadly consequences. Second, James and Taylor do review the relationship between personality (among other things like domain skills, situations, and culture) and creativity.[28] The complexity of these relationships is illustrated in studies they review: creativity and openness to experience are positively related, but creativity and conscientiousness (impulse control, planning, and organization) are negatively associated with creativity. Hostility, self-acceptance, and impulsivity have all been found to be positively associated with creativity.[29]

Even though it is taken as a cultural assumption that creativity is a desirable trait in individuals and a resource in organizations, there is recurring evidence that creativity is associated with dishonesty. One study directly tested the "creativity increases dishonesty" hypothesis. In five separate experiments, the authors "... show that participants with creative personalities tended to cheat more than less creative individuals and that dispositional creativity is a better predictor of unethical behavior than intelligence."[30] Other researchers have also found this connection between creativity and dishonesty.[31]

Similar unintended negative patterns are observed in firms and CEO behavior. According to Resick, Whitman, Weingarden, and Hiller[32]: "...[for] 75 CEOs of Major League Baseball organizations over a 100 year period...dark-side personality characteristics (narcissism) of CEOs were negatively related to contingent reward leadership...[which in turn was] negatively related to manager turnover and ratings of influence."[33] Jonason, Richardson, and Potter[34] found, "Those high in narcissism reported being more creative than most people, an association that may reflect narcissistic self-delusions of popularity and charm."[35]

They studied 207 individuals and their self-reported innovative characteristics and dysfunctional personality traits, and report that:

> ...Those who reported innovative characteristics also [were more likely to be] Arrogant, Manipulative, Dramatic, Eccentric; and [to exhibit] lower levels of Cautious, Perfectionist and Dependent. A representative approximation of the higher order factor "moving against people" was positively associated with innovative characteristics.[36]

Journals have devoted special issues to the topic. In 2004, the *Journal of Organizational Behavior* did just that. The editors focused primarily on individual innovation and reviewed the effects of moderating variables such as co-workers, supervisors, organizational context and national culture, group tenure, diversity, group processes like participation and management of competition between ideas, and external demands on the group, with mixed results.[37]

Researchers have been active at the organizational level, where finance and economics scholars have explored the role of restricting information, which has resulted in limited analyst coverage of innovation,[38] the hiding of information about innovative securities to exploit uninformed investors,[39] and the role of trust and its restraints on innovative performance.[40] In fact, some theorize that unintended, negative consequences are the norm for most forms of financial innovation.[41]

Given the importance of innovation systems to regional and national aspirations, there is active policy literature on innovation systems and their processes.[42] This is especially salient given the globalization of firm- and industry-level innovation systems. This trend and the parallel emergence of more open innovation models are of particular interest. Research on interorganizational innovation arrangements is seeking to move beyond moral hazard issues focused on supply-chain innovation. For example, Noordhoff et al. studied 157 joint innovation projects in Holland and found that embedded ties often weaken how much benefit suppliers achieve from customer innovation.[43] Social capital appears to follow an inverted curvilinear relationship between the buyer's objectivity and supplier opportunist behavior.[44] The supply chain can suffer obsolescence of product offerings when it incorporates high technology but has a long life cycle.[45] This literature has been extended to online co-creation. Similarly, Gebauer and his colleagues found that co-creation communities online often experience perceived unfairness and dissatisfaction, which has a ripple effect, such as negative word-of-mouth.[46] Online communities seem vulnerable to conflict outcomes rooted in the dark side: "... the results challenge the direct influence of co-creation experience on members' actions [and sense of community]...."[47]

The article further shows that dealing with such critical situations and managing conflicts in co-creation communities mean an open dialog in the public sphere, which requires co-negotiation and co-moderation.[48] It appears that in practice, time metrics and organizational forms contribute to these problems in new product development, at least according to expert opinion.[49]

Supplier-buyer relationships also seem especially vulnerable to curvilinear effects of relationship quality. Villena, Revilla, and Choi studied buyer–seller relationships and found that:

> …social capital impedes value creation… Either too little or too much social capital can hurt performance [in BSR, buyer-seller relationships and] confirms that building social capital in a collaborative BSR positively affects buyer performance, but that if taken to an extreme it can reduce the buyer's ability to be objective and make effective decisions.[50]

Clearly, the unintended effects of structuring buyer–seller relationships for co-development need to be examined.[51]

Service innovations are equally exposed to the dark-side problem, especially in areas of financial innovations. Henderson & Pearson found that structured equity products average 8% greater-than-fair-market value using option pricing methods.[52] These products do not provide tax, liquidity, or other benefits, taking advantage of uninformed investors because of complexity. The authors report that the greater number of analysts covering firms, the fewer patents and patents with lower impact.[53]

The dark side of innovation gives rise to a number and variety of urgent, intersecting issues calling out for attention. There is a critical need for action, new policy, and decision-making based on the best theory-based research on these topics. Universities over the past 30-plus years have taken on a greater share of the innovation/R&D duties and are now seriously considering engagement as an important strategic goal. The recognition of the interdisciplinary nature of much of the high-impact publications, and the potential for new research, are central to these timely goals. For example, the University of Michigan has an extensive autonomous vehicle testing and educational program, which is a clear example of joint and interdisciplinary action research.[54]

Notes

1 Tsay-Vogel, M., Shanahan, J., & Signorielli, J. (2018). Social media cultivating perceptions of privacy: A 5-year analysis of privacy attitudes and self-disclosure behaviors among Facebook users. *New Media and Society, 20*(1), 141–161. Article first published online: August 2, 2016; Issue published: January 1, 2018.
2 Kang, C. (2019, May 5). A severe penalty awaits Facebook, but how severe? *New York Times*, 1, 24.
3 Metz, C., & Isaac, M. (2019), It's never going to go to zero. *New York Times*, Business section, pp. 1, 6–7.
4 Lambert, F. (2018, June 7). NTSB releases preliminary report on fatal Tesla crash on Autopilot.
5 Fortin, J. (2017, April 7). Does Uber really prevent drunk driving? It depends on the study. *New York Times*.
6 Fleetwood, J. (2017). Public health, ethics, and autonomous vehicles. *American Journal of Public Health, 107*(4), 532–537.

7 Eidelson, J. (2019). D.C. isn't Uber's biggest problem. *Bloomberg Businessweek*, Issue 4600, pp. 21–22.
8 Kessendies, D., & Begun, B. (2019). Uber wants the law on its side. *Bloomberg Businessweek*, pp. 18–20.
9 Chee, F. M. (2018). An Uber ethical dilemma: Examining the social issues at stake. *Journal of Information, Communication and Ethics in Society, 16*(3), 261–274.
10 Driebusch, C., & Farrell, M. (2019). Uber's high-profile IPO slips in weak first session, *Wall Street Journal, 273*(110), A1, A2.
11 Ferré-sadurní, L. (February 2019). Inside the Rise and Fall of a Multimillion-Dollar Airbnb Scheme. Retrieved from https://www.nytimes.com/2019/02/23/nyregion/airbnb-nyc-law.html.
12 Bimber, B. A. (1996). *The politics of expertise in Congress*. Albany, NY: State University of New York Press.
13 Cropley, D. H., Cropley, A. J., & Kaufman, J. C. (Eds.). (2010). *The dark side of creativity*. New York: Cambridge University Press.
14 Miller, D., & Friesen, P. H. (1982), Innovation in conservative and entrepreneurial firms: Two models of strategic momentum. *Strategic Management Journal, 3*, 1–25.
15 McLaren, R. B. (1993). The dark side of creativity. *Creativity Research Journal, 6*(1–2), 137–144.
16 Gino, F., & Ariely, D. (2012). The dark side of creativity: original thinkers can be more dishonest. *Journal of Personality and Social Psychology, 102*(3), 445–459.
17 Zibarras, L. D., Port, R. L., & Woods, S. A. (2008). Innovation and the "dark side" of personality: dysfunctional traits and their relation to self-reported innovative characteristics. *The Journal of Creative Behavior, 42*, 201–215.
18 Khoo, H. S., & Burch, G. S. J. (2008). The "dark side" of leadership personality and transformational leadership: an exploratory study. *Personality and Individual Differences, 44*(1), 86–97.
19 Janssen, O., van de Vliert, E., & West, M. (2004). The bright and dark sides of individual and group innovation: a special issue introduction. *Journal of Organizational Behavior, 25*(2), 129–145. doi:10.1002/job.242.
20 Gonzalez-Roma, V., & Hernandez, A. (2016). Uncovering the dark side of innovation: the influence of the number of innovations on work teams' satisfaction and performance. *European Journal of Work and Organizational Psychology, 25*(4), 570–582.
21 Plucker, J. A., & Dakwa, K. D. (2012). The dark side of creativity. *The International Journal of Creativity and Problem Solving, 22*(2), 109–112.
22 Cropley, D. H., Cropley, A. J., Kaufman, J. C., & Runco, M. A. (Eds.). (2010). *The dark side of creativity*. New York: Cambridge University Press.
23 Akinola, M., & Mendes, W. B. (2008). The dark side of creativity: biological vulnerability and negative emotions lead to greater artistic creativity. *Personality and Social Psychology Bulletin, 34*(12), 1677–1686.
24 Niepel, C., Mustafić, M., Greiff, S., & Roberts, R. D. (2015). The dark side of creativity revisited: is students' creativity associated with subsequent decreases in their ethical decision-making? *Thinking Skills and Creativity, 18*, 43–52.
25 Dahmen-Wassenberg, P., Kämmerle, M., Unterrainer, H. F., & Fink, A. (2016). The relation between different facets of creativity and the dark side of personality. *Creativity Research Journal, 28*(1), 60–66.
26 James, K., & Taylor, A. (2010). Positive creativity and negative creativity (and unintended consequences), pp. 35–36, chapter 3 in Cropley et al. (2010).
27 Ibid., p. 36.
28 Ibid., pp. 38–41.
29 Ibid., p. 40.
30 Gino, F., & Ariely, D. (2012). The dark side of creativity: original thinkers can be more dishonest. *Journal of Personality and Social Psychology, 102*(3), 445–459.

31 Liu, L., & Ye, M. (2015). The dark side of creativity. *Open Journal of Social Sciences, 3*(9), 190.
32 Resick, C. J., Whitman, D. S., Weingarden, S. M., & Hiller, N. J. (2009). The bright-side and the dark-side of CEO personality: examining core self-evaluations, narcissism, transformational leadership and strategic influence. *Journal of Applied Psychology, 94*(6), 1365–1381.
33 Ibid., p. 1365.
34 Jonason, P. K., Richardson, E. N., & Potter, L. (2015). Self-reported creative ability and the dark triad traits: an exploratory study. *Psychology of Aesthetics, Creativity, and the Arts, 9*(4), 488–494.
35 Ibid., p. 488.
36 Ibid.
37 Janssen, O., Van de Vliert, E., & West, M. (2004). The bright and dark sides of individual and group innovation: a special issue introduction. *Journal of Organizational Behavior, 25*(2), 129–145.
38 He, J., & Tian, X. (2013). The dark side of analyst coverage: the case of innovation. *Journal of Financial Economics, 109*, 856–878.
39 Henderson, B. J., & Pearson, N. D. (2011). The dark side of financial innovation: a case study of the pricing of a retail financial product. *Journal of Financial Economics, 100*(2), 227–247.
40 Molina-Morales, F. X., Martínez-Fernández, M. T., & Torlò, V. J. (2011). The dark side of trust: the benefits, costs and optimal levels of trust for innovation performance. *Long Range Planning, 44*(2), 118–133.
41 Henderson and Pearson (2011).
42 Diaz-Rainey, I., & Ibikunle, G. (2012). A taxonomy of the 'dark side' of financial innovation: the cases of high frequency trading and exchange traded funds. *International Journal of Entrepreneurship and Innovation Management, 16*(1): 51–72.
43 Noordhoff, C. S., Kyriakopoulos, K., Moorman, C., Pauwels, P., & Dellaert, B. G. (2011). The bright side and dark side of embedded ties in business-to-business innovation. *Journal of Marketing, 75*(5), 34–52.
44 Villena, V. H., Revilla, E., & Choi, T. Y. (2011). The dark side of buyer-supplier relationships: a social capital perspective. *Journal of Operations Management, 29*(6), 561–576.
45 Gravier, M. J., & Swartz, S. M. (2009). The dark side of innovation: exploring obsolescence and supply chain evolution for sustainment-dominated systems. *The Journal of High Technology Management Research, 20*(2), 87–102.
46 Gebauer, J., Fuller, J., & Pezzei, R. (2013). The dark and the bright side of co-creation: triggers of member behavior in online innovation communities. *Journal of Business Research, 9*, 1516–1527.
47 Ibid., p. 1516.
48 Ibid.
49 Cooper, R. G., Edgett, S. J., & Kleinschmidt, E. J. (2002). Optimizing the stage-gate process: what best-practice companies do—I. *Research-Technology Management, 45*(5), 21–27.
50 Villena, V. H., Revilla, E., & Choi, T. Y. (2011). The dark side of buyer-supplier relationships: a social capital perspective. *Journal of Operations Management, 29*(6), 561–576.
51 Ibid., p. 561.
52 Henderon, B. J., & Pearson, N. D. (2011). The dark side of financial innovation: a case study of pricing of a retail financial product. *Journal of Financial Economics, 100*(2), 227–247.
53 Henderson and Pearson (2011).
54 Zhang, Q., Na, D., Robert, L. P., & Yang, X. J. (2018). Trust in AVs: the impact of expectations and individual differences. *Presented at the conference on autonomous vehicles in society: Building a research agenda.* May 18–19, East Lansing, MI.

11
INNOVATION RENAISSANCE

A renaissance is at its core a revival. This book is a threefold call to revive a more objective, informed, and politically neutral Weltanschauung or worldview of a very complex and multi-disciplinary view of the field of innovation studies. This is why we picked the sundial for the cover of this book. The sundial was invented by the Greeks but eventually was made obsolete by the invention of clockworks in the Renaissance. But now and then, clocks were recalibrated with sundials. Sundials take on a revived (renaissance) meaning as decorative motifs. See the picture I took of the sundial below at Eastview Mall in Victor, NY (Figure 11.1).

There is understandable resistance to adopting this view of the field because it is challenging. While others want us to live in the moment or be mindful, innovation requires one to live in the future, and this is not an easy way to go through life. In part, this is what leadership is about—seeing the future and making the future real in a way that motivates action.

The threefold call of the book is this:

1. Much of what is easily available in the media on innovation is incorrect. The first three chapters of the book focus on debunking and demystifying this complex subject. Disruptive innovation is not radical innovation. Open innovation is not working better with suppliers, and maybe crowdsourcing is not for everyone. Like many other myths that have become "streetwise" interpretations of the rubric, creative individuals do not necessarily thrive in a calculated risk-taking organizational climate.
2. Theory matters an even if most theories outlive their usefulness, empirical science eventually will dominate a field that creates the raw material for policy decisions.

FIGURE 11.1 Eastview Mall Sundial, iPhone 6, taken at 1 pm EDT, April 2019, John E. Ettlie

3. What endures is worth documenting in the aftermath of the original contribution if reinforced by subsequent work. Synchronous innovation has been shown to underpin successful adoption of innovation in thousands of cases and hundreds of empirical tests. Under weak appropriation conditions, such as the adoption of a new operations-information technology system, it is organizational or administrative innovation that becomes the critical explanatory construct. This is not merely an academic exercise. Billions of dollars are spent every year on purchased new technology that can easily go south. Successful adoption of new technology is just as important as an effective R&D portfolio for strong appropriation benefit capture.

What remains to be considered for readers that have made it this far and are at least modestly interested in the prospects of enlightened views of the field is an informed debate on the truly critical issues emerging as of this writing. Three issues are paramount, and they are taken up separately below.

First, there is a critical need for the revival of a theory-based, empirically valid view of a multi-disciplinary innovation studies field. The non-critical, politicized view of this issue contends that all things bright and beautiful are multi-disciplinary. We contend that some, but not all problems, are more easily solved with a multi-disciplinary approach to innovative problem solving.[1] The debate about rigor versus relevance is very much at the heart of this issue.[2]

Second, the gap between practitioners and academics is wide but closing due to a number of factors. Enlightened practitioners engage leaders in the innovation field directly through consulting. A practitioner colleague I met with frequently, for example, has questioned the usefulness of crowdsourcing in his high-technology environment. This is enlightened thinking. A very successful consultant, former student, and friend of the author has asked many times: why survey our clients on an issue when there are thought leaders in universities (and elsewhere) that have spent entire careers researching? Eric von Hippel is an example of one such practitioner. Another critical force at play, which appears to show promise in reversing the polarity between academics and practitioners, is online EMBA programs. In my own experience, seasoned online class members collaborate almost immediately on the innovation topics critical to the field like the synergy of product and service innovation. They are engaged from the first synchronous session in our online innovation courses.

Third, there is a studied neglect of the unintended, negative consequences of the innovation process. Some of these examples already have been presented in previous chapters, but perhaps one in-depth case will serve to sharpen focus on the dark side of the innovation process: Uber. There once was a government agency, the Office of Technology Assessment (OTA), designed to monitor and study the potential unintended consequences of new projects, but it no longer exists and is a story in and of itself.[3]

We've had a run of articles on Uber, all bad, as of this writing. Founder and CEO, Travis Kalanick was called by the *NY Times*[4] "famously combative" and "facing business challenges—a tarnished image, legal difficulties, and competition from rivals like Lyft...."[5] *Automotive News* called Uber a "pirate" for using "Greyball" software to avoid sting operations in cities where Uber operations have been restricted. Complaints abound of drivers being underpaid and misclassified as contractors instead of employees, and of Uber having a "toxic" work environment.[6] Also, the company is being sued for technology theft.

In a recent issue of the *New Yorker*, Sheelah Kolhatkar chronicled with great eloquence how the Uber moral compass has gone haywire.[7] "Toxic patterns," including sexual harassment and continued scandals with no reform forthcoming from the top to change the culture of Uber, got Travis Kalanick fired (he "resigned," of course). It took four months of continuing problems before he stepped down. Uber is "at war with its drivers,"[8] has an intellectual property lawsuit with Waymo, and is under investigation by the Justice Department for evading regulators in two cities where the ride-sharing service was introduced. The question raised in the article is whether or not it is possible to innovate without all the (non-Christensen) disruption and the better-to-ask-forgiveness-than-ask-permission practices. The article reviews contentions that Uber can only make money if it becomes a monopolist in at least some of its markets, and that clearly is not the case. Most major airports now have docking curbside placement for Uber and Lyft. Nearly a half million potential customers have deleted the Uber application from their smartphones.

Uber made the front page of the *Wall Street Journal* with more bad news. Apparently, Uber has been leasing unsafe cars to drivers.[9] "Chasing growth, the ride hailing giant bought SUVs in Singapore subject to recall—then one caught fire." Uber has no CFO or COO, and the chief safety officer left a year ago. Local, gray-market dealers supplied SUVs passed on by authorized Honda dealers and saved the company an estimated 12% and at a delivery rate of 200 per month. All these moves were in the name of growth, not in the name of driver and passenger safety. Local Uber managers urged the company to take defective vehicles off the road, but Uber's general manager, Warren Tseng, said in an email that it would cost 1.4 million Singapore dollars a week (about 1 million USD) in wages for drivers, rental, and parking fees. Of course, these vehicles were not removed, and the company waited for replacement parts. Even after the SUV fire, drivers were only told there was a recall and directed them to a website but never mentioned overheating and fire dangers advised in Honda's recall notice.[10]

Airbnb is suffering similar issues while being challenged as an unregulated hotel. Not only has Airbnb faced problems concerning regulations of private hosting and subletting in major cities like San Francisco and New York, the hotel tax issue tends to be quite important to local administrators.[11] Airbnb has been hacked,[12] renters are primarily interested in tourist sites, and the service generally does not serve an entire city.[13] Most recently (as of this writing), Airbnb is being sued by a guest that claims she was sexually assaulted by her host, on the grounds that Airbnb failed to do a background check.[14] In spite of these issues of illegal rentals, taxes, and security, the company (like Uber) has grown dramatically.

Not surprisingly, this unethical management style has created competitors. Cabs in Washington, DC, are switching to app-based meters by regulation using Square Inc. to process transactions.[15] Drivers are be able to discount fares when traffic is light. Companies won't be able to increase fares in busy times as with Uber technology surge pricing. Links with local merchants for delivery of meals and groceries and carpooling are under consideration.

Uber is an example case, coming full circle from Chapter 10, for a more balanced treatment of the subject of innovation, which includes the unintended negative consequences of innovations on small and large scales. The truth of the renaissance in creativity and innovation is that we are now paying a social price for the misguided national opinion that innovation is always desirable; damaging have arisen. There used to be an Office of Technology Assessment in Washington, DC. It was an arm of the US Congress, and its purpose was to oversee technological innovations. When this office was done away with, important oversight was lost.

If Congress remains deaf and blind to the unintended consequences of innovation, then the states and local government will have to step up and fill the void.

A concerted effort to focus business ethics and engineering ethics on a better understanding of this American blind spot will be required for successful human capital development that is so drastically needed in many industries. This is a clear opportunity for multi-disciplinary research. Consider the advent of autonomous vehicles and MRIs, which are digital imaging of the brain. Engström argues that we have arrived at state-of-the-art of medical imaging whereby digital images are interpreted as pictures of the brain, but in fact they are the result of a typically proprietary, commercially motivated technology that translates the brain into statistical aggregates. "The driverless car...raises a usefully analogous concern regarding the ethical as automated, as a built-in statistical utility function...."[16] There is no comprehensive or accumulated evidence that autonomous vehicles or even Uber or Lyft have eliminated or even reduced DUIs or DWIs, which was one of the ethical or moral arguments for their adoption (see Chapter 10 for a detailed discussion). Engineers are not satisfied with autonomous technology grounding, especially sensor technology and prevention of external hacking of control software. Would it be too much to ask the engineering ethics community to start considering concerns about issues, such as deliberation and operation of a development process in a vacuum?

Lest we think academe is above this concern about the dark side, or unanticipated negative consequences of the innovation process, as introduced in Chapter 2 (e.g., "toxic environment for women in economics"),[17] it is worth looking at one final example of applied research on academic entrepreneurs. Using a sample of 105 research universities and 73,603 scientists, Gianiodis, Markman, and Panagopoulos[18] report that "scientists privately leak discoveries invented while working for their universities"[19] and that universities "often do not retaliate even when having knowledge of such opportunistic behavior...."[20] It seems clear that academic entrepreneurs routinely circumvent the rules and policies under which they conduct their research, which not only benefits the scientists but also the region for economic development. That is, the ecosystem tends to dominate decision-making and start-up activity outside the university. Extant incentive systems do not appear to have any impact on these "backdoor" activities.

Technology commercialization offices (TCO) on the campus are often not up to the daunting task of overcoming this opportunism due to resource constraints, or skills and capabilities of TCO personnel. Much work needs to be done to understand overt opportunism at the individual, departmental, college, and university levels, which in turn are embedded in a typically complex ecosystem. Further, the authors interviewed faculty and students in firms, federal research institutes, medical research facilities, and hospitals and found that overt opportunism "is rampant" in the private and other public sector organizations. The broader issue of entrepreneurism embedded in a complex ecosystem ultimately becomes the focus of future research. Perhaps the academic entrepreneur becomes the poster child for the unintended negative consequences of the innovation process.

Notes

1 Ettlie, J. E., & Sanders, N. R. (2017). Discipline boundaries in innovation studies: Operations management and allied fields. *Journal of Strategic Innovation and Sustainability,* *12*(1), 41–54.

2 Tushman, M., & O'Reilly, C. (2007). Research and relevance: Implications of Pasteur's quadrant for doctoral programs and faculty development. *Academy of Management Journal, 50*(4), 769–774.

3 Bimber, B. A., (1966). *The politics of expertise in Congress: The rise and fall of the office of technology assessment.* Albany, NY: SUNY Press, and Kunkle, G. C. (1995). New challenge or the past revisited?: The office of technology assessment in historical context. *Technology in Society, 17*(2), 175–196.

4 Isaac, M. (2017). Uber's C.E.O. plays with fire. *The New York Times,* p. B1.

5 Ibid., p. B6.

6 (March 2017). Even disruptors must play by the rules. *Automotive News, Mobility Report,* p. 12.

7 Kolhatkar, S. (2017). Uber's opportunistic ouster. *The New Yorker,* July 10 and 17, 2017 Issue, p. 27.

8 Ibid., p. 27.

9 MacMillan, D., & Purnell, N. (2017, August 4). Smoke, then fire: Uber knowingly leased unsafe cars to drivers. *The Wall Street Journal.*

10 Ibid.

11 Nieuwland, S., & Van Melik, R. (2018). Regulating Airbnb: How cities deal with perceived negative externalities of short-term rentals. *Current Issues in Tourism.*

12 Perlroth, N. (2016, October). Hackers used new weapons to disrupt major websites across U.S. *The New York Times.*

13 Nieuwland and Melik (2018).

14 Vora, S. (2017, August). Airbnb sued by guest who says a host sexually assaulted her. *The New York Times, Travel Section,* p. 2.

15 Brustein, J. (2017, May 17). Square will replace meters in Washington taxis, *Bloomberg Businessweek.*

16 Engstrom, T. H. (2016). Making and managing bodies: The computational turn, ethics and governance. *Proceedings, Sixth Annual International symposium on Digital Ethics.*

17 Wolfers, J. (2017). Evidence of toxic environment for women in economics. *New York Times,* August 18, 2007, BU3.

18 Gianiodis, P., Markman, G. D., & Panagopoulos, A. (2016). Entrepreneurial universities and overt Opportunism. *Small Business Economics, 47*(3), 609–631.

19 Ibid., p. 609.

20 Ibid.

12

INNOVATION BY DESIGN

The call for entries for the "Innovation by Design" competition appeared on the cover of the May 2019 issue of *Fast Company*. The call included 21 categories, 30+ judges, and it was billed as the "The World's Most Prestigious Design Competition."[1]

The difference between this chapter and the *Fast Company* call for a design competition is that here we concentrate on the means to an end, not the end itself. How does one design an organization that is capable of winning design competitions?

Prescriptive theories in the applied sciences can be tricky. The innovative science in any industry consists of theories and empirical evidence that is constantly evolving. In an eclectic field like innovation studies, the rubrics change quickly because the subject matter and emerging lexicon is controlled by many disciplines. Take the recent example of digital manufacturing or the adoption of technology in services.[2]

Somehow, just a summary of the book in Chapter 11 did not seem a fitting way to finish off these varied topics that could inform action. The term "capstone" doesn't really do any activity justice because there is always something that follows, in this case, the epilogue chapter. Further, the design thinking movement is just gathering steam in management literature, if one includes MIS and big data. For example, Antons and Breidbach review 641 articles on service research and service design research while illustrating the application of topic modeling and machine learning.[3] They advance four research directions in their findings: (1) link disconnected topics within the service research stream, (2) increase generalizability of service innovation and design, (3) expand theoretical scope of service innovation and design, and (4) advance the methodological repertoire of service innovation and design. The most germane of this new literature are the contributions linking design, strategy, and innovation such as Foss and

Saebi's article, which reviews business model innovation,[4] and Cagnin's paper, which argues for transformative business strategy by linking design thinking and future literacy.[5]

What causes innovation?

An appropriate starting point for a prescriptive theory of the innovation process seems to be asking the question, "What causes innovation?" The best approximate answer to this important question was probably provided by Danny Miller. He coined the term "entrepreneurial orientation."[6]

Importantly, Miller made the formal connection between actors and strategy in his research. For both weak and strong appropriation conditions, leaders as actors in their roles throughout the organization are really the genesis of consequences of the innovation process. The notion that goal orientation is necessary for radical innovation is consistent with making leadership first among equals in consideration of what causes innovation.[7]

Leaders see problems that need solutions or technological opportunities that need to be exploited and in some cases are able to reconcile the technological push and market pull economic terms. To come full circle from earlier chapters of this book, what has often been forgotten is the Miller and Friesen warning of the downside of the innovation process—which implies that too much growth too fast can be just as risky as early, successful innovation.[8] There is recent empirical evidence to support this curvilinear effect in the empirical finding that the degree of co-development has a diminishing return relationship with new product frequency (Relationship between Co-Development and New Product Frequency, p. 213).[9]

Robert Burgelman[10] adds significantly to Miller's work and dwells on the connection between senior leaders and strategy. His work is reintroduced in a later section of this chapter because it is relevant to the causal link in the causal model introduced there: integration.

Other writers have contributed to our understanding of how innovation leaders and entrepreneurs have done a good job of demonstrating this link between technological opportunity and market challenge. John Howells makes the following important distinction:

> ...value of distinguishing between two types of market concept used by the innovating firm. These are the "reference market" which is a traded product that is a principal source of "use" ideas for the mental construction of the "innovation market" concept. It is the latter that can be thought to guide the construction of innovative production technology.[11]

Network centrality moderates the role of individuals in the innovation process. Ibarra[12] reports that this research focuses on relative impacts of individual attributes, formal position, and network centrality on the exercise of individual power.

This is measured as involvement in technical and administrative innovations. It turns out that centrality was important for administrative innovation roles but has little relationship to technical innovation roles. Centrality mediates the impact of individual attributes and formal position on administrative innovation. An organization's informal structure may be more critical when power requires extensive boundary spanning.

Ibarra's work is directly relevant to our work—reported in Chapter 9 and summarized in this new prescriptive lens below—concerning balanced thinking style. The link between cognitive theory and innovation action has important implications for selection and development of people in new roles in innovative start-ups and incumbent firms.

Leadership and strategy: what endures

Two of my own articles address causality directly, although no prescriptive theory was offered formally in these publications. The first addresses the link between policy or strategy and innovation among a sample of food processing equipment suppliers.[13] Summarizing from a modified abstract, "... context [environmental uncertainty] causes policy, which causes innovation.... Increasing organization size up to a point and an aggressive technology policy emerge as the two key variables in this model of organization and innovation."[14]

My second article, which prescribes action, appeared in 1990.[15] Summarizing from that abstract extends the particulars of the synchronous innovation (SI) framework covered throughout the book. The article focuses on the simple question of why some manufacturing firms are more likely to successfully adopt new processing technologies. Part of the answer is significantly associated with the experience profile of general managers. Here is what I found:

1. CEOs with manufacturing experience also are significantly more likely to implement an aggressive manufacturing technology policy. What is an aggressive manufacturing policy? These firms are the first to try out new methods and equipment. They are also more likely than others to actively recruit new technical talent or develop this talent in-house, and demonstrate a commitment to technological forecasting. Further, these CEOs make sure customers are aware of how modernizing the firm will benefit them. CEOs take calculated risks when they have manufacturing experience.

2. Commitment to training during modernization is much greater when senior vice presidents and divisional general managers have manufacturing experience. This suggests that training and development are still very much a strategic concern in domestic manufacturing, although not as much as technology policy. Commitment is reflected in plans and practices for training and budgets for modernization. If training budgets do not reach at least 10% of project cost, commitment may be lacking.

3. Direct labor savings resulting from modernization and automated assembly operations are more likely to be emphasized by traditional senior managers. Divisional managers with manufacturing experience are less focused on labor savings during the modernization process.
4. The use of new manufacturing systems is much greater when divisional managers have manufacturing experience. These same managers are also likely to support administrative experiments to implement new flexible automation modernization projects. This was not the pattern for senior management.

In 1990, it was evident that there was a role and a critical need for general managers with manufacturing experience at all levels of the firm. At the top, that experience is necessary for creative policy formulation and implementation. On the C-level management team, it is crucial for commitment to training and development, and at the divisional level for administrative experimentation.

We followed up this study to focus on middle managers, with interesting complementary results. It is obvious that middle managers have an important role to play in new product development (NPD) and strong appropriation conditions. We studied eight manufacturing firms using in-depth, open-ended interviews, but we were surprised to find that most of these companies were beginning to develop products that are new to the firm, industry, and world (nearly half, or 10 of 21 new product projects). This was a distinct break from their past actions.

These newer products likely are driven by a combination of market and technology forces, with distinct roles for middle and top management. As would be expected, incremental new products required less mustering of resources, but when middle managers became responsible for driving the conversion of general requirements into specifications, resource issues had typically not been resolved. We also replicated much of what was in the literature at the time concerning how rare radical product innovation was. Of the 17 new products currently being used by the customers of these firms, only 5 (29%) were new-to-the-world or new-to-the-industry.

There was a clear pattern in how general requirements were derived in these data. Market forces were the primary driver from external sources as opposed to competition. Top-down requirements tended to be driven by a combination of technology push and market pull factors. Top managers exerted the greatest pressure to reconcile market and technology factors in these eight firms. Specifications that resulted from general requirements came after the firm was able to marshal resources needed to proceed, and barriers blocking progress, such as clarification from customers about what was truly needed in new offerings, were removed. Middle managers are in charge of this conversion of general requirements to specifications.

A total of 17 of the 21 new products we studied had already been introduced, and we found there was a significant correlation between external influences on the NPD process (e.g., markets and customers) and success ($p = 0.014$). That is, three were failures, ten were pending, and eight were successful (six of the eight were driven by customers). Following up on two of the new-to-the-world products, we found a 50–50 split on success. Only two of these products experienced direct input from top managers to convert general requirements to specifications, ten were converted by middle managers with the help of professional staff, and nine products benefited from customer input to convert ideas into specifications. Overall, these results show a clear demarcation between general and middle managers in the NPD process.

A recent article in the *Academy of Management Journal* echoed these findings.[16] What the authors found for a sample of Swedish firms is that when one focuses on measures of educational diversity, middle management teams and top management teams are quite different. For top management teams, educational diversity determines whether firms will engage in strategic innovation activities, and middle management teams with educational diversity are more likely to predict the actual outcome of these processes, such as successful product innovations and market novelty.

An important extension to this successful adoption of manufacturing technology prescription appears in our work on service innovation, another example of weak appropriation because of the lack of intellectual property protection of most services. Although, Barras[17] proposed a "reverse product cycle" for services involving three stages of technology adoption and development in services. Steve Rosenthal and I found that top managers actually substitute for the role or R&D in successful service offerings.[18]

We have done considerable work on service innovation and the differences between this process and NPD.[19] In one study, we conducted a comparative study of 38 new products and 29 service innovations and found that how these firms formalize development of new offerings is quite different. Manufacturing is more likely to document new strategies and structures when products are new to the industry or new to the firm. However, when a service firm has a truly novel idea, it is more likely to be successful. Services are substantially more likely to have a short beta testing process and to exploit general manager (internally sourced) ideas for new offerings, which appears to be an alternative to formal innovation structures. Perhaps since service firms rarely have a formal R&D function, top managers appear to substitute for this function.

In our second study of service innovation, Rosenthal and I conducted in-depth interviews over a period of two years in nine manufacturing firms that had launched significant new service innovations representing important diversification moves for the firm.[20] Both strategies going forward require CEO/president sponsorship, but are founded on different corporate cultures. The engineering culture path to successful commercialization is a driver and well-spring of concepts new to the firm. These novel ideas require multi-functional strategy-making and prevail when champions from operations have deep knowledge of the conversion process in the respective industry. This finding replicates what we reported earlier and noted above in the 1990 article on general manager experience and successful adoption of process innovations. This is relevant because this chapter is devoted to prescriptions that span the gulf between strong (new products) and weak (adoption of new processes and information technology) appropriation conditions.

The entrepreneurial orientation path to commercialization is aligned with concepts new-to-the-industry or new-to-the-world, and these are paired with sole champions from R&D or engineering. Both strategies can work well but are clearly dependent on development history and corporate culture as well as available resources. For manufacturing firms considering making the transition to significant service offerings, the findings here indicate at least two viable approaches to commercialization, but both depend significantly on chief executive sponsorship regardless of the initial conditions and context. These two paths are summarized in Figure 12.1.

The theme of this chapter continues to be illustrated by leadership for innovation in that it applies to both strong and weak appropriation. Service innovation is an easy fit into the weak appropriation category because it tends to be easily imitated in the absence of intellectual property protection. Another critical example of weak appropriation is the adoption of hardware–software innovation from outside the firm. Take for example our study of the adoption of enterprise resource planning (ERP) systems,[21] where we found in 80 cases that for implementation of these complex hardware–software systems, leadership

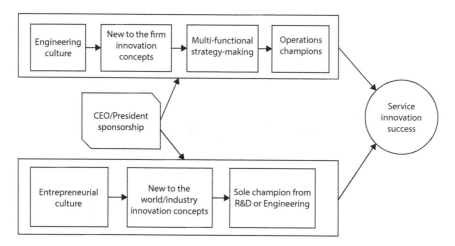

FIGURE 12.1 Two shining paths to successful new service venture creation (From Ettlie, J. E., & Rosenthal, S. R., *J. Serv. Manag.*, 23, 440–454, 2012.)[22]

(five dimensions) was the most important predictor of on-time/on-budget performance, along with three other factors[23]:

> Leadership (social learning theory), business process reengineering (change the company not the technology), and acquisition strategy (buy, do not make) were found to be significant predictors of adoption performance (final model $R^2 = 43$ percent, $F = 5.5$, $p < 0.001$, $df = 7,52$), controlling for industry (manufacturing versus service), <the absence of EDI legacy> project start date, and scale (sales).[24]

Leadership consisted of five highly reliable dimensions, including hands-on use of ERP or modeling the behaviors by divisional managers, which were seen as needed by all firm or business unit members for successful adoption and negotiation of third-party contracts. Leadership is the common ingredient to innovation success regardless of appropriation conditions. Note that "on-time and on-budget" does not include customer satisfaction, showing the way for continuation of this research stream.

Although there is no direct evidence of the successful process evolution of SI, it is valuable to share general observations about directed change when investments in new technology are significant. What we have observed is a pattern of dependency that managers tend to follow when they do achieve success in adopting new technology. The next diagram below ("Generalized SI Process Model") is a schematic of this four-step process. The SI model has not changed, but the path to the sweet spot is now followed in this summary schematic in Figure 12.2.

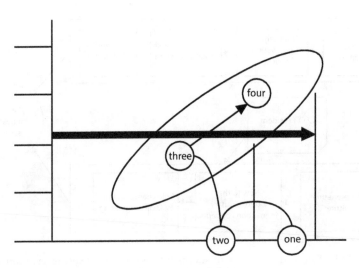

FIGURE 12.2 Generalized synchronous innovation process model (y-axis is organizational or administrative innovation and the x-axis is technological innovation)

Managers tend to underestimate the challenge of adopting a technology and often retrench their commitment to the "big bang" approach to technological change. So the first step in this path dependency is to reduce or stage the adoption process. This is represented by circle one→circle two.

The next stage of this process that we observe is the "synchronous" realization. In serious, well-managed implementation teams, technology alone will not solve this challenge, and the introduction of organizational innovations, becomes the focus of the effort. New strategies, tactics, organizational structures, job descriptions, etc. become the preoccupation of an administrative experiment to make things right. Since these new strategies and structures tend to be modest at first, only incremental performance is typically realized. This path from circle two→circle three becomes the template process model. Then as confidence in the process builds, changes become bolder and more expansive. Thus, moving up the sweet spot from circle three→circle four becomes possible and eventually a reality. Typically, participants in this evolution won't even recognize the changes as anything other than an extension of what a strong culture can do to foster successful adoption, and that is why directed human capital is the key to this SI process model. Next, we take up the second common factor in causal model prediction: integration.

We turn to capabilities, which also create boundaries of effective innovative action. The capacity to act when new capabilities are needed often becomes the reason for open innovation initiatives like crowdsourcing or crowdfunding. This represents a significant upgrade of the resource-based view (RBV) of the firm, especially as it relates to innovation.

Capability enhancement

Start-ups (which typically begin with a small team of people, not one person),[25] newcomers from other industries, and incumbents all have to be both willing and able to satisfy customers and compete against rivals. It should come as no surprise that capabilities are part of the prescriptive model introduced in this chapter. Three contemporary authors come to mind when new capabilities emerge in the innovation literature: David Teece for dynamic capabilities, and Wesley Cohen and Daniel Levinthal for absorptive capacity.[26]

The most important contribution of these authors and their followers as a link to the prescriptive model of this chapter is the human and social capital needed to reconfigure and absorb technology-driven change. One of the lesson-successful innovators learn early: the new product, service, or process is not the ultimate benefit of innovating; rather, it is an increased capacity to be a better innovator. The goal is to be in a better position than competitors in the labor markets to recruit the exceptional talent needed to transcend generations of new dominant designs. This is the capability that matters.

The key difference between this third dimension of a prescriptive model of successful innovation and other candidates is that it applies to both strong and weak appropriation conditions. For strong appropriation, it should be obvious: R&D budgets are dominated by the cost of human capital. For the latter, it may not be obvious, but a few studies show how people moving across organizational boundaries have a very positive impact on adoption of technology and its subsequent implementation. Flows of people across organizational boundaries are critical to the acquisition and deployment of human capital. There is a series of three studies from my research streams that are relevant to this issue.

In 1980, the first study of three in this research stream was published on the impact of acquisition of key personnel and adoption of process innovation.[27] The overarching assumption of the initial line of research is that information flows alone cannot account for the differences in innovation outcomes, and that the movement of people across organizational boundaries represents an important adjunct to the information theory of innovation.

In the first article, seven propositions were developed from various literature streams including: personnel turnover of especially creative people, policies impacting human capital recruitment and development, absorption of new personnel through structural adaptation, and impacts on radical versus incremental technology projects. Five case studies were compiled, including three technical success cases and two commercial success cases all drawn from one firm in the industrial gas sector, where the product is always the same, but the application varies across customers. Even with this small sample of case studies there was a trend approaching statistical significance (Kendall $tau = 0.60$, $p = 0.117$), supporting the notion that the more significant projects were measured by potential impact on forecasted sales and the observation of an important staff addition or turnover.

In the second study,[28] which focused on the food processing sector and packaging innovation, we found that personnel flows had an important impact on innovation decisions, but positive gains of new people are a relatively rare occurrence. Only 23 (41%) of these 56 firms report any significant, innovation-impactful personnel additions, and 15 of these involve management positions. We only found support for the idea that net gain personnel flows are more likely to be related to radical, as opposed to incremental process adoption. Evidence suggests that there is an inverted U-shaped relationship between net personnel flows and innovation outcomes. New blood seems to stimulate innovation up to a point, after which there is a negative impact on the innovation process. Adding too many creative people at once who all have a significant influence on the process may be unwise.

We also found that the impact of employee flows on innovative outcomes seems to be moderated by organization structure and the availability of slack resources for innovating. In particular, net personnel flows were significantly more likely to be positively correlated with the sum of the staged adoption behaviors for one of the important flexible packaging technologies we studied (the retort pouch) in decentralized ($p \leq 0.05$) and complex ($p < 0.01$) organizations. This suggests that autonomy and new job titles with substantial visibility help innovation.

The availability of resources strengthens the relationship between the adoption of the retort pouch and net personnel gains, although the effects were not as strong ($p < 0.10$) as for the structural moderators. Resources allocated to new personnel were counted on for innovation payoff.[29]

In the third study[30] we focused on advanced manufacturing technologies like flexible manufacturing systems in 50 US plants over a period of three years. Personnel flows follow a two-stage process, whereby senior managers acquired by the firm promote adoption of new process technology, and as the sample of modernizing plants illustrates, intrafirm mobility of primary manufacturing engineers promotes implementation of computer-integrated manufacturing systems. The interfirm mobility rate was 41%, and 22 of the 39 cases (56%) experienced intrafirm mobility. Most ($n = 11$) involved manufacturing engineers promoted to manager or ($n = 5$) rotation of manufacturing engineers to facilitate implementation.

We found a significant correlation between the use of administrative innovations and intrafirm personnel flows during modernization, $r = 0.32$ ($p = 0.03$). These administrative innovations included: new job descriptions, technology agreements between unions and management, new strategy or policy, new organizational structures, and in two (rare) but very important cases, engineer/blue-collar teams. These teams are important because most union contracts would not allow engineers and blue-collar workers on a new job site in a plant at the same time. There was a meaningful correlation between corporate involvement in the plant modernization project and a line item in the budget for manufacturing R&D, $r = 0.44$ ($n = 33$, $p = 0.005$). This was not the case for R&D helping to design the new manufacturing system, or for corporate manufacturing engineering helping to coordinate the project. Up until this time, it was unusual to see manufacturing and design engineers hired and promoted in the same pay-grade scales, and it was about this time in US manufacturing (early 1990s) that this began to change to greater parity. Clearly, there is a relationship between leadership and capability enhancement in most of the more remarkable cases of both strong and weak appropriation. This reinforces the notion of SI, or the simultaneous adoption of hardware–software systems and organizational innovations.[31]

The alternative to human capital solutions to the challenge of dynamic capabilities needed to prepare for the future of the enterprise is to import information that enhances existing capabilities. This is now referred to as the open innovation approach started by Henry Chesbrough.[32] Open innovation existed many decades before Chesbrough named it. Working with suppliers in manufacturing continues to be the hallmark of prosperous Japanese firms over the last four decades. Crowdsourcing is not new; consider the following examples[33]:

> **1714: The Longitude Prize.** In 1714, the British government was searching for a solution to what they called "the Longitude Problem," which made sailing perilous (thousands of seamen were killed every year). Seeking

innovation, the British government offered £20,000 (about $4.7 million in USD in 2010) for people to invent a solution. This is possibly the first ever example of crowdsourcing. The contest was won by John Harrison, the son of a carpenter. Harrison invented the "marine chronometer" (i.e., an accurate, vacuum-sealed pocket watch). The aristocrats were hesitant to award Harrison the prize but eventually paid him the £20,000. This is a fantastic one because it highlights one of the principles of crowdsourcing—innovation and creativity can come from anywhere.

1936: Toyota Logo Contest. In 1936, Toyota held a contest to redesign its logo. They received 27,000 entries. The winning logo was the three Japanese katakana letters for "Toyoda" in a circle, which was later modified by Risaburo Toyoda to "Toyota."

1955: The Sydney Opera House. In 1955, Joseph Cahill, the Premier of New South Wales, Australia, ran a contest offering £5,000 to design a building for part of Sydney's Harbor. The contest received 233 entries from 32 countries around the world. The winning design is one of the most innovative landmarks ever. Architectural contests continue to be a popular model for getting buildings designed.

In our work, we have found that there are at least two generic types of innovation predicted by Chesbrough and actuated by competing firms. In our study of the banking industry in Iberia, we found that either inside-out or outside-in open innovation strategic initiatives can work, depending upon the goal of the firm.[34] Although open innovation has enjoyed a burgeoning stream of academic awareness in applied or trade publications, the theoretical underpinning of these strategies and practices has been relatively scant. We conducted an in-depth comparative study of two global banks with home bases in Spain to test the usefulness of one of the micropractices and microfoundations of the two firms. Although all organizations practice some combination of internal and external sourcing of innovation, we used the Chesbrough distinction between inside-out open innovation and outside-in open innovation. We found that the two banks' deployment of open innovation processes produced strong results including greater top-line growth and bottom-line efficiency gains, depending upon the beneficial implementation of two different strategies.

The overall message of our study is that BBVA became the most successful bank in Europe using inside-out open innovation. Santander (the red bank) became the fastest-growing bank at the time using outside-in alliances with specialized information technology.

In the continuation of this research stream, we have attempted to resolve the great paradox of openness posed by Kenneth Arrow[35]: if you open up to outsiders, you risk technological spillovers.[36] In our most recent conference paper, we have found the beginnings of the one potential reconciliation of this paradox. From the abstract of a study of the US automotive industry and external versus internal networks for ideation we found the following:[37]

> We studied 75 US automotive R&D projects focused on upgrading powertrain technology and used two theories: competitive dynamics and boundary issues in open innovation. We concluded that firms that target single competitors are significantly and directly associated with greater success (lagged year/year sales and validated and projected project success) and incremental technology projects while protecting internal core technology projects. These results suggest that future research ought to test the notion that external boundaries are more important in open innovation when firms target competitors, and internal boundaries are more important when the competitive landscape dominates strategy.

Not only do these findings corroborate earlier conclusions from offshoring R&D[38] and competitive dynamics, they point the way to potentially significant convergence of theory and empirical findings on the importance of distinguishing between radical and incremental technologies. This is also a step forward in resolving the open innovation paradox.[39] Given that incumbent firms often complain about the potential of technology spillovers in their open innovation experiments, the empirical evidence actually suggests that there is a way to cope with this challenge by keeping radical technology in-house and sharing incremental technology developments with outsiders.

Integration

One of the most meaningful legacies of the Industrial Revolution was the concept of division of labor. The more specialization, the greater the need is for coordination. If novelty is tossed into the mix, integration challenges become even more daunting. New strategy driven by leaders begets new structure. Integrating structures are the overarching category of new structures needed to implement a new strategy.

One of the compelling convergences in innovation studies literature is the concept that integration is a necessity for both strong and weak appropriation. Two of the giants in our field, Al Rubenstein and Robert Burgelman, both concluded that this rare commodity is the essence of successful innovation processes in R&D-investing firms.[40] Ernesto Reza published findings that indicated that integration is also essential for successful adoption of new technology. Integration combines with leadership to cause successful innovation, regardless of intellectual property protections or other mechanisms typically employed to protect the rights of the innovator.

Burgelman[41] makes the connection between leadership and integration, arguing that firms require two things to maintain viability: diversity and order. "Diversity results primarily from autonomous strategic initiatives of participants at the operational level. Order results from imposing a concept of strategy on the organization. Second, managing diversity requires an experimentation-and-selection approach."[42]

Burgelman emphasizes the need for supervisory middle management roles to support the strategic initiatives that need implementation in the capabilities and operations of the firm. By delegating and endorsing entrepreneurial activities to achieve a strategic vision, top managers allow the middle managers to redefine strategic context. Only top management can balance diversity, as in our study of eight manufacturing firms, combining market and technology forces in NPD. General managers can direct structure toward "… innovative administrative arrangements … required to facilitate the collaboration between entrepreneurial participants and the organizations in which they are active."[43]

Our first real test of the integration hypothesis was in our 50-plant study.[44] The preliminary findings of this project, which spanned three years, were first reported in 1990. These initial results proved quite helpful in framing additional projects and replications of the SI model of successful adoption of hardware–software systems. We found a significant differential pattern of the impact of integration on unique performance outcomes of these new hardware–software systems, all using some form of advanced manufacturing technology. Hierarchical structural innovation was correlated with throughput time reduction, whereas design-manufacturing structural adaptations were correlated with utilization (two-shift basis) of these new production systems. Supplier integration was correlated with two performance indicators: cycle-time performance and reduction in lower scrap and rework (which averaged 30%). The one market-directed innovation (forming new customer alliances) was correlated with new system flexibility (as measured by part-families scheduled), which was strong evidence supporting the manufacturing scope theory of plant modernization.[45] We later went on to establish that part families were the most reliable measures of scope, as opposed to just part numbers.[46]

We focused on integration in another collaborative project examining both strategic and functional coordination that links directly to capabilities. Sandy Rothenberg and I published an article relevant here because it recommends action for both strong and weak appropriation in the automotive industry. We prescribe two types of integration linked to two types of uncertainty (market and technological). The two dimensions of uncertainty are value-added functional (like R&D and marketing) and platform integration (early versus late stage of product development).[47] See Table 12.1.

One proviso should be added to this section of the prescriptive model: culture will always create the boundaries of what is possible when it comes to effective implementation of strategy. If the culture supports the new moves, and if the moves represent administrative experiments, then, as Burgelman says, all is possible.[48] Fixed plans with no alternatives are rarely effective. It is interesting to note that David Obstfeld[49] in his recent book "places an important emphasis on understanding coordination processes among people who are already acquainted

TABLE 12.1 Functional versus platform integration in the global automotive industry

	Platform integration	Functional integration
Market uncertainty	• Existing technologies • Existing Markets • Short term response	• Discontinuous Innovation • New markets (especially emerging) • Longer term response
Non-market uncertainty	• Political (i.e. lobbying) on incremental social change • Incremental Environmental Performance improvements	• Expecting radical social demands for environmental performance • Greater focus on technologies for large environmental performance improvements.

Source: Rothenberg, S., and Ettlie, J.E., *Calif. Manage. Rev.*, 54, 126–144, copyright © 2011. Reprinted by Permission of SAGE Publications; Ibid., p. 133.

and may already be working together."[50] New, as yet unpublished, work of our own compares different types of collaboration in buyer–seller relationships. The preliminary findings are quite promising, as reported at a recent conference.[51] The preliminary report uses path-dependency theory to guide the investigation of the structuring of partnership relationships (supplier and customers) and their impact on a wide range of NPD outcomes.

We used a survey sample of 223 manufacturing firms and focused the analysis on three structuring dimensions: synchronizing, integrating, and coordinating. As it turns out, all three dimensions were significantly correlated with new product commercial success rates (mean = 60.4%, replicating earlier surveys). Only synchronizing partnerships, entered stepwise, in a significant regression equation to predict new product success rates (Beta = 0.293, $p = 0.001$). We then substituted commercial success with profitability percentage as the dependent variable (mean = 54.3%) and found that coordinated partnerships were the only significant dimension to enter the equation (Beta = 0.256, $p = 0.004$) controlling for scale and other variables. These results suggest strong preliminary support for the overall notion path dependency of this process, since integration does not enter either regression equation stepwise. There was one additional remarkable finding. We found that suppliers are significantly more likely to attempt to control the timing and method of co-development (e.g., synchronizing and coordinating) as compared to their customers. Validating regressions taking a 12-outcome scale of the NPD process (e.g., lead-time reduction) suggests an even more complex path dependency underlying the causal process, which would be an excellent extension of this research stream.

Summary

This chapter has been focused on a prescriptive model of the innovation process. Three key dimensions with nuances were presented: leadership, integration, and capability management to increase the odds of successful development and adoption of new technological ventures. A summary figure is offered below to capture this prescriptive theory.

Leadership→capability enhancement→integration→successful development and adoption of new technology is the simplified version of this theory. The nuances are important and were chosen because the empirical evidence strongly suggests that regardless of appropriation regime, strong or weak, they apply. These nuances of the leadership dimension include the notion that C-level managers are not alone in the guidance of successful new technological experiments. There is a vital role for middle managers in the leadership process as well.

Capability enhancement is directly in line with the growing popularity enjoyed by open innovation advocates. The proviso that new capability needs to apply in both weak and strong appropriation requires close examination of the adoption theories and empirical record in this field, as well as new product and new service development. The resolution of the potential tug-of-war between the various ways in which open innovation processes enhance capabilities versus signaling customers remains to be enlightened by future research. Will it be crowdsourcing as some have predicted? Will it be a matter of a blend of approaches and theories? We are on the path of studying open ambidexterity as one avenue toward future understanding. We believe that if one compares M&A history of a firm or business unit and calls for information to enhance NPD processes, there is a clear pattern of a combination of these two strategies with a path dependency favoring open innovation first, followed by acquisition.

Integration of effort is perhaps the hardest concept to appreciate, with the proviso that any dimension of a successful prescriptive theory of innovation would have to apply to both strong and weak appropriation. A parsimonious model as the guide to action must include the general idea that the two-step action plan of a new strategy needs to be followed by a new structure,[52] which is the overarching justification and underpinning of this theory. Figure 12.3 summarizes these effects.

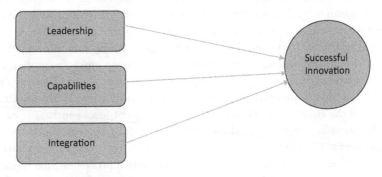

FIGURE 12.3 Prescriptive model of the innovation process

Notes

1 The Fast Company, Issue 232 (May, 2019).

2 The idea for this chapter resulted from an anonymous comment from one of my students in the on-line course evaluations in fall semester, 2017, for which I am grateful.

3 Antons, D., & Breidbach, C. F. (2018). Big data, big insights? Advancing service innovation and design with machine learning. *Journal of Service Research, 21*(1), 17–39.

4 Foss, N. J., & Saebi, T. (2018). Business models and business model innovation: Between wicked and paradigmatic problems. *Long Range Planning, 51*(1), 9–21.

5 Cagnin, C. (2018). Developing a transformative business strategy through the combination of design thinking and futures literacy. *Technology Analysis & Strategic Management, 30*(5), 524–539.

6 Miller and Friesen (1982) quoting their abstract: "Two very different models of product innovation are postulated and tested. The *conservative* model assumes that innovation is performed reluctantly, mainly in response to serious challenges. It therefore predicts that innovation will correlate positively with environmental, information processing, structural and decision making variables that represent, or help to recognize and cope with these challenges. In contrast, the *entrepreneurial* model supposes that innovation is always aggressively pursued and will be very high unless decision makers are warned to slow down. Thus negative correlations are predicted between innovation and the variables that can provide such warning. Correlational and curvilinear regression analyses revealed that each model was supported by conservative and entrepreneurial sub-samples, respectively, in a diverse sample of 52 Canadian firms."

7 Alexander, L., & Van Knippenberg, D. (2014). Teams in pursuit of radical innovation: A goal orientation perspective. *Academy of Management Review, 39*(4), 423–438.

8 Miller, D., & Friesen, P. H. (1982). Innovation in conservative and entrepreneurial firms: Two models of strategic momentum. *Strategic Management Journal, 3*(1), 1–25.

9 Maria Stock, R., Zacharias, N. A., & Schnellbaecher, A. (2017). How do strategy and leadership styles jointly affect co-development and its innovation outcomes?. *Journal of Product Innovation Management, 34*(2), 201–222.

10 Burgelman, R. (1983). Corporate entrepreneurship and strategic management— Insights from a process study. *Management Science, 39*, 1349–1364.

11 Howells, J. (1997). Rethinking the market-technology relationship for innovation. *Research Policy, 25*(8), 1209–1219.

12 Ibarra, H. (1993). Network centrality, power, and innovation involvement: Determinants of technical and administrative roles. *Academy of Management Journal, 36*(3), 471–501.

13 Ettlie, J. E. (1983). Organizational policy and innovation among suppliers to the food processing sector. *Academy of Management Journal, 26*(1), 27–44.

14 Ibid., p. 27.

15 Ettlie, J. E. (1990). What makes a manufacturing firm innovative?. *Academy of Management Perspectives, 4*(4), 7–20.

16 Schubert, T., & Tavassoli, S. (2019). Product innovation and educational diversity in top and middle management teams. *Academy of Management Journal.* doi:10.5465/ amj.2017.0741.

17 Barras, R. (1986). Towards a theory of innovation in services. *Research Policy, 15*(4), 161–173. Abstract: The paper sets out some foundations for a theory of innovation in service industries, and indicates the role that such innovation may play in the generation of growth cycles.

18 Ettlie, J. E., & Rosenthal, S. R. (2011). Service versus manufacturing innovation. *Journal of Product Innovation Management, 28*(2), 285–299.

19 Ibid., 2011.

20 Ettlie, J. E., & Rosenthal, S. R. (2012). Service innovation in manufacturing. *Journal of Service Management, 23*(3), 440–454.

21 Ettlie, J. E., Perotti, V. J., Joseph, D. A., & Cotteleer, M. J. (2005). Strategic predictors of successful enterprise system deployment. *International Journal of Operations & Production Management, 25*(10), 953–972.
22 Ettlie, J. E., & Rosenthal, S. R. (2012). Service Innovation in Manufacturing. *Journal of Service Management, 23*(3) 440–454.
23 Ibid., p. 953.
24 Ibid.
25 Ruef, M., Aldrich, H. E., & Carter, N. M. (2003). The structure of founding teams: Homophily, strong ties, and isolation among U.S. entrepreneurs. *American Sociological Review, 68*(2), 195–222.
26 Teece, D. J. (2009). *Dynamic capabilities and strategic management: Organizing for innovation and growth* (Vol. 4). Oxford, UK: Oxford University Press, and Cohen, W. M., & Levinthal, D. A. (1990). Absorptive capacity: A new perspective on learning and innovation. *Administrative Science Quarterly, 35*(1), 128–152.
27 Ettlie, J. E. (1980). Manpower flows and the innovation process. *Management Science, 26*(11), 1086–1095.
28 Ettlie, J. E. (1985). The impact of interorganizational manpower flows on the innovation process. *Management Science, 31*(9), 1055–1071.
29 Ibid.
30 Ettlie, J. E. (1990). Interfirm mobility and manufacturing modernizaiton. *Journal of Engineering and Technology Management, 6(3–4)*, 281–302.
31 Ettlie, J. E., & Reza, E. M. (1992). Organizational integration and process innovation. *Academy of Management Journal, 35*(4), 795–827.
32 Chesbrough, H., Vanhaverbeke, W., & West, J. (Eds.). (2003). *Open innovation: Researching a new paradigm.* Oxford, UK: Oxford University Press on Demand.
33 This article was written by Alec Lynch founder of graphic design crowdsourcing service DesignCrowd. https://blog.designcrowd.com/article/202/crowdsourcing-is-not-new-the-history-of-crowdsourcing-1714-to-2010.
34 Gianiodis, P. T., Ettlie, J. E., & Urbina, J. J. (2014). Open service innovation in the global banking industry: Inside-out versus outside-in strategies. *Academy of Management Perspectives, 28*(1), 76–91.
35 Arrow, K. J. (1962). Economic welfare and the allocation of resources for invention. In C. K. Rowley (ed.), *Readings in industrial economics* (pp. 219–236). London, UK: Palgrave.
36 Ibid.
37 Working paper, July 2019, Ettlie et al.
38 Ettlie, J., & Hira, R. (2018). *World scientific reference on innovation: Volume 2: Engineering globalization reshoring and nearshoring: Management and policy issues.* World Scientific Publishing.
39 Arrow (1962).
40 Rubenstein, A. H. (1989). *Managing technology in the decentralized firm.* Wiley-Interscience, and Burgelman, R., Christensen, C., & Wheelwright, S. (2009). *Strategic management of technology and innovation.* New York: McGraw-Hill.
41 Burgelman, R. A. (1983). Corporate entrepreneurship and strategic management: Insights from a process study. *Management Science, 29*(12), 1349–1364.
42 Ibid., p. 1349.
43 Ettlie, J. E. (1990). What makes a manufacturing firm innovative?. *Academy of management perspectives, 4*(4), 7–20.
44 Ettlie and Reza (1992).
45 Ibid.
46 Ettlie, J. E., & Penner-Hahn, J. D. (1994). Flexibility ratios and manufacturing strategy. *Management Science, 40*(11), 1444–1454.
47 Rothenberg, S., & Ettlie, J. E. (2011). Strategies to cope with regulatory uncertainty in the auto industry. *California Management Review, 54*(1), 126–144.

48 Burgelman (1983).
49 Obstfeld, D. (2018). *Getting new things done: Networks, brokerage, and the assembly of innovative action*. Palo Alto, CA: Stanford University Press.
50 Kauppila, O. P., Bizzi, L., & Obstfeld, D. (2018). Connecting and creating: Tertius iungens, individual creativity, and strategic decision processes. *Strategic Management Journal, 39*(3), 697–719.
51 Ettlie, J. E., Carnovale, S., & Duhadway (2019). Path dependency and structuring partnerships in new product development, presented at the POMS National Meeting, Washington, DC.
52 Amburgey, T. L., & Carroll, G. R. (1984). Time-series models for event counts. *Social Science Research, 13*(1), 38–54; Ettlie, J. E., Bridges, W. P., & O'Keefe, R. D. (1984). Organization strategy and structural differences for radical versus incremental innovation. *Management science, 30*(6), 682–695; and Rubenstein (1989).

INDEX

Note: Page numbers in italic and bold refer to figures and tables, respectively.
Page numbers followed by n refers to notes.